MW00607861

WAR, WINGS, AND A WESTERN YOUTH, 1925-1945

Also By Ted C. Hinckley

In addition to a wide range of articles and book-length anthologies dealing with American history, the author has written three histories on frontier Alaska:

The Americanization of Alaska, 1867-1897
(Palo Alto, California, 1972)

Alaskan John G. Brady, Missionary, Businessman, Judge and Governor, 1878-1918
(Columbus, Ohio, 1982)

The Canoe Rocks: Alaska's Tlingit and the Euramerican Frontier 1800-1912
(Lanham, Maryland, 1995)

WAR, WINGS,
AND A
WESTERN YOUTH
1925-1945

Ted C. Hinckley

Adjunct Professor of History
Western Washington University
Bellingham, Washington

Pentland Press, Inc.
England • USA • Scotland

PUBLISHED BY PENTLAND PRESS, INC.
5124 Bur Oak Circle, Raleigh, North Carolina 27612
United States of America
919-782-0281

ISBN 1-57197-009-6

Copyright ©1996 Ted C. Hinckley

All rights reserved, which includes the right to reproduce this book or portions thereof in any form whatsoever except as provided by the U.S. Copyright Law.

Printed in the United States of America

For my three granddaughters that they may
more fully honor the men of Navy Air
who took their final flight across the Pacific,
1941-1945

TABLE OF CONTENTS

PREFACE

Anyone who writes a book about his or her own early years quickly discovers two inescapable realities. The portrait that emerges is self-serving, despite the narrator's best efforts to thin out ego's varnish. Secondly, there is the dispiriting sense of melancholy that accompanies writing about one's distant childhood through adolescence. Like fingering dust-covered toys in a grandparent's attic, each scribbled sentence sparks a chain of memories. And whether happy or sad, all are as ethereal as Alice's Wonderland or Christopher Robin's Pooh Corner.

Veterans and academicians who have successfully mined their own military service, men like Douglas E. Leach and Frank F. Mathias, have taken some comfort that the young men they are describing are so remote as to be virtual strangers. In the present instance, and for whatever psychological reason, this unfortunately has not been the case, and objectivity can only have suffered.

This autobiography examines the widening perspectives of a Southern California lad on the approaching Second World War. Raised in a comfortable, upper-middle class Pasadena environment, the author reflects what is today condemned as a patronizing outlook. For post-Vietnam Americans who prefer to focus on Uncle Sam's warts, his confident, mid-20th century patriotism will prove disturbing. Likewise, his prudishness on sexual matters can only produce exclamations of disbelief two generations removed from the 1940s. Although this account deals with "the good war," it is less a war book than a small piece of social history. The essence of this story is how a privileged WASP (White Anglo-Saxon Protestant) youth grew up and reached manhood with wartime duty as a Navy flyer.

The author has tried to get his facts straight, if only out of respect for the historical profession which has been so generous to him. Names have not been changed, nor is any episode fiction. That thousands of formative forces, large and small, are never noted is unavoidable. Particularly troubling are the youthful friends and associations whose names never appear in these pages yet whose affectionate counsel and laughter often meant so much to the emerging Southern California lad a half-century ago.

To the unnamed adults whose patient guidance enabled the author to finally grow up and become an educated American, all he can mutter now is a profound thank you for their hope and faith. For the Pasadena youth who flew away from 1211 Avoca Avenue, life has been far more fulfilling than he ever could have imagined, immensely more rewarding than he either earned or deserved.

ACKNOWLEDGMENTS

In one sense an autobiographical account is itself a narrative acknowledgment. To thank all those many good people whose guidance assisted with this memoir is now quite impossible.

During 1994, four loyal friends assisted me with my emerging manuscript and supplied both corrections and constructive suggestions: Professor Gerald Wheeler, Commander (USNR); Jack Goddard, Captain (USNR); Roderick C. Johnson; and Dennis Garrison. Because each approached my work from quite different perspectives, their contributions proved invaluable. Those errors that remain must be blamed on "cockpit trouble."

Librarians and archivists without whose support my account could never have become airborne deserve special recognition. Among them are: Bernard F. Cavalcante, Naval Historical Center, Washington, D.C.; Melinda Ellis, Pasadena Public Library; Steve Ewing, Patriots Point Naval and Maritime Museum, Mt. Pleasant, South Carolina; Mary Beth Hayes, Arcadia Public Library, Arcadia, California; Robert B. Harmon, San Jose State University; Audrey Herman, Sonoma County Library, Santa Rosa, California; Noel C. Holobeck, St. Louis Public Library, Missouri; G. M. LaRiviere, Hawaii State Public Library System, Hilo, Hawaii; James C. Marshall, Toledo Public Library, Toledo, Ohio; Raymond G. McInnis and Frank Haulgren, Western Washington University Library; Richard M. Schrader, National Personnel Records Center, St. Louis, Missouri; Pam Taranto, Metropolitan Cooperative Library System, Altadena, California; Charles Verrastro, Broward County Historical Society, Ft. Lauderdale, Florida; Kristen Vickerman, U.S. Naval Academy Alumni Association, Annapolis, Maryland.

The following individuals awakened dormant ideas and offered specific help on various chapters: D. C. Allard, H. R. Anderson, Dirk A. Ballendorf, Louis Blatterman, Deane Bottorf, John F. Burcham, Charles Burdick, Forrest F. Crane, Ray Crow, James P. Delgado, Roger Daniels, R. L. DeLorme, James F. Downs, Charles Fortlage, Richard F. Gentzkow, Sue and Stephen George, Thornton Hamlin, William S. Hanable, Mark A. Hardisty, Richard Harmer, Robert Harmon, Robin Higham, James Hitchman, Lawrence E. Hoyt, Samuel Hynes, Edgar G. Irwin, Morton and Jane Johnson, James B. Katke, Susan and Tom Koester, Douglas E. Leach, Bernard J. Lewis, John B. Lundstrom, Philip Marshall, Ruth Martin, Patrick McLatchey, Dan McLaughlin, Stephen T. Millikin, Robert Molleston, Raymond O'Connor, A. W. Olson, Herschel A. Pahl, Otis Pease, David L. Reineman, Clark G. Reynolds, Kevin Short, George L. Stimson, Marcell F. Varner, Richard Wartinger, Donald Whisenhunt, Paul White, and Austin Woodward.

Surely a thank you is due to the American Studies program at Indonesia's Universitas Gadjah Mada and its director, Djuhertati Imam Muhni. It was a generous Fulbright appointment there during the fall-winter 1994-1995 that permitted a polishing of this manuscript.

My industrious wife, Caryl Chesmore Hinckley, has tolerated more military history than she ever wanted to hear about. Perhaps she realized this book was a statement her husband had to make. *Terimah kasih banyak, isteri sayang.*

Ted C. Hinckley, Adjunct Professor
Western Washington University
Emeritus Professor
San Jose State University

CHAPTER I

"They'll never take my son to die in a foreign war."

"Lindbergh's gone, lady."

"He took off some time ago," commented another disappointed well-wisher.

Carrying their not yet two-year-old baby, the smartly-dressed couple returned to their auto. About them a milling crowd of fellow New Yorkers likewise deserted Long Island's Roosevelt Field. Understandably the Hinckleys' thoughts ascended to the silver *Spirit of St. Louis* monoplane and its popular pilot, the boyish, grinning Charles Lindbergh. His ambition to fly alone across the Atlantic had captured columns in the New York press.

On 20 May 1927, millions of Americans discovered just how irresistible were "Lucky Lindy's" youthful good looks and modesty. Having mastered the intricacies of the gasoline engine, a Promethean power for car-crazed 1920s Americans, Lindbergh affixed triumphant wings on that exalted symbol of individual freedom. To his countrymen's jubilation, and Europe's as well, "the mechanic who mastered the skies" had successfully completed the first solo, nonstop transatlantic flight, a hazardous feat that previously months had killed a number of veteran aviators.

In a decade famous for ephemeral newspaper celebrities, Lindbergh attained an enduring adulation. Ultimately sixty-nine countries honored him with gifts worth over two million dollars. Enthralled by the flyer's daring, the Theodore C. Hinckleys may have sensed in "America's bird man" an uplifting symbol for the future awaiting their late-in-life baby, Theodore Charles, Jr. Didn't Edison, Ford, and now Lindbergh assure dominant technological leadership for the United States? Hadn't the "war to end wars" been fought and won? Teddy's mother—a few years earlier Miss Eunice Marguerite Platt from Carthage, Missouri—glowed with optimism about her nation's future. With marriage she had promptly traded her hard-earned R.N. pin for a housewife's duties. Soon she was preparing herself for four or five children.

Neither of the Hinckleys had graduated from college. Thanks to their adventurous inclinations, and a prosperous and expanding America, each had achieved a socio-geographic mobility denied their small-town Illinois-Missouri parents. At the beginning of the century, first as a lawyer in the Philippines and then at the Panama Canal Zone (law firm of Hinckley and Ganson), Theo had traveled a lot of the world. In 1916 he had visited his sister, Louise Chopin, wife of the San Francisco

Examiner cartoonist Oscar Patrick Chopin. Eventually, Theo vowed, he too would settle in their hospitable Golden State.

By December 1927, having accumulated an estate in excess of $200,000 and weary of Manhattan's frenzy, the forty-seven-year-old attorney-businessman bade Gotham good-bye. Somewhere among southern California's numerous citrus grove-insulated communities and its sun-warmed rolling hills and rock-strewn arroyos, the Hinckleys would discover a retiree's Eden in which to raise their family. Eunice called it "the promised land." After due investigation, they settled on Pasadena for its very real cultural advantages as well as its proximity to burgeoning Los Angeles.

Before fixing on California's genteel "City of Roses," the Hinckleys spent a few months in San Francisco visiting the Chopins. The Chopins had named their own daughter after Oscar's mother, the gifted but then vaguely appreciated novelist, Kate Chopin. They rejoiced at Eunice's second child, San Francisco-born Jane Leverich Hinckley, no doubt named by her mother after the outspoken peace advocate, Jane Addams. In a few years "Uncle Pat" Chopin became a beloved figure for Teddy and Jane. He quickly won Eunice's heart by using her wavy-haired son as a model for his 1927-28 New Year cartoon, "Lindbergh, Writ in the Sky" (2 January 1928). Eunice squirreled away Chopin's original *Examiner* sketch only extracting it some years later for her son's edification.

Did she suffer a mother's anxieties when Theodore purchased Teddy his first airplane ride, a fifteen minute biplane flight out of San Francisco's Crissy Field? Belted way down in the open cockpit of the fabric-wrapped fuselage and strapped against his father, the three-year-old saw almost nothing of the Bay cities spread out below. However, he did touch California's special heaven.

Prior to their motoring across the continent to the West Coast, Theo had assured his wife he would pass the California bar examination. "Our savings might someday disappear," she warned him. Both had been born in the 1880s; the years were getting away from them. But her husband never found an auspicious time to challenge the bar. Perhaps his ego could not accept the possible sting of failure. Like too many of his peers, the illusory permanence of the twenties' prosperity had mesmerized him.

America's 1929-1933 collapse hammered the Hinckleys' Pasadena lifestyle. Swept away by the Great Depression were such accustomed luxuries as a live-in maid, seasonal opera tickets, a country club membership, and aspirations for foreign travel and a second auto. Luckily they never suffered penury. Nor did their blue-eyed towhead and his kid sister Jane ever bear the physical and psychological pain endured by millions of 1930s youngsters. Nonetheless, sobering proof that America hurt and hurt bad was commonplace. Instead of shielding their two children from the nation's harsh social dislocations, their parents—inveterate Sunday afternoon drivers—purposely acquainted them with a Los Angeles County migrant "Okie" camp, food lines for "unemployed

So what if the cruel Depression scaled back the "Major's" Pasadena retirement dreams? Here he poses with Eunice, Jane and Teddy for a 1933 portrait at their new home.

drifters", and once, inadvertently, a violent labor jurisdictional dispute on Spring Street, Los Angeles.

With little to do except manage his shrinking portfolio and care for his attractive 1211 Avoca Avenue residence, retiree Theodore Hinckley relished familiarizing his son, as well as Teddy's pals, with sporting events of every imaginable kind. Significantly the senior Hinckley's enthusiasm for organized athletics utterly failed to match his son's swelling fascination for mankind's survival game.

Periodic rings at their home's front door announced unshaven tramps requesting temporary work in exchange for "eats." Unfailingly Mother Hinckley responded with make-work and a large tray of hot food. Concurrently her husband became a pro bono publico resident attorney for the down-on-their-luck clientele wandering through neighboring taverns. Occasionally these somber, silent men would come to the Avoca Avenue house with papers for "the Major" to fill out. Having served as a captain in the Army Quartermaster Corps during the World War (in Pasadena by the 1930s the term "Great War" was fading away), Theo found it agreeable to be addressed "Major Hinckley." Teddy sensed that this denoted respect; being an Army officer and a lawyer empowered one to assist others. One evening, probably in 1933 or 1934, after the typical unsmiling man in the usual worn out clothes departed, the Major informed his son that their guest had been a soldier in the Spanish-American War. "Both of my older brothers volunteered for that war; I wanted to, but my mother wouldn't hear of it." And then with reflective pride, "No one in this family has ever been drafted." Only later would his son grasp the distinction between volunteering to get oneself killed and being drafted.

At about this same time guns, armies, battles, wars, nations, and heroic men slowly began to coalesce in his childish mind. From infancy,

Teddy had distinguished himself from other living humans; his "me" and "mine" were normal enough. A far-sighted mother made certain he benefited from nursery school and an abundance of playmates of both genders. Among his earliest memories vicariously thrusting him into a social context far beyond the immediacy of home were Bible stories and fanciful fables of every description. How comforting that menacing goblins and witches were always defeated by beautiful fairies and beneficent magical forces. To his highly impressionable mind, some of these fictional creations were as vivid as the living creatures—chicks, rabbits, guinea pigs, and kittens—which his parents randomly brought home to enliven their children. His own expanding bedroom shelf of enchanting picture books further reassured him that good boys and girls need not fear the clutches of wicked beings. But with reading mastery—belated like just about everything in his mental development—fairyland's reality dimmed, particularly after Teddy Jr. discovered the diverse miscellany shelved in Ted Sr.'s study.

Like no other place among the boy's special sanctuaries, this high-ceilinged room with its book-lined walls and commanding John Singer Sargent-like portrait of his father sparked soaring flights for Teddy's imagination. Although lacking the compelling color illustrations so commonplace today, his father's turn-of-the-century hodgepodge of dilapidated magazines, gold-embossed sets of books, and his sepia-tone photo collections provided tickets to every part of the world. Merely rustling a few pages in this paper jungle promised a profusion of foreign travel scenes. Readily available were dramatic accounts of men exploring exotic lands, and capturing wild animals. Especially seductive to the child were the tales of uniformed men challenging each other on famous battlefields.

Among the cardinal picture lessons learned by Teddy within his father's library was the universality of human violence. Beyond Pasadena, life balanced on a precarious teeter-totter. Photographs taken in Asia featured dismembered Chinese "Boxer fanatics"; other photos mingled dead, twisted bodies of American soldiers with "Filipino Insurgents." Scenes of slaughtered soldiers strewn across endless trenches recalled Europe's 1914-18 bloodbath. Books on nature, inventions, picturesque trips to Spain, Holland, and Japan, even the forever intriguing volumes on archeology never quite thrilled the lad as did the cruel, ambivalent attraction of yesterday's wars.

Old engravings in his father's *Messages and Papers of the Presidents* (James D. Richardson's compilation) of nineteenth century urban eruptions in places like Baltimore and Pittsburgh duplicated contemporary news photos of infuriated strikers appearing in his parents' daily newspapers. Beyond the security of his home, school, and familiar surroundings, all was not well in Teddy's "sweet land of liberty." Manifestly human discord was global, yesterday and today. And tomorrow? And why did petty discord turn so destructive and such baneful disputes explode into the horror of war?

Although disappointed for her Theodore and acutely mindful of his Depression-battered ego, Eunice Hinckley avoided the swamp of despond. A rural Midwesterner's practicality, powerfully reinforced by her muscular Calvinism, enabled her to perceive how really lucky was the Hinckley family. Wealth had eluded their grasp. Nonetheless, their spacious two-story, white-shingled, green-shuttered home was paid for; so was their Dodge sedan. And if the financial columnist Roger Babson was correct, Theodore's stock holdings—just as well to forget his now worthless foreign bonds—protected them from joining America's poor. That her husband had proved a faithless spouse, found a sexual partner in Los Angeles, and at times talked divorce shook her. The love denied her in marriage was compensated for in the affection she shared with a small group of women friends, and especially in the absolute devotion given to her son and daughter.

Eunice, perhaps due to the boisterousness of her own two younger brothers, rejected the over-protectiveness increasingly practiced among middle class mothers. Between the ages ten through twelve, Teddy came to realize, "You must fight your own battles." Before then, Eunice's loving solicitousness for her two children evidenced itself in all the caring traditional ways: explanations why Teddy and Jane must eat such and such food; numerous classroom visits; a plethora of reassuring hugs and kisses; and nightly bedtime stories capped by lights-out prayers. Yes, Eunice Hinckley enjoyed being a mother, but then she had been well-trained for the task.

Age twelve when her own mother died in 1899, Eunice Platt had become a surrogate mother for her three younger siblings. Disciplined by adversity, intelligent, verbal, and as stubborn as a Missouri mule, the robust young woman surprised the parochial men in her family. Big sister became not only a registered nurse but a Progressive Age woman willingly casting her future with America's booming cities. Despite the metropolis' economic and cultural allurements, her values remained rock-solid, small-town Bible belt. Unlike some regions of the United States which had enthusiastically supported President Woodrow Wilson's 1917 summons to defeat German militarism, many of Missouri's village rustics lived up to their "show me" antecedents. Some months after America entered the Great War, the pull of patriotism overcame her inherent suspicions of foreign entanglements; nurse Platt's tour of duty with the Navy was spent at New Orleans fighting the deadly influenza epidemic.

By the time of her mid-1920s marriage to a quite worldly attorney, her latent, Midwestern skepticism at "sacrificing American doughboys in a futile war" had reemerged. In heartfelt agreement with the rising isolationist crescendo, she damned the day that "Uncle Sam pulled England's chestnuts out of the fire." Ignoring her husband's insistence that Great Britain was "probably America's best friend in an increasingly hostile world," she informed anyone who would listen, "They'll never take my son to die in a foreign war."

Certainly her salubrious, self-centered Teddy had no itch to die in a foreign war; nevertheless, and much to his mother's regret, his fascination for war's indispensable tools was growing. Sometime in the mid-thirties, he accompanied his parents on a Sunday afternoon Los Angeles visit with General Robert E. Wood. Theo had first become acquainted with the Army officer in Panama, later serving under him in New York City during the war. Arriving at the Biltmore Hotel, and well-scrubbed for the occasion, Teddy, Jane, and their parents were warmly welcomed by General Wood. Much to the boy's disappointment the General had shed his uniform for mufti. In fact he was now president of America's gigantic Sears Roebuck Company.

Shortly after launching into old-times reminiscences, the retail titan observed the lad searching about his apartment. "What is Teddy looking for, Theo?" he inquired.

"Guns," the lad piped up.

Male laughter and a mother's groans. And then before her husband could short circuit his Eunice, General Wood heard, "The merchants of death are never going to take my son to die in a foreign war."

By the mid-1930s, with the expanding Japanese invasion of China, Major Hinckley found himself caught in a crossfire between an isolationist spouse and Avoca Avenue's armchair nationalists. Required to assist his father in the Saturday morning leaf-raking and curbside leaf-burning ritual, his son overheard a range of spirited exchanges. On the Democratic occupant of the White House discussion seemed unnecessary. Most everyone agreed with the Major that Franklin D. Roosevelt and Eleanor were disasters. On how to deal with "the Japs," numerous opinions surfaced. One neighbor urged halting Japan's brutal treatment of China with a flight of America's new, all metal, B-10 Martin bombers. Merely dropping bombs on ramshackle Tokyo and thereby creating a gigantic conflagration could stop their aggression. "Disastrous metropolitan fires were nothing new to Japan," the Major retorted. Perhaps armed American intervention might dissuade the Japanese military, but "waging a war all the way across the Pacific would be crazy."

The retired attorney's opinions were not without weight. After all, he had lived and worked in East Asia; his first law partner had been a Manila Chinese. Indeed, the Major dared acquaint his listeners with the fact that Japanese soldiers were extremely sturdy, hardened to survive under conditions no American soldier ever could. At that assertion, the Major ignited almost as much heat as that provided by Avoca Avenue's pungent burning eucalyptus leaves.

Fortunately for Teddy and his sister Jane, their elementary school years were for the most part filled with the carefree experiences enjoyed by children in their social class. Their special Pasadena was a WASP Pasadena. Although an acronym of later vintage, it fits. Excluding those ruined by the Depression, Pasadena's certified upper middle class WASPs shared a comfortable if rather complacent society. Eunice Hinckley fretted about this condition as well as "public ignorance." Hearing from teacher friends that there were a surprising number of children who had no idea why Christmas was actually celebrated, she built a shallow 3 X 4 foot open box, filled it with sand and miniature sheep. Behind the nativity figures a cardboard back drop displayed twinkling stars and a large angel heralding the birth of Jesus. Every Christmas thereafter, Arroyo Seco School featured "Mrs. Hinckley's crèche" just inside its front entrance. If there were protests, Teddy would surely have heard of them.

Certainly boys residing between Fair Oaks and South Orange Grove Avenues never suffered from any lack of tomfoolery. In good weather there was bicycling, tree climbing, taunting cranky oldsters, and exploring up and down the Arroyo Seco—its indigenous biota then extended all the way to Los Angeles. Empty corner lots invited dirt clod fights, digging pit forts, and the slam, bang of tackle football. For an unsurpassing thrill, nothing quite equaled sneaking up on some neighbor's home after nightfall and "pulling their switch"; a lot of older Pasadena residences retained electric switchboxes mounted on an exterior wall. To reach the power lever often necessitated climbing up on the back of a fellow culprit. Suddenly causing the victim's house to be cast into absolute darkness and then eluding punishment by flight over a back fence promised hilarious derring-do. And should rainy weather confine the miscreants, 1211 Avoca offered piles of *Famous Funnies* and *Popular Comics*, construction of wooden guns from old broom handles, playing chess or cards, swapping foreign stamps or bubble gum cards, and casting lead soldiers.

Pasadena's cavernous civic auditorium featured all-city children's musical programs consisting of selections from some of the world's finest symphonic music. Like much else in the 1930s cultural realm, these superb professional performances were paid for by Roosevelt's New Deal, legislation paradoxically damned by Pasadena's prosperous WASPs. Ballroom dancing lessons at the Huntington Hotel and the recently completed Vista del Arroyo likewise mixed genders. Along with church and school pageants, the Pasadena Playhouse supplied delightful adaptations of children's classic literature. Appreciated by all the Hinckleys were the occasional inspections of the treasures displayed at the nearby Southwest Museum and the Los Angeles Natural History Museum. For their son it was no contest when given the choice of visiting San Marino's decorous Huntington Art Gallery or nearby Zane's Lion Farm.

A summer activity exceeded in pure pleasure only by the fireworks mayhem of the Fourth of July was swimming at Brookside Municipal Park's "plunges." Frequently, but never often enough, a carful of Teddy and his pals would be let out there at midday, and following an afternoon of boyhood ecstasy, granted the privilege of walking home. The hike from the park down the length of Orange Grove Avenue all the way to Columbia Street, the border between South Pasadena and Pasadena and the neighborhood where most of his friends lived, was a long one. Munching licorice sticks and chattering about Orange Grove Avenue's most imposing residences and their legendary occupants—Did Mrs.

Wrigley's comatose body still quiver within her magnificent chalk-white mansion?—capped off a perfect day.

It was probably "Negro Day" at the Brookside pools which first forced Teddy to personally acknowledge Pasadena's legacy of racial discrimination. Previously his father had driven him through the city's African-American enclave north of California Street, carefully pointing out the numerous shiny new autos parked in front of homes with trash-strewn front yards. Dumped at Brookside Park by a hurried parent, he and his pals abruptly recognized that the forever inviting swimming pools were thrashing not with white bodies but exclusively with black ones. Was the gatekeeper half-asleep or did he appreciate that these Caucasian boys represented the "dominant race"? Whatever, the white kids paid up, went through the turnstile, and had a perfectly marvelous time. Afterward Teddy asked his parents why the separation of Pasadenans. His father mumbled something about health codes. More shamefacedly, his mother replied, "To avoid trouble." Their son had only the foggiest understanding of lynchings, race riots, and other vicious manifestations of black-white tensions. Previously racial antagonisms had been abstractions located in his father's books detailing Negro slavery in Africa and throughout the Americas. Henceforth arbitrary distinctions between human beings were recognized not only as economic and regional but racial.

From at least his seventh year, Teddy had played cowboys and Indians with his friends. Saturday afternoon movies more often than not portrayed American Indians as the bad guys. Like grizzly bears, they usually got killed. However, the boys living around the intersection of Avoca Avenue, Oak Lawn Avenue, and State Street frequently preferred being Indians. Indians could sneak up better and knew how to survive in the wilderness. Lucky them, they didn't have to conform to WASP strictures. Being a "wild savage," at least until dinner time, afforded an infinity of "let's pretend." Was it by parental design or mere chance that a family outing cast a grim, haunting Indian shadow across the boy's conscience?

Set in a large natural amphitheater at Hemet, California, the annual "Ramona Pageant" (drawn from Helen Hunt Jackson's novel *Ramona*) captivated Teddy and, to a degree, his not unsophisticated parents. The tragedy exuded an almost classical Greek determinism. Alessandro, the pageant's central male figure, was a mission Indian. Notwithstanding his best efforts to acculturate, including his marriage to a ranchero's lovely daughter Ramona, Alessandro was, in the pageant's climactic scene, gunned down by land-grabbing Americans. Gentle Alessandro's spectacular death at white hands not only ruined Teddy's savage Indian stereotype but compelled him to evaluate his own culture. This was not a fresh exercise. Parents and teachers had already probed "with liberty and justice for all." *Ramona*'s intermingling of Native American, Hispanic, and Yankee values, the pageant's spectacular setting and its colorful dramatization evoked an unforgettable respect for California's grinding, historical human cost.

That a durable Christian morality might take root within her children must surely have been among Eunice Hinckley's commonest prayers. In the 1930s, Pasadena was blessed with a truly outstanding number of church leaders. Embellishing their pulpits were the impressive church edifices in which these pastors preached. For over a half a century American Protestantism had been promoting large multifaceted churches equipped to serve swelling congregations. Colorado Street's Pasadena Presbyterian Church (PPC) had it all: an indoor roller skating rink and a basketball court for kids and marriage counseling and scholarly classes for adults. PPC even included its own KPPC radio station. At its pastoral helm was scholarly Dr. Robert Freeman; his equally gifted wife Margery taught at nearby Occidental College. Indeed, some described Oxy and even the city's popular YMCA as extensions of PPC.

This church assured the Hinckleys' son a happy Sabbath refuge from the onerous demands of public school labors. Sunday school always began with an ivory-pounding, middle-aged female pianist exuberantly playing one of three peppy hymns: "When Morning Gilds the Skies," "For the Beauty of the Earth," or "This Is My Father's World." Dr. James Leishman, PPC's co-pastor, exhibited a saintly patience repeatedly tested by Teddy and his errant Sunday school chums. One Lord's day, the pranksters launched three or four airplanes from the fourth floor of the Christian education building. Crafted from that morning's Bible lesson, one of them landed almost squarely on Dr. Leishman's snow-white head. Fearful of the scowls and a shaking fist certain to be directed at them, the paralyzed miscreants looked down in utter befuddlement upon an upturned, smiling Franciscan face. Gently waving his hand, he collected the boys' handiwork and strolled away.

Within this Presbyterian community, John Wesley's triumphant confidence in man's inherent goodness easily eclipsed John Calvin's harsh strictures. Its membership was exclusively Caucasian. If there were poor Pasadenans among PPC's congregation, and surely there were, the overwhelming atmosphere generated by its Sunday school teachers was one of upbeat Christian success. Within Teddy's boyish mind the love personified by Jesus and the verity and practicality of his message was absolute. Thank God for a Christian indoctrination. That religious anchor may have prevented a future loosening of both his mental and moral moorings when the sensitive lad faced the cannon's mouth about which he so foolishly fantasized.

Early on, Mother Hinckley had also begun brainwashing Teddy and Jane that their bodies were "holy temples given on loan by God." By high school, Ted had developed the usual hearing difficulty where his parents were concerned, but of the dozens of maxims which Eunice had pounded into her son's sluggish brain, "the body is a holy temple" had fortunately become ineradicable. Anything that might seriously impair his body was to be prudently weighed. When a prominent and extremely persuasive Pasadena Junior College athlete appeared at church and cogently condemned tobacco and liquor in any form, Teddy joined the water brigade. Because his beer-drinking father occasionally lighted up a Lucky cigarette, he deemed these less hazardous, but liabilities nonetheless.

Since nursery school strange notions had agitated him. Periodically the troubled child sought his mother's counsel about what she labeled "evil" or "bad" thoughts or conduct. Bragging, selfishness, envy of others, an itch to steal, to lie and cheat, the Devil's fatal allurements discouraged him. Condemnation of such attitudes and actions by parents, housekeepers, relatives, and an expanding circle of adult associations continued to fortify his widening moral sensibilities, if not his behavior.

To punish misbehavior became "Eunice's responsibility." Whether laying on with the children's discarded balloon sticks or her own durable yardstick, she never flinched when duty demanded her son be whipped. Only twice did his father thrash him. In both instances a quite thorough beating occurred after insulting the opposite gender. In the first instance his licking came after he used a garden hose to soak an unoffending woman neighbor through her kitchen window. The second thrashing took place at about sixth grade after he deliberately flaunted his sexual organs before his sister.

He must have been about ten when those inevitable Dionysian pulsations first beset him. Peering through the keyhole separating his room from his sister's in order to discover what Jane and her friends were up to, he discovered they were preparing to take a bath. Much to his astonishment, his penis grew. The following day he asked his mother why this hardening had taken place. An unprecedented silence followed. The mystery was only solved a few days later when his father recounted an abbreviated and revised version of Carlo Collodi's *Pinocchio*. In this instance Pinocchio's nose grew longer as his eyes repeatedly violated the privacy of others. Not until junior high school when Teddy's peers supplied him "the truth about sex" did he feel entirely sure about his nose. Of course by that time the periodic flights of his penis were a petty torment neither fable nor father could resolve.

One of the numberless axioms and proverbs endlessly repeated by Eunice Hinckley was, "An idle mind is the devil's playground." Her son's generally idle mind at Pasadena's Arroyo Seco Elementary School can only have depressed her. She could not blame his lethargy on the school's teachers who were, by and large, excellent. Amiable enough and generally polite to his teachers, her Teddy unfortunately surrendered to sloth whenever demanding study reared its frowning face. Reading proved acceptable; writing was generally disagreeable. In almost any form, arithmetic added up to agony. Mercifully, playground recesses and class singing of "Anchors Aweigh" and "My Bonnie Lies over the Ocean" interspersed joyful release from desk drudgery.

Perhaps because he too had been a poor pupil, the lad's father rarely if ever rebuked him for his lackluster class work. Possibly his son's pack rat enthusiasm—shelves of "Big Little Books," United States and international stamp books, matchbooks and soda bottle caps, Wild West and Pirate bubble gum cards—and Teddy's swelling aviation and war news scrapbooks may have indicated all was not lost. Like his spouse,

Theo missed few opportunities to expand the horizons of his children's minds. Summertime meant regular visits to Pasadena's outstanding public library; books were checked out by every family member. Eunice fantasized her son as A. A. Milne's Christopher Robin; however, he much preferred to mingle with the exotic menagerie filling the pages of L. Frank Baum's Oz books.

In mid-1932, eager to show off her two children to old friends and family, Eunice journeyed with them back to her Missouri hometown. The warm hospitality accorded the three Hinckleys more than matched Carthage's hot summer weather; some citizens may have suspected that Eunice Platt's seemingly successful marriage had become wobbly. Nearly as important as the message delivered to Theodore by that train trip east was her determination to acquaint Jane and Teddy with the virtues of small town, Midwestern life. Swimming and fishing at Carthage's mill pond and leaping from an abandoned hay loft into what had become a flivver's stable remained unforgettable delights. Quite different synapses responded when his mother arranged for "Uncle John," a distant relative, to familiarize Teddy with farming and "the people who made America great." That four-day farm experience alerted the boy's senses to the yeoman myth long before historians discovered it. A twelve-hour work day, an utter lack of electricity, voracious chiggers, and the redolent stench of squishy, shoe-clinging sheep and cattle manure—who in their right mind would freely join "God's people"?

Family movie-going took off during the mid-1930s, only ebbing when high school-age exclusiveness asserted itself. For musical romance, there was Ruby Keeler and Dick Powell, Ginger Rogers and Fred Astaire, and especially entrancing, Nelson Eddy and Jeanette McDonald. Schlock? If so, it was harmless schlock. At about sixth grade, McDonald along with Olivia DeHaviland and Sonja Heine formed an odd constellation in Teddy's unreachable galaxy. Laughter, sometimes a tear or two, accompanied Mickey Rooney's *Andy Hardy* series. Watching the mirth of his usually sober-faced parents enjoying Will Rogers and Charlie Chaplin movies warmed Teddy almost as much as his mother's post-show strawberry shortcake. Realistic motion pictures such as Hollywood's powerful *The Good Earth* and the Martin and Osa Johnson African travelogues guaranteed lively suppertime discussions.

Only once did the Hinckleys expose son and daughter to a horror movie. Halfway through King Kong their eight-year-old son hid under his seat; not until the giant ape finally toppled from the Empire State Building did the thoroughly frightened boy return to his seat. Nor did he appreciate parental chuckles at his nighttime protests about the "goblins hiding under my bed." Teddy's refusal to take out the garbage after dark, particularly when his kid sister suffered no qualms whatsoever, did perhaps disconcert them. Eunice didn't want her son to be a soldier, but a coward?

On national holidays, 1211 Avoca Avenue proudly displayed the Stars and Stripes. Mealtime grace only occasionally included public figures; the Hinckleys' palpable dislike for "that man in the White House" discomfited Teddy. Prayers for peace and the less fortunate were common enough. Just as Theo's children never saw him in church, they never heard him pray. Religious practices, like public school activities, were Eunice's charge. Among his paternal duties, the Major sought to familiarize his son with the sacrifices necessary for maintaining American independence. Eunice reluctantly agreed that the arrival at San Pedro of America's venerated Old Ironsides, the USS *Constitution*, called for a family outing. Here was indeed living history; a three-masted fighting vessel launched when George Washington was president, this frigate had repeatedly defeated British warships during the War of 1812. On these very decks had strode Navy greats like Decatur, Bainbridge, and Hull.

For Teddy it was a heady experience, made even more exciting by the sky-filling presence of the recently-completed dirigible, the USS *Macon*. In bad repute due to the crashes of earlier sister airships, the Navy was bending every effort to convince skeptical taxpayers that the huge 785-foot long *Macon* combined observation, antisubmarine surveillance, and a bombing potential like nothing in the fleet. The Hinckleys missed an actual demonstration of this immense mother craft bringing aboard her four hook-on F9C-2 Sparrow Hawks. Nevertheless, Teddy's vigorous imagination had no trouble visualizing the biplanes' cloud level trapeze act. Two years later on 12 February 1935, the Pacific Ocean claimed the *Macon* and her fighter plane protectors. Good luck and good training enabled all but two of the eighty-three officers and men aboard to scramble to safety. The *Macon*'s demise spelled the end for the Navy's rigid airship program. Uncle Sam, however, had only begun his naval buildup.

Bad enough the ceaseless killing in China, but the possibility of yet another terrible European war appeared increasingly likely. Different generations utilized different sources for comprehending America's slide into a Second World War. After the *Los Angeles Times* published a large brown-tone map detailing Italy's invasion of Ethiopia, ten-year-old Teddy thumbtacked it to the wall of his back porch room. Correspondence and conversations with old Panama friends had about persuaded his father that another world war was indeed coming. Unless the United States prepared itself, "We might get an awful drubbing."

Curious about naval preparedness, for it was the U.S. Navy that must protect his old Panama and Philippine haunts, the Major selected Navy Day, 27 October 1935, to inspect what some purported to be America's most powerful maritime weapon. Utterly unaware of the saltwater thrills awaiting them, his son accompanied him. Joining the dockside crowd of school children and parents celebrating the Navy's 160th birthday, the two Hinckleys were soon skimming across San Pedro harbor. Anchored offshore lay an immense gray structure. Had it not been for the aircraft carrier's concave bow, Teddy might have presumed the almost 900-foot vessel was a towering steel castle. The USS *Lexington* (CV-2), like her sister leviathan, *Saratoga* (CV-3), had originally been laid down as a battle cruiser in 1921. Seven years later the *Lexington* joined the West Coast fleet at San Pedro, thereafter participating each year in fleet maneuvers about the Hawaiian Islands, in the Caribbean, off the Panama Canal, and in the eastern Pacific.

In 1910, a barnstorming American pilot named Eugene Ely had first flown an airplane off a war vessel. Planes launched from a British warship had actually bombed German dirigible hangers during the World War. Theo had heard a lot about General "Billy" Mitchell's struggle to convince America's military leaders that aerial bombardment must radically affect naval warfare. But on that ebullient 1935 Navy Day, graced by warm southern California weather, even Neptune himself would have had difficulty envisioning this "Queen of the Flattops" bombed and blazing, desperately struggling to remain afloat.

An ecstatic Teddy joined the hundreds of other children surging through the *Lexington*'s labyrinthine passageways. Eagerly he devoured a big sugar cookie extended him by a grinning Navy cook. A huge elevator for transferring aircraft from the hanger deck to the flight deck returned the chattering, laughing throng topside. Parked on the carrier's vast flight deck, were a flock of freshly-painted Grumman F2F-1 war birds of Navy Air's Fighting Two squadron (VF-2B). Suddenly a loud speaker squawked. Deck personnel scrambled and parents grabbed their kids. Abruptly Teddy found himself half-lifted, half-thrown onto the net catwalk bordering the port side of the flight deck. Saltwater sparkled far below the wiggling, yelling children, and their not exactly happy parents. Across from them a stubby, bi-winged fighter plane coughed impatiently, and then with a roar from its engine, shot off the bow. Everyone cheered.

A wave-splashed Navy liberty boat returned father and son dockside. An hour or so later an intoxicated ten-year-old, reached his own Pasadena home port. Did Eunice Hinckley discern the rusting futility of a mother's vow? How easily, how very easily the male weld of military membership could supplant a woman's steely protest, "They'll never take my son to die in a foreign war."

CHAPTER II

"Japan has attacked Pearl Harbor."

Bullets from the attacking Japanese airplanes repeatedly ripped into the American gunboat. Topside, the doomed vessel's crewmen bravely if futilely manned their old-fashioned Lewis guns and continued hammering away at the diving, roaring warplanes. It was December, a month in which Americans traditionally give thanks for the year's blessings and prayerfully prepare for a good new year. Japan's surprise attack sent shock waves across the United States. Who had ordered these Japanese pilots to bomb the USS *Panay* as well as the three Standard Oil tankers? Especially reprehensible was the strafing of the survivors seeking a shelter along the Yangtze's river bank.

Four months earlier, in mid-September 1937, the eleven-year-old had carefully penned his full name, Theodore Charles Hinckley Jr., on the form admitting him to Pasadena's McKinley Junior High School. From now on, he informed his parents, it would be, "Ted, no more Teddy."

With McKinley friends planning father and son banquet.
(left to right: Jim Stoddard, David Monsen, Vice-principal A. L. Howell, author, and Austin Woodward.)

Seated in South Pasadena's Rialto Theater, the four Hinckleys, like millions of other American families viewing the latest newsreel at their local movie theater, watched in angry amazement. Slowly the United States gunboat *Panay* sank into the Yangtze's muddy waters. Her clearly marked stars and stripes put the lie to Japan's initial explanation that its pilots were confused. Would the gunboat's destruction ignite a war with the far off island nation? Japan had recently seized China's capital; sensational reports of her soldiers' rape of Nanking filled the newspapers.

President Roosevelt's "Quarantine Address"—an attempt to create war hysteria in America, snapped an infuriated Eunice Hinckley—had preceded the "nonsensical *Panay* war talk." "Protecting the Rockefellers' Far Eastern oil," she fumed, "is not worth the life of a single American." Husband Theodore reacted more realistically. Had the retiree kept a diary, he might well have agreed with the nation's Secretary of the Interior who did keep one. "I am becoming imbued with the idea," wrote Harold L. Ickes, "that sooner or later the democracies of the world, if they are to survive, will have to join issue—armed issue—with the fascist nations."

But Japan was not yet ready to fight a transpacific war with the United States. For the *Panay*'s loss of two men and some thirty wounded, the Tokyo foreign office quickly tendered its most profound apologies while paying full monetary compensation, $2,214,007.36. The sight of hundreds of smiling, peace-seeking Japanese school children waving American flags touched Ted Jr. What impressed his father was the remarkable speed with which Nippon's government voiced its regrets and the effusive follow-up amends from leading Japanese citizens.

Seeking an explanation for the grisly *Life* magazine photo of Japanese soldiers testing their bayonets on rope-bound, live Chinese prisoners, Ted consulted his father. Theo recalled his own East Asian experiences. "Life is cheap there; quite likely the Chinese are practicing equally barbarous acts." Ted had just read the award-winning 1930s children's book, *Young Fu of the Upper Yanqtze*; Young Fu's grinding struggles included cruelty at the hands of Chinese soldiers. Patently there was no reason to dispute the elder Hinckley's solomonic wisdom.

Ted's continued abhorrence of mental discipline easily defeated any real classroom victories. Fortunately, centrally located McKinley Junior High (grades seven through ten), like the lad's Arroyo Seco Elementary School, possessed an unusually strong faculty. But scholarly respectability simply could not compete with his own joyful exploratory reading, his kaleidoscopic collections and hobbies—the most current being the tedious fabrication of balsa wood model airplanes. Ted's mantra: freedom from dutiful responsibilities. Outranking virtually every other abstract value was his emerging quest for peer approval; funtime participation in youth groups, organized and disorganized, compensated for his poor classroom performance. Blissful ignorance shielded the self-complacent juvenile from the variant ambiguities balancing social responsibility and individual power. But he was discovering that power had many faces.

By eighth grade parental punitive power meant not only economic loss but a denial of weekly radio shows featuring America's "gangbusting G-Men." In fact, parental leverage for directing their son's life was waning. Steadily, exquisitely supplanting this dependency were the gentle tentacles of junior high's peer friendships. Theo and Eunice wisely, if hesitantly, recognized that their love must inevitably be compromised by a teenager's consuming school and community socialization. Within him, adolescent friendships were generating mysterious emotional gratification; from without they interposed authentic, applicable explanations for life itself.

Anglo pupils formed McKinley's dominant majority; fortunately Pasadena's mid-city 1930s ethnic mix was reflected in the school's student body. Mexican-Americans, African-Americans, and Japanese-Americans mingled freely in most aspects of on campus life.

If the African-American teenagers excelled in disproportionate numbers in athletics, they appeared invisible in almost everything else. Sporadic in classroom attendance, sometimes disappearing for an entire semester or even a year, they formed a seemingly happy-go-lucky group. Never having before associated with Negroes, Ted identified with their usual good-naturedness, although at first bewildered how even a mindless reference to their skin color incited anger. Luckily his father, as well as older white youths, had previously warned him, "Don't rub them the wrong way; Negroes have explosive tempers." Twice during his four McKinley years, Ted witnessed bloody knuckles after school fights in which they gave an admirable account of themselves.

The industrious Tommy Kelly, an African-American classmate, stereotypical in every physical feature, repeatedly matched his ablest white classroom competitors. Thankfully Kelly and some talented Negro girl students disabused their WASP associates of any notions that black people were inherently inferior. Male or female, few if any of them participated in upper-middle class, WASP, off campus, evening social functions. At school, the history of Negroes—never "Blacks"—was limited to social studies discussions of slavery, abolitionism and post-Civil War figures like George Washington Carver and Booker T. Washington. Alert teachers made certain that disgraceful contemporary outrages such as the Scottsboro Boys' injustice were not excluded.

In stark contrast with the generally unmotivated African-American pupils were the Nisei, virtually the sole representatives of East Asian immigrants in McKinley's class of 1941. Cosmopolite Theo never tired of ruminating about the energetic, tightly woven Asian family. Summertime Hinckley family beach excursions required driving through market gardens southeast of Alhambra; invariably these trips found the Major alerting his youthful passengers to the Japanese-American stoop labor sweating among their truck crops in nearby fields. In one form or another he habitually remarked, "While we play, they work. Someday they won't be in those fields." For Ted Jr., the predicted someday was now. The teenage Asians' competitiveness in the classroom and in sports was as consistent as their upbeat, wisecracking repartee. Well before Ted's tenth grade graduation, one of them won election as president of the entire student body. Ted's conclusion: "These guys are winners."

McKinley's Mexican-Americans were neither winners nor losers. In part, they escaped the invisibility customarily cloaking African-American students because their California roots went deeper than those of any other non-Indian ethnic group. Since elementary school, in reading assignments and playground pageants, Ted's public school teachers— themselves predominantly WASP—repeatedly alluded to the "Spaniards," rarely "Mexicans," chronological seniority. The educators' proof might include: Los Angeles' historic Olivera Street; less than a century ago Rancho San Pasqual (Pasadena) had been Mexican territory; and the popular movie star Leo Carrillo was a direct descendant of Mexican California's governing aristocracy. Predating even the rancheros' pastoral California was the enduringly impressive architectural heritage of Father Serra's missionary labors; nearby missions San Gabriel and San Fernando provided frequent excursion sites for the Hinckleys' out-of-town guests. And Old Mexico itself lay just south of San Diego.

Ted cherished the Mexican-American kids' melodic speech, but never enough to advance his fluency much beyond, "¿Como esta usted? " Why large numbers of them lived in rundown houses and relatively few participated in school activities rather perplexed him, doubly so since, unlike Negro teenagers, and even the Japanese-Americans, the soft-spoken Latinos, their bilingual ability excepted, appeared so WASP-like. Indeed, one Hispanic contemporary had the improbable name of George Hinckley. Cheerful personalities like Gus Fernandez, Paul Garcia, and Angel Contraras generally brightened Ted's day; like himself, they smilingly, silently suffered through their studies. Ted had been admonished, "The moochies carry knives and fight in packs; don't cross one." He did witness a couple of Latino fights—one with a quite wealthy Anglo—fierce, slugging contests, but he never saw a knife. Like all of McKinley's bloody-nosed boys becoming men, they "fought fair."

Heaven knows why the Hinckleys' son felt obliged in seventh grade to provoke a fight. He carefully selected a quite benign peer, a WASP youth who could make it a fair fight. Insisting he had been insulted—some ridiculous argument in wood shop class—they agreed to meet after school, each with his seconds. After wrestling around a bit, and drawing not a drop of blood and neither able to best the other, the fight—it was hardly that—ended. Reflecting on this inanity afterward, the Hinckleys' son shamefully confessed to himself that he had brought no honor whatsoever on himself; doubly humiliating, he had failed to win a contrived fight.

Grievously more corrosive was his daily rejection of academic accountability and the disappointment he knew this brought his parents. Possibly Eunice Hinckley took heart in that her beau ideal, Charles Lindbergh, had at first been a poor student, an uninspired

school dropout. Pleased that her son's savings had enabled him to purchase a worn but workable toy sixteen millimeter movie projector for
thirty-five cents, she presented him with a ten-minute film featuring
Lucky Lindy. Hearing that her son had given a film talk on America's
"Lone Eagle" to some very patient neighbors, she located a used copy of
Lindbergh's *We*. To the budding adolescent the famous pilot's literary
description of his relationship with his *Spirit of St. Louis* proved less
appealing than the media-hyped aftershocks of the sensational
"Lindbergh kidnapping."

Fortuitously propping up Ted's uninspired learning was the
more zealous schoolwork by his neighborhood friends. Of the
dozen or so bright, animated young men
whose company he so
highly prized, pals with
whom he had bonded
since early elementary
school and whose
friendships he continued to cherish until
military service spun
them off into adulthood, three influenced
him profoundly.

Singularly consequential in shaping his
mind and character
was Larry Hoyt and his
mother, Eleanor Hoyt.
To each of her three
sons—Larry was the
middle lad—she endowed elevated intellectual gifts and a personal commitment to
secure a superior education. Ultimately Ted

*Another mother for the author, the remarkable Eleanor Hoyt
pictured here with her gifted son, Larry, challenged Ted to
"stop fooling around and measure up." In her Red Cross
Auxiliary uniform, "Mom" Hoyt radiates justified pride in a
second naval officer son.*

would act upon her
challenge, but refractively, thanks to pal
Larry.

Eleanor Fitch Hoyt was a product of Smith College and the recipient
of a modest family inheritance; indeed, the Hoyts were in an exclusive

minority who still enjoyed a live-in maid and country club membership. With her blazing smile, athletic salubrity, and delightfully supple mind, "Mom" Hoyt provided a refreshing change from Ted's own portly, unglamorous mother. Both women were certified WASPs; but while one fiercely defended Victorian values, the other welcomed the new age of accelerating change. Staunch Republicans, they nonetheless disagreed on how to confront the looming specter of another world war. Ted was the beneficiary of their differing opinions and philosophies.

Even after England stood steadfast and alone before Hitler's juggernaut, Eunice Hinckley remained adamantly isolationist. Urbane Eleanor Hoyt voiced a vigorous dissent. Correctly discerning that the rampaging Nazi conquests mandated arms aid for embattled England, support only stopping short of a congressional declaration of war, she boldly insisted that advances in aviation had compromised the Atlantic moat. Reflecting a midwestern, middle-class, small-town America, Eunice voiced a religious fundamentalist's inherent pessimism about the human condition. Mom Hoyt, in contrast, exuded a refreshing joie de vivre acquired from her comfortable East Coast upper middle-class antecedents. It made little difference whether the woman was playing golf, singing Jerome Kern tunes at her piano, discussing politics, or poking fun at one of the four Hoyt males she so nimbly juggled, Eleanor Hoyt enlivened her associates. Deftly combining a society matron's charm with a diplomat's analytical perspective of public affairs, her opinions counted among Pasadenans who mattered.

Like Ted, Larry enjoyed an attractive, confident personality. In sports, as with the fair sex, they were well matched; in the classroom it was no contest. Larry won honors; his pal doodled. In part, Ted's aimlessness may explain his affection for Lawrence Stimson.

As a son of George L. Stimson, a prominent Southern California architect, Lawrence, like Larry and Ted, never tasted the Depression's bitter broth. For Ted he provided a Huck Finn friendship that the far more predictable Tom Sawyer, Larry Hoyt, shunned. Lawrence was not a "bad boy"; lawbreakers were lepers in the eyes of the

Stimmy dared his peers, worried all adults, and grew up to become a hot-shot Army Air Corps pilot.

Hinckleys' son. "Stimmy" simply had to reach further to fulfill boyhood to manhood's expectations. Whether risking his life emulating Tarzan in Pasadena's abundant trees, climbing precipitous cliffs along the Arroyo Seco, or designing finger smashing explosives, Lawrence's imagination never ran short of escapades to worry young and old. The rapidity with which this errant youth recovered from the stern senior Stimson's whippings astonished his playmates. More protracted than the thrashings administered in other homes, each whop of the architect's razor strop was echoed by a depressingly mournful howl. Then after what seemed an eternity, a red-eyed Lawrence would come dashing out of his handsome Oak Lawn home as eager as ever to join the gang in yet another frolic. Upon his dad's sudden death, he ran away. Four days later, after wandering around nearby Monrovia's tiny airport, the hungry lad returned home. Among Ted's comrades it was Stimmy who first possessed his own gun, his own radio, his own auto, and first flew an airplane. He also became the torchbearer who first dared enter the mysterious door unlocked by "not nice girls."

Like Ted, Jim Downs lived in the National Geographics's world. Life offered so much to do and see; why so little time?

If the two Larrys formed Twain's classic counterparts, Tom and Huck, Jim Downs can be cast as Nigger Jim. A Caucasian, Jim was definitely not an upper-crust Pasadena WASP but lived in one of Avoca Avenue's small, weathered little bungalows. Jim's dad had been a Navy enlisted man in the "war to end wars." From his barrel chest extended two exceedingly muscular arms; the right forearm was properly tattooed, terminating at a hand with no thumb. Even attired in a snappy, white shirt and a rainbow necktie, the proletarian's gnarled, mangled hands protruded like menacing bear traps. Rembrandt, better, Van Gogh, and definitely not Sargent, should have painted him. Stocky, shorter than his lighthearted wife, and gifted with a rich loquacity, Jim's "old man"—an apt expression but one none of Ted's other pals ever employed when referring to their fathers—stridently defended the goodness of Roosevelt's New Deal. His wrath fell on America's malignant bankers. Within this laboring man's home, Roosevelt, the premier wealthy WASP from Hyde Park, became a mixture of St. Francis and Robin Hood.

A romantic like Ted, Jim found Clio's charms irresistible. Surely history's Muse must have smiled at their boyish babble as the two youths refought military history and vicariously explored the world of transpacific peoples. Perhaps Ted's freest adolescent hours were those meandering hikes on nearby Raymond Hill accompanied by his handsome Dalmatian, Beau Geste, and pals Jim, Stimmy, and Larry. Nature had refashioned the slopes surrounding Pasadena's vanished Raymond Hotel with grass carpets perfect for kite flying and youths' soaring flights of fancy. Unlike Ted, Jim's socio-economic background denied him the niceties of hotel cotillions, expensive summer excursions, and the soirees at South Orange Grove Avenue's spacious homes. Like sports awards and classroom scores, life's inequalities, in Ted's complacent eyes, remained a given.

What about life's physical agony as well as its cruel brevity? By his frosh year of high school, sorrowfully, unavoidably, Ted had learned these lessons. Dreams of football glory evaporated when Osgood-Schlatter disease attacked his knees and necessitated months of painful, plaster cast-encumbered recuperation. A happy-go-lucky McKinley classmate heroically attempting to save three sisters from drowning joined them in death. Deaths of Grandmother Hinckley (Fanny Maddox Hinckley) and beloved Uncle Pat snapped irreplaceable branches from the family tree. Doubly sobering was the sudden death of next door neighbor Gregory Marshall. Father of Gregory Jr. and Philip, two of Ted's pals, the senior Marshall was a beloved figure on Avoca Avenue. Forever laughing, he invariably found time to chat and even to romp with the fledgling adolescents. But the Depression's crushing woes topped by his own business burdens eventually proved just too heavy to bear. His suicide met with Eunice's disapproval; Theo called it "a brave act."

Certainly Ted's and Jane's mother never had any reluctance about articulating moral judgments. On occasion, serendipity reinforced her commitment to shape within her children a "Christian conscience." One Saturday morning, itching to try out a friend's newly fashioned sling shot, Ted spotted an inoffensive neighborhood girl some distance off. "See if you can hit her." The weapon snapped, the rock sped at its target, and there was a scream. Grace Peter's cheek had been pierced just below her eye; almost immediately her gentle face became blood red. Fortunately the wound quickly repaired itself; regrettably, its scar refused to disappear. For years thereafter Ted's conscience flinched whenever he saw the victim of his mindless impetuosity.

Reflexive humanitarian actions by Theodore and Eunice reminded their next generation what civitas meant. On one occasion, while motoring down Fremont Avenue, the Major abruptly braked his auto, jumped out, and broke up a quite uneven juvenile sidewalk fight. Less dramatically, Eunice Hinckley periodically halted the family car beside a neighborhood bus stop where middle-aged cleaning women sat. "Going our way?" If she was, the part-time maid saved a dime, and in the thirties a dime could buy two large candy bars or a thin cheese sandwich at a "greasy-spoon" restaurant. Pro forma, "civic duties" by the Hinckleys generally included voting, paying taxes, and participation in diverse community improvement functions, involvements which tacitly reminded their progeny that youth was definitely not the axis about which the world turned.

For Ted's gang, Headlee L. Blatterman perfectly demonstrated how the mid-twentieth century world was being transformed. With his large, round pocket watch and bespectacled countenance, amiable Blatterman, chief engineer at Los Angeles' radio station KFI, typified America's confident technologists. The respected inventor's gadget-filled home, situated on State Street five houses removed from the Hinckleys', was an applied laboratory of the rapidly dawning electronic age. His son Noodles—by junior high it was Louie—introduced Avoca's youngsters to television entertainment; almost as enthralling were the fine musical recordings and theatrical productions emanating from the senior Blatterman's large, oversized disks and impressive array of sound systems.

Armed with their slide rules and drawing boards, Southern California's electronic wizards, like the state's cocky airplane designers, smiled triumphantly as they shriveled planet Earth. Mild-mannered, serenely confident, technocrat Blatterman never imagined anyone would object to the sky-piercing, eighty-foot transmission pole he implanted in his side yard; after all, it was his property and it did point upward to the future. Attorney Hinckley reacted otherwise. Following a gentlemanly confrontation, the shaft assumed a profile in proportion with its surrounding palms.

Among the adult Hinckleys, Hoyts, Stimsons, Marshalls, Blattermans, and yes, Downs, there existed an unwritten but firmly adhered to social contract. Its elementary tenets: adults were wiser than children; work preceded pleasure; those in public authority must be respected; and all Humankind could claim an inherent dignity. Predictably, kids violated their seniors' contract. Just as predictably, they paid a price for doing so. Most of their urbanite parents, men and women, so well served by man's mechanical marvels gave only passing thought to an earlier age's assiduous "glorification of God." But if their tacit social contract excluded the Almighty, the indispensability of the Judeo-Christian golden rule remained solid enough.

Neither by the Avoca Avenue gang nor by most of their associates were pejorative ethnic slurs commonly employed. Living so comfortably in a predominantly white Christian cocoon, why should they have been? Jew, depending on its usage, was a human category of periodic interest around the Hinckley dinner table. The Jew Jesus accounted for some of this, as did relevant tidbits of Old Testament history. "Jews," noted the evening meal's magistrate, "have suffered the greatest persecution; that's why they have developed such a rich sense of humor"; Jewish radio comedians like Joe Penner, Gracie Allen, Jack Benny, and Eddie Cantor left the attorney's paradox unassailable. Nevertheless, suspicions of Jewish commercial acumen compelled him to caution his children about Hebrew dexterity at driving hard bargains.

Nazi Germany's night of terror, *Kristallnacht*, shook Ted's parents. Ugly new words like "scapegoat," "abominable," and "pogrom" entered Ted's vocabulary; familiar concepts like "exodus," "martyrdom," and "the crucified Christ" took on a relevancy as never before. Among his maturing teenage friends at school, church, summer camps, everywhere, the brutality of Europe's dictatorships was awakening a latent appreciation for democracy. Technicolor footage of Japan's aerial assault on Chungking reminded West Coast residents of all ages of the evaporating security of America's Pacific moat.

Concurrently capturing the attention of Ted and his pals was the successful "final leg completion" of Pan American World Airway's China Clipper route. The transpacific passage promised "safe and comfortable flights" between Hong Kong and San Francisco. Islands such as Guam, Midway, and Wake won a currency heretofore monopolized by Oceania's Hawaii and the Philippines. Quickly assembled pine wood China Clipper kits became the rage, and miniature replicas of the Glenn L. Martin Company's graceful M-130 four-engined "flying boat" were soon dangling from many a lad's ceiling. In this matter Ted won a neighborhood pre-eminence when cousin Esther Kleffel, a member of Shanghai's American community, mailed him a China Clipper first day cover. The Major framed the Chinese-stamped envelope with its red notation "Hold For First Flight," adding it to the military pictures and war maps expanding across his son's bedroom wall.

Two years later in August of 1939, the Hinckley family joined the throngs visiting San Francisco's Golden Gate International Exposition shimmering on Treasure Island. Located in the middle of the Bay, the almost one-mile square man-made island with its exotic sculptures and pageantry, heralded "America's Pacific century." Eunice insisted her son view the priceless on-loan fifteenth century masterpiece, "The Birth of Venus" by Botticelli; reluctantly Ted did so. What did instantly capture his admiration was an all metal, silver-winged Venus incongruously parked within a cluster of white plaster buildings. Three times he waited in the long line to inspect the interior of Boeing Corporation's gleaming Army Air Force B-17 bomber; *Life* magazine aptly called it a "Flying Fortress."

Hardly had the vacationing Hinckleys returned home before Germany smashed into Poland and another World War had begun. And before long, just as the Major had predicted, "Germany, with the best Army in the world" overran its hapless neighbors. By June of 1940, the doom of valiant England appeared inescapable. Previously a majority of Pasadena's WASPS had bemoaned "China's fate" before "militarized Japan." Now the swelling succession of German victories bought at so cheap a price challenged public credulity. Throughout the United States during the 1930s, hungry communities had drawn closer together. With the forties' exploding fury, an endangered nation drew closer. Ridicule of President Roosevelt, even after he announced for an unprecedented third term, seemed less shrill. "How long," people asked, "before Americans would once again be 'Over There'?"

Not since the fourteenth century's Black Death had Asians and Europeans found themselves engulfed in such catastrophe. Unbelievably, one of the world's most sophisticated nations was busily perfecting the Holocaust's mass executions. However for Ted Hinckley, those frightening 1939-1941 years, his first two years of high school, brought happiness and inward satisfaction. Like millions of males before him, the catalyst was a lovely young woman.

Sister to two wild and woolly brothers, Mother Hinckley had early on made quite certain that her children's elementary sexual differences were demystified. Not until his first year of junior high, when handed a "dirty" comic book featuring a copulating Jiggs and Maggie, did Ted realize why his own parents periodically locked their bedroom door. Concurrent sex seminars among playground pals enlarged the teenager's lascivious curiosity; like them, he was titillated by verbal smut. Beyond that, he had little if any desire to actually investigate Eros' realm; to him, that small number of McKinley girls and boys existing behind the libidinous curtain seemed pitiful.

One year later, during eighth grade, Ted's lackadaisical sexuality turned an abrupt biological corner. With almost no forewarning, his raging hormones rose up and threatened to drive him over a cliff that all his heretofore moral instruction had warned him against. Art books in his father's study only partially placated his burning desire for enlightenment on naked women. Ignorant of puberty's manifestations, aghast and ashamed of the lecherous devils racing around in his head, he didn't know where to turn. Then it struck him. One of his pals, Norman Newcomb, had stacks of old medical books stored in his dad's garage. Gang gossip described Dr. Frank Newcomb's volumes as invitingly salacious, filled with "lots of photographs of naked people." What the overheated youth had not heard was that while the physician's moldy tomes contained a plethora of graphic illustrations of naked humans, each and every such photo—mercifully the photographs were in black and white—exhibited some gruesome disease. In a number of cases these doomed syphilitic men and women had been photographed front and back from their knees to their foreheads to reveal the victims' horribly infected anatomy. Surgeon Newcomb's Seventh Circle of Hell rogues' gallery effectively cooled Ted's frenzied libido.

Providentially, Cupid arrived as Eros fled. Pretty girls had previously brightened Ted's educational landscape. Indeed, as early as elementary school, infatuations with first grader Shirley Ross and then fifth grader Beverly Thompson had left bittersweet wounds from Cupid's arrows. Then came McKinley's lovelies: Phoebe Lind, Florence Fussell, Nina Hess, Mary Van Orden, Anne Scott, Susan Larwill, and so many more accelerating his merry pulse. But it was blue-eyed, blonde-haired Frances Alex who in May of 1939 dazzled him with a springtime that probably no female ever had or could.

For Ted, Frances was never reality. Her mirthful laughter and quick wit bewitched and bewildered him. No doubt she realized she could play him as a marionette, but instead, for two wonderful years, her affection

warmed him with a personal and academic ambition heretofore quite lacking. His grades advanced, he became
a class president, and even won election to McKinley's student council.
Ted and Frances shared an adolescents' world of simple pleasures: bicycling, bowling, playing badminton,
surfing and hiking, and most of all,
dancing scintillating swing time at
Pasadena's civic ballroom. For
Frances it was fun; too often for her
worshiper, it was a trapeze act in
space. Theirs was never anything but
a platonic relationship. In truth, his
lips never touched hers; to kiss a
dream was impossible, even though
she coquettishly invited same.
Conscious that their daughter had
found a safe sweetheart, Mr. and Mrs.
Max Alex kindly shared with him the

*Every young man should be so lucky as
to romance a lovely like Frances Alex.
Unquestionably her kindnesses and intelligence powerfully uplifted the author
during those restless teenage years.*

finest dining and dancing attractions Los Angeles could boast.
Understandably, Eunice and Theo likewise rejoiced.

Fortunately for Ted and Frances, their two mothers hit it off.
Frances' father had flown with the German Air Force in the First World
War; indeed, a number of his relatives resided in Hitler's Third Reich.
Little wonder, then, that the Alexes concurred with Mrs. Hinckley's rigid
isolationist opinions, convictions that had recently led her to affiliate
with the America First Committee.

On 20 June 1941, the two mothers, accompanied by their "going
steady" high schoolers, drove to the Hollywood Bowl to hear an address
by Colonel Charles Lindbergh. In Ted's boyish roster of American
heroes, the Colonel didn't quite rank with Captain John Paul Jones,
General George Armstrong Custer, or Captain Eddie Rickenbacker.
However, Ted had never been to the Bowl, and the evening promised
holding Frances' hand under starlit skies. For some months previously,
he had accompanied his information-hungry mother to a stimulating
series of Pasadena Junior College lectures reviewing world trouble spots.
To his surprise he had thoroughly enjoyed each speaker.

By 1941 Lindbergh had emerged as a paramount voice countering
the interventionists who would defend America by defending England.
Since the mid-1930s, the famous flyer and his devoted wife Anne
Morrow had resided in England, seeking escape from the relentless pub-
licity surrounding their baby son's kidnapping and death. Although living abroad, the "Lone Eagle," remained a steadfast patriot; in a wide
range of public and private activities he served humankind. When in
1938 he accepted a decoration from Reich Minister Hermann Goering for
his contributions to world aviation, the heralded hero promptly found

himself stigmatized "a Nazi tool." "His albatross," Anne labeled the medal. Lindbergh defended himself: to have rejected it would have insulted the Germans whose government Washington officially recognized. But it was the Lone Eagle's blunt warnings—all too accurate as it transpired—about the rapid buildup and technical acceleration of Hitler's Air Force, that really angered powerful politicos at home and even in France and England. Regrettably Germany's booming economy beguiled Lindbergh. In marked contrast to the technocrat's fascination with German efficiency was his horror of Stalin's Soviet Union. "Russian life," he wrote in 1940, "is as close to hell on earth as it is possible for human beings to come." "Let Hitler and Stalin fight it out," shouted the America Firsters. Russia's assault on little Finland further convinced isolationist Americans how dangerous was the interventionists' folly.

So swollen with antiwar protesters was the Hollywood Bowl that spectators excluded by the jam-packed multitude had climbed up into the huge amphitheater's fringing trees. Instead of a decorous city college audience, the Hinckleys and Alexes found themselves immersed in a restless crowd; for Ted it was like a Rose Bowl football contest, except that this bowl's membership seemed old and cranky instead of young and exuberant. Sharing the stage with Lindbergh were his wife, Senator D. Worth Clark of Idaho, the novelist Kathleen Norris, and silent screen star Lillian Gish. Clark and Norris briefly condemned Europe's war, but it was Lindbergh whom the crowd wanted to hear.

"As Lindbergh came to the battery of microphones," reported the *Los Angeles Times*, "the audience as one leaped to its feet waving hats, flags, coats and anything else with which it could express its enthusiasm." His uninspiring delivery, especially following a thunderous three-minute ovation, disappointed Ted; the speaker's belief that Hitler was winning the battle of the Atlantic chilled him. That America was "unprepared for war and it would take us years to prepare adequately for the type of war we now consider entering," echoed his father's opinions. Lindbergh predicted that an entrance into the conflict must turn "this country into a military nation that exceeds Germany in regimentation"; he pleaded for the audience to put its "support behind a negotiated peace in Europe."

In less than twenty-four hours, the absurdity of trying to negotiate peace with Hitler was manifest. "Herr Hitler's invasion of Russia," mused the Major, "will meet the same fate that destroyed Napoleon." At last solitary England had a mighty fighting ally. Concurrently across the Atlantic, America's burgeoning "arsenal of democracy" was rapidly supplanting the Depression's dreariness with a warmly welcomed armaments boom.

That same month Ted graduated from McKinley. Alarmed by the stories of PJC (Pasadena Junior College) "drinking parties"—at that time the last two years of high school were spent on the junior college campus—his mother transferred him out of the Pasadena Public School System to South Pasadena-San Marino High School. Dumbly aware of his absolute helplessness before his goddess, he returned Frances' sorority pin, requesting that she keep his club pin. His pals had been at no pains to remind him of his ridiculous infatuation. Sensitive to her brother's pain, his sister gave him a copy of Osa Johnson's best-selling autobiography, *I Married Adventure*. He promptly devoured it, afterward wondering whether someday he could find a woman with an enthusiasm for life to equal Osa's. Not until erased by war's cruel intoxication would the ache of Ted's lost love pass away.

Throughout the summer of 1941, Germany once again showed the world what blitzkrieg meant. But could "the world's finest Army" swallow the Soviet Union's prodigious Eurasian land mass stretching from Central Europe to the Pacific Ocean? By November, and aware that a violent break between Japan and the United States was coming, Esther Kleffel's husband Julius Kleffel, a veteran resident Shanghai businessman, loaded up a freighter with East Asian exports and prepared his family for a hurried departure. A German citizen imprisoned by the Japanese in 1915, trader Kleffel—now an American citizen—had no desire to spend another three or four years interned in a Japanese prison. Eunice, while seething over the likelihood of war, assured her cross-Pacific cousin that 1211 Avoca could accommodate the Kleffels. Yet even with a "War Warning" cautioning them that there was a dangerous increase in the likelihood of war with Japan, Hawaii's military commanders could not fully grasp their peril.

Relaxing in his back porch bedroom with three of the Avoca Avenue gang, playing Monopoly or reading magazines, Ted wished the year would hurry up and end. Sixteen years of age was too young for military service, seventeen seemed a long way off. And which branch of the service would he enter? Army? Navy? Or the Marines? If they wouldn't have him, what about the Royal Canadian Air Force?

Aware that his father was standing in the doorway that led to his sister's room, he looked up. His pals broke off what they were doing, waiting for the Major to speak. His face twitching with a broken grimace, he half choked out the words, "Japan has attacked Pearl Harbor."

CHAPTER III

"Body, Mind, and Spirit"

Why his father had picked a foggy week night for the family to roll out their Plymouth completely buffaloed Ted Jr. It was doubly perplexing with all this post-Pearl Harbor talk about conserving gasoline for the war effort. The semi-blacked out drive to Arcadia's Santa Anita race track seemed nutty! The family's sedan slowed as it began a half circuit of Southern California's famous horse racing park.

By his sixteenth birthday Ted no longer had any confusion about life's daily, indeed, deadly, roulette wheel. His swelling absorption with the Second World War news from Europe, from China, from Africa, and now from across the Pacific was pelting him with sanguinary words and pictures. Survival was humanity's perpetual gamble.

Their Plymouth, like the other autos behind and in front of them, no doubt containing other curious Californians, slowed way down. None of the Hinckleys spoke as each passenger attempted to penetrate the thin fog moving across the sprawling, shadowy recreational area. "Somewhere in there," Theo reminded his family, "are Japanese-Americans awaiting forcible relocation."

Whether on racing or non-racing days, daytime or early evening, the grounds and buildings of Santa Anita Park generally imparted a Golden State charm. Enjoying the San Gabriel Mountains for a backdrop, with multiple, variegated banks of flowers bordering its well-maintained facilities, the Park hardly fit Eunice's description of "the devil's handiwork." Adjacent to the racetrack's highway approach was a vast asphalt parking lot, on Sundays a favorite place for teaching one's kids how to drive. Indeed, it was here that Ted's father had instructed him in urban America's rite of passage and then ill-advisedly denied him membership in the legion of licensed California drivers.

Wartime's blackout added to the hushed, unusually static atmosphere of the acclaimed race track now become a somber "assembly center" for Issei (first generation) as well as the Nisei (second) soon to be shipped off to "relocation camps." Journalists hardly dared stigmatize these internment sites as "concentration camps," although they were located in some of the bleakest parts of the arid West, desert regions intensely hot in the summer and freezing in the winter.

"Look, Theodore, they've put up barbed wire and searchlight towers. Isn't that a soldier with a gun over there?"

The Major remained coldly silent. Shaken from their adolescent reverie, his two teenagers, if only for a few minutes, witnessed wartime's harsh reality.

"Where have they put the Tatsubos and Fukutakis?"

"I have no idea," Theo replied, "but I am told that a lot of the evacuees are being temporarily housed in the horse stables."

Afterward Ted remembered how strangely mute that evening's homecoming. Did he also reflect on the fact that these "relocated" Japanese Americans—eventually 112,000 men, women, and children from California, Washington, and Oregon—were innocent wartime victims, and like Ted's and Jane's cousins, the Kleffels in Shanghai, interned along with other hapless civilians, threatened no one? Unlike the Kleffels in Shanghai, however, those incarcerated within Arcadia's race track were not people residing in a foreign land but American citizens, most of whom had been living in Eunice's promised land well before the Hinckleys had arrived there.

It troubled Ted that school friends from McKinley, and more recently kids from his junior class at South Pasadena-San Marino High School, all native-born Nisei were locked behind those high wire fences. In his selfish shortsightedness, he was almost as vexed at the abrupt closure of their parents' floral shops, California Avenue stores which in recent years had supplied him lovely fifty-five cent gardenia corsages for high school dates. Nor was Ted's equating of disappearing Japanese-American classmates with vanishing, sweet-smelling corsages utterly incomprehensible. At both Pasadena and South Pasadena, the atmosphere surrounding the bus departures of the forever zestful Nisei had exuded a festive quality, or so it seemed to the Hinckleys' callow son. If there were long faces, he remembered none. Yes, there had been some prolonged hugs, but instead of an accompaniment of tears, all the young people—WASP and Asian alike—had cheered as though they were leaving for a sporting event, a track meet with nearby Glendale or Monrovia. Older and wiser, the parents and teachers donned smiling masks. Surely some must have sensed the grim irony behind the farewell charade: barbed wire imprisonment for a Pasadena elite.

Like most Pasadenans in the days immediately following Japan's successful sneak attack, the residents along Avoca Avenue conjectured about the likelihood of a Japanese air raid on Southern California's mushrooming war-born factories. Informed that the Pasadena Civil Defense Council needed air raid wardens for the South Orange Grove area and was holding a meeting at Arroyo Seco School, Ted happily forewent his homework and attended. To his surprise only a couple of adolescents were present within the crowded room. Speaking to the all-male audience, the Defense Council representative confessed how remote the probability that the City of Roses would be targeted. "Nonetheless," he warned, "a crippled aircraft or jettisoned bomb load is always a possibility." Ted found himself appointed temporary warden of District Five, Precinct Three; shortly afterward he received his Defense Council card designating him an official fire watcher.

For a few exciting hours on the night of 24 February 1942, Avoca Avenue's fire watcher thought "the Japs had come." The shooting had begun the previous night when the *I-17*, a large Japanese submarine, surfaced off Goleta adjacent to Santa Barbara. While locals listened to President Roosevelt's reassuring words celebrating the birthday of George Washington, the Japanese skipper surfaced and slammed some two dozen shells into and around a coastal oil pumping facility. Total damage for the Signal Oil Company was a few hundred dollars. If California's military were humiliated and angered at Captain Kozo Nishino's audacity, too many of the state's citizens looked about for a panic button. On the following evening they found it, pressed it, and Ted Hinckley joined the thousands of Southern California civil defenders called out to protect the Republic from Japanese bombers. Although a blacked-out Pasadena saw or heard no "Jap bombers," spectators atop downtown Los Angeles buildings witnessed quite a light and sound show. Along the blacked-out coast brilliant shafts of coast artillery searchlights crisscrossed the sky; irregular blasts of antiaircraft fire confirmed the enemy had penetrated America's defenses.

The following morning below huge headlines—40% of its front page— the *Los Angeles Times* summarized in frightening copy what had NOT occurred. "Roaring out of a brilliant moonlit western sky, foreign aircraft flying both in large formation and singly, flew over Southern California early today and drew heavy barrages of antiaircraft fire—the first ever to sound over United States continental soil against an enemy invader." In light of the crushing losses in sailors, ships, and soldiers which America and its allies were then being subjected to in the South Pacific, perhaps spooked Southern California's "Battle of Los Angeles" supplied some comic relief.

The all-night fiasco left the Major's sleepy son half-bewildered, half-bemused. Not so the Arroyo Seco schoolhouse meeting of serious-faced middle-aged men which had preceded it; that modest gathering of Pasadenans determined to defend the motherland had magnified Ted's own growing awareness of ascendant manhood. Mr. Marc Leigh, an admired family friend who had for years traded Sunday School chauffeuring with Theo, had also attended that meeting. Spotting the Major's son, he had crossed the room, warmly greeted Ted, and conversed with him as an equal. That had never happened quite that way before. For a teenager earnestly trying to grow up, to be a man respected by men, Leigh's cordiality as well as that of other adult neighbors, proved little short of intoxicating.

Ted's pleasurable satisfaction from all male socialization had begun years earlier; potent in fueling this joy of comradeship was the Pasadena and South Pasadena Young Men's Christian Association.

Adjacent to Pasadena's strikingly handsome Civic Center, the Y's main branch was a mecca for men and boys from all over the city. Among its 1930s administrators was Paul Somers, a man's man if ever there was one. Somers exuded a contagious enthusiasm for living fully, living the Y way, "Body, Mind, and Spirit in service of Christ." To the men and boys with whom he laughed, preached, played, and patently cherished, his broad grin and dynamic leadership were a perpetual tonic. Theo and Ted had enjoyed Somers' inspirational officiating at various father and son gatherings. His hard-hitting moral messages, while refreshing his listeners, goaded them "to do better." When Somers led the singing of "Onward Christian Soldiers" or "Follow the Gleam," Ted itched to follow him anywhere. Of all his uplifting admonishments, one stood out: Christianity and masculinity could and should reinforce each other.

McKinley's Hi-Y club was probably typical of the all-boy YMCA clubs scattered throughout the Southern California public high schools: WASP leadership dominated. Indeed, the Christian-affiliated clubs' use of tax-supported gyms and classrooms seems not to have raised an eyebrow. To his delight and surprise, Ted was invited to join McKinley's Hi-Y; he had no illusions that anything he had done on the playing field or in the classroom had achieved this. His benefactor was Larry Hoyt's older brother Bill.

McKinley's Hi-Y sponsor was Al Renner, an extremely popular biology teacher. He had played football with the acclaimed University of Southern California eleven. Although lacking Somers' pyrotechnic vitality, Renner shared his affection for young people and understood how to be one of the boys without ever being a boy. Disturbed by the club's harsh physical initiation—severe paddling, massages employing smelly chicken guts, supplemented with a plethora of stinking limburger cheese—he eventually terminated that rite of passage. One suspects that the club's almost exclusive Anglo composition likewise troubled him. But in the early 1940s the challenge of rearranging Pasadena's well-established WASP dominance of the public schools remained a matter for future resolution.

Perhaps a few of Ted's fellow Hi-Y friends worried over that inequity, but it's doubtful. Somewhat mitigating this condition was an all-city Hi-Y meeting held on the first Wednesday evening of every month which included representatives from two schools with a much larger African-American student component than McKinley's. Convening at the city's main branch, the program began with a banquet, followed by group singing and a rousing speaker, more often than not a current sports personality, a wisecracking sports journalist or an athlete conspicuous in yesterday's sports columns. To these extroverted males, a female speaker within that dining hall would have been as welcome as Carrie Nation at a brewers convention. Who cared if the meat loaf tasted like baked sawdust? Who cared if the dessert was a pudding gruel? Here squeezed into the main branch's gym were "Pasadena's finest," prominent business leaders eager to subsidize the banquet for a chance to hear an illustrious speaker, Y directors, respected teacher-sponsors, and above all, the well scrubbed, white-shirted young men of varied ethnic hues wearing their school sweaters, singing, shouting, and cheering their leaders' jokes, and applauding the brief, buoyant talks by he-men.

Four years prior to his McKinley Hi-Y initiation, Ted had started attending Pasadena's Camp Orizaba on Catalina Island. Not until after America entered the Pacific War did this Catalina Island YMCA summer camp become off limits for Ted and his pals. Nestled within a secluded cove, gifted with one of the island's rare sand beaches, Camp Orizaba was a paradise for youths aged nine to eighteen. Ted usually spent the regular nine allotted days there, but if his parents wished to take an extended vacation, he joyfully repeated the camp's swimming, sailing, rifle-range shooting, racket games, and nature study. Campfire capped off each fun-filled day with exuberant singing, and here again, as at Orizaba's outdoor chapel, songs and inspirational talks aimed to uplift the campers' ethical principles and conduct. There were positive memory montages that stuck: Dick Reineman, the one-armed counselor daily performing five-fingered miracles at the arts and crafts center; the night when fifteen counselors across the valley formed a cross with their flashlights and sang "The Old Rugged Cross"; and that glorious morning when Ted dumbfounded himself and swam the mile test permitting him to check out any boat he wished. There were also negative flashbacks just as soon forgotten: stealing his tent leader's firecrackers and inserting them in the dry logs well pyramided for the evening campfire; and quitting on the senior mountain climb when his knees gave out.

Affiliation with South Pasadena High School dictated shifting Ted's membership to a new Hi-Y club, one in which he possessed little if any status. At McKinley his restricted athletic participation had posed no peer barrier; at South Pasadena he acutely felt the absence of a letter sweater and the honored clan membership thereby denied him. Severance from old McKinley friendships, especially a girl friend about whom he cared a great deal, and his father's refusal to let him get that sacred driver's license, all compounded by his turbulent adolescent restlessness—what am I doing in these classrooms while my country's fighting a global war—threatened to becalm if not wreck him on the shoals of dejection. He flunked a math class, got a D in Spanish, a subject which he usually enjoyed, took a swing at a classmate, and found himself being chastised by the boys' vice principal. Unknown to him, his father wrote California's National Guard. No, not until he was eighteen could Theodore Hinckley's son qualify for the Guard.

Nor did it lift his declining self-respect when his mother informed him that her sister's oldest son, Nelson Upthegrove, had been accepted at Michigan and before long would enter Annapolis. Ted and Jane had never met their Ann Arbor cousins, two of whom had suffered from polio as children and then bounced back to enjoy remarkable records both as students and as swimmers. Had he applied himself, could Ted have attended a United States military academy? For a day or so the thought troubled him.

Ironically, at the very moment when male approval counted for so much, it was the opposite gender that reinflated his sagging morale. Diminutive Miss Amy Rachel Foote, "South Pas' redheaded wildcat" drama teacher, asked him to stay after school and try out for one of her theatrical productions. Having trod the boards off and on since elementary school, Ted did so, and while his subsequent accomplishments on the stage were a long, long way from scoring on a football field, building sets and acting did keep him out of the vice principal's office.

What he really wanted was out of high school. But if he couldn't don a uniform, South Pasadena's Public Library's *Illustrated London News*, *Time*, and *Newsweek*, along with his father's *Life* and *Liberty* subscriptions, did permit an empathetic participation in the war. Of all the Allied fighting men, Ted especially identified with the airmen. Nothing could equal the *Illustrated London News* for enabling "Walter Mitty" Hinckley to soar heavenward with England's valiant fighter pilots, men whose Spitfires and Hurricanes were winning the Battle of Britain against Goering's Luftwaffe. *Liberty* published a serialized biography of the First World War Allied ace of aces, William Avery "Billy" Bishop; equally captivating was the publication's serialized war novel abruptly terminating the Second World War slaughter by the use of an atomic bomb.

Life magazine's superb Pacific War combat pictures and later use of facsimile photos of miniaturized warships, enabled Ted, and doubtlessly tens of thousands of other news-hungry Americans, to fly into battle with their Navy's airmen. Confirming that henceforth it was the carrier not the battleship which would dictate victory on the seas was the 7-8 May 1942 Battle of the Coral Sea. Five months earlier, Japanese land-based planes had sunk Britain's *Repulse* and the *Prince of Wales* battleships. The audacious successes of British carrier aircraft at Taranto, Italy (11 November 1940) and the Japanese at Pearl Harbor had been achieved against moored warships. But the Coral Sea contest was exclusively a carrier battle. Photos of America's "Queen of the Flattops" staggering from her internal gas line explosions, mortal wounds inflicted by Japanese airmen, recalled Ted's boyhood tour of the proud *Lexington*. Somewhat compensating for her death were combat photos of the burning and doomed Japanese carrier *Shoho*. Had Japan's astounding six-month string of triumphs finally been broken as the "war propagandists" claimed?

"War propagandists" was Eunice's term. Although uncomfortable with the word propaganda, many people realized their war news was being manipulated. While Japan's December 7 bombing of Hawaii had effectively silenced the isolationist clamor, nothing could eradicate Eunice's revulsion to war and antipathy for those who directed it. Resigned to "the calamity," she fervently prayed that her son might somehow be spared war's horrors.

Much to the discomfort of Jane and Ted, their parents' heated disagreements on family finances and politics occasionally degenerated into shouting matches. For the Major, dissuading his wife that a "warmongering Roosevelt" had caused the Pearl Harbor attack proved futile. The evening the family's radio informed her that America's President had insulted none other than Charles Lindbergh, a good soufflé supper collapsed. A year earlier, and appreciating his equivocal position as an America First spokesman, the aviator had resigned his reserve commis-

Despite the parental squabbles over shrinking income, 1211 Avoca's diverse delights provided its occupants, and Ted's numerous neighborhood friends, unmatched hours of pleasure.

sion. However, once the shooting began, Lindbergh's skills became important tools for the war effort; FDR's treatment of him was uncharacteristically mean-spirited.

Given her abhorrence of war, yet living within a nation relishing the dazzling phenomenon of wartime full employment, Eunice Hinckley inevitably, if irately, accepted reality. She certainly suffered no illusions about Hitler or Tojo. "Devils incarnate," she branded them. Nevertheless, it bothered her that Pasadena Presbyterian Church's highly-regarded minister, Dr. Eugene Carson Blake, employed a war novel, John Steinbeck's somber *The Moon is Down* to dramatize mankind's unquenchable desire for freedom.

It was the 4-5 June 1942 Battle of Midway that swept up the Hinckley's foolishly romantic son into his own special heaven from which he could dive down on an evil armada. Of all the different types of airplanes that excited Ted's fertile imagination, he particularly fancied the Devastator torpedo bomber, the Navy's first all metal, low-wing carrier plane. Flouting the barrage of enemy antiaircraft fire, these Douglas TBDs had flown right at Admiral Isoroku Yamamoto's flattops, dropped their deadly torpedoes, and then miraculously, the surviving aircraft had skimmed over the sea back to their mother ship. Well after the Midway battle had ended, its costs were released. Unquestionably America had won an extraordinary victory: four enemy carriers sunk with one U.S. carrier lost, but the sacrifice of torpedo bomber pilots and their gunners was grim. Every Devastator in Torpedo Squadron Eight (VT-8) had been shot down. Only four of the fourteen planes in Torpedo Squadron Six (VT-6) made it back to the *Enterprise* (CV-6). Excellent Japanese ship handling, and perhaps malfunctions, had denied every torpedo its mark.

Douglas Devastators of the USS Enterprise's Torpedo Squadron Six (ca. late1941).
Note the unlucky logo.

The loss of the Devastators had not been in vain. Their low level assault had attracted the circling Japanese Zeros, thus enabling the screaming SBD Dauntless dive bombers to place their deadly loads right on the Japanese flattops.

Ted could hardly get enough of the details related to this epic air-sea battle. The squadron insignia of VT-6, a giant albatross with a fish in its bill flying toward a distant waterspout, intrigued and perplexed him. Later its symbolism was explained to him. The albatross was a torpedo plane. Its fish formed a six ("fish" was Navy lingo for torpedo); the threatening funnel-shaped cloud embodied the battle pandemonium into which the solitary sea bird was headed. After *Life* printed a group portrait of VT-8's doomed aviators (one pilot survived), it too became an icon on Ted's sleeping porch wall. To his mother this wall, now almost entirely covered with war's pictorial debris, can only have inflicted pain.

Resolutely determined that her son must survive the war, even though keeping him out seemed less likely everyday, Eunice punched away at war's futility. Assured that he had read Eric Remarque's foreboding *All Quiet on the Western Front*, she took him to see its equally unyielding film version featuring Lew Ayres. Mars did suffer a few bruises. However Ted's enthusiasm for joining him remained intact. As it transpired, external forces were complementing his mother's pacifist designs.

Without informing his parents what he was about, Ted boarded the Pacific Electric's big red trolley for downtown Los Angeles; his destination was the Federal Building's Marine recruiting office. In less than fifteen minutes deft questions by a recuperating veteran of Guadalcanal revealed the Hinckley's son was neither rugged in physique nor mind, not an athlete but an actor, in truth, merely a Christian romantic. "Son, with your knees you should try the Navy or the Army Air Corps." Despite this rejection, the sergeant's advice did make sense. Another experience at about this same time further convinced the Major's son he could never be a saber-waving Custer, notwithstanding that he and pal Jim had repeatedly ridden with Errol Flynn in his thrilling reenactment of "hell-bent for leather Custer." One afternoon while out shooting BB guns with Stimmy, Ted winged a sparrow—a feat heretofore never accomplished. Incapable of dispatching the crippled creature hopping helplessly about, he begged his chum, "Kill the damned thing." Jerking out his sheath knife, Stimmy did precisely that while snorting, "A helluva warrior you'd make!"

It was dawning on the Hinckleys' feckless son that for all war's hypothetical spell, neither his body nor his mind really possessed the special qualities required for soldiering. Bad enough to be cursed with unreliable knees, but frequent bouts of severe sinusitis dictated repeated agonizing insertions of "the hook" to cleanse his easily-infected skull cavities. The inherent fragility of the human anatomy was undeniable. Grim descriptions of war's ghastly purposelessness coincided with other despairing scenes, among them word pictures implanted from Ted's recently acquired *Diary of an Unknown Aviator*. In its final pages the gallant, foredoomed World War I pilot scribbled his disillusionment. "War is a horrible thing, a grotesque comedy. And it is so useless. This war won't prove anything. All we'll do when we win is to substitute one sort of Dictator for any other. In the meantime we have destroyed our best resources. Human life, the most precious thing in the world, has become the cheapest . . ."

What prescience. Mussolini, Stalin, Hitler—all were products of the First World War. With the end of this second conflagration would mankind blindly repeat the cycle of substituting "one sort of dictator for any other"?

Ted's despondent, frustrating two years at South Pas High might well have occurred without a war. In part his petulant personal insecurity was a willful male's quite normal biological evolution. The youth's surging, conflicting emotions and storm-tossed intelligence sought an anchorage where men, and yes, women, might laugh and freely work together. However, like millions of men before him, for better or for worse, Ted's elusive anchorage could never be reached until he first sailed his own uncharted seas.

Like McKinley, South Pas boasted an abundance of lovely young women, quite a number mature beyond their years. Three of these smiling, sophisticated chatterboxes, gentle Virginia Beach, skeptical Nancy Huggins, and good-natured Althea Ames, patiently endured his well-intentioned fumbles trying to exit from adolescence. But Ted kept his dates to a minimum; the pain from one severed infatuation remained all too real. Furthermore, he distrusted his wild horses.

Observing their friend's retarded sexuality and aware that he had never even experienced the delights of necking, pals Stimmy and Jim pondered what to do. Larry had gone off to prep school, Fountain Valley School in Colorado, and had written of his conquests—foolishly Ted believed him—while a bemused Stimmy cautioned him, "It's fun, Ted, but don't light that damn thing if you can avoid it."

Immensely proud of his dilapidated old Chevy two-door—paid for thanks to after school part-time work at Lockheed Corporation—and eager to show it off, Jim confronted his gauche friend. "Ted, you need to grow up. My girl friend has just the number for you." Quite familiar with the wiles of a seductress, due to his surfeit of reading, Ted happily agreed to accompany Jim on a blind double date to the big city. Rumble seat necking followed a Grauman's Chinese Theater flick. Not surprising, the intimacy proved exciting. Two weeks later Ted again found himself with the same company, but in a pitch-black West Los Angeles residence. His only link to the outside world was Frank Sinatra crooning "That Old Black Magic." After two hours of heavy necking, and his testicles about to burst, Ted discovered as every man doing "what comes naturally" must: protracted necking is not only hard on the male anatomy but enables a woman to grow extra arms. No matter how he maneuvered his "hot garters" date, his hands simply could not penetrate her defenses. Afterward he thanked Jim for this adventure, and thanked God that he was still a virgin. Probably he should also have thanked "hot garters," but then he never saw her again. Stimmy was right, "Don't light that damned thing!"

Ted had discovered the worldly thrills of canoeing above Niagara; infinitely more exciting, the galactic universe of ideas was expanding before him. Of course, this vast heaven of abstractions, abstractions that in fact determine each human's future, had been twinkling over him since his parents first attended him in his Long Island cradle. No single, paramount revelation blasted-off Ted's love of learning; propulsion for that voyage required additional years. It was often English teachers—perforce distrusted for they demanded he work—whose learning first enlivened his appreciation for life's paramount ideas.

Among those persevering pedagogues was McKinley English teacher Ernest Bishop. Permanently crippled from German artillery fire in 1918, Bishop's rather stumbling classroom manner was more than compensated for by his droll humor and uncanny ability to weave together each work's historical setting, the specific author's mixed abilities, and what the prose or poetry might or might not say to contemporary Americans.

At South Pas, and despite Ted's lethargy and well-justified mediocre grades, the chemistry in his English classes proved just right. A Pomona College music major, the slim, short Richard Wooton hardly fit the masculine he-man mold. Wooton's strength lay in his obvious affection for American literature, and the soul his mellifluous voice breathed into his classroom readings. Thanks to Wooton, Washington Irving, Emerson, Poe, Twain, and other great American writers became Ted's companions for life.

A proper WASP, Ted had been taught to show respect for his elders. But typical of a society that increasingly emphasized youthfulness and incessant change, Ted could only pity, certainly not venerate anyone over sixty; veneration of the elderly was a quality practiced by enfeebled Chinese. Venerable Miss Rebecca Hayslip wrecked that stereotype. His admiration for her and her World Literature class awakened an esteem for word meanings that he would have ridiculed just a few years earlier. Ted doubted that the wee, white-haired woman, so worn out physically that she had to remain seated during most of her class, could last another semester. Yet before the first week ended, he reluctantly admitted to his mother, "You were right. Miss Hayslip is terrific." And then for his senior year he faced Miss Madge Hill's dreaded Senior English. Here again Ted's thorough dislike of work—library research, writing, rewriting, and still more rewriting, and the especially onerous fussing over grammar—dogged the pleasure he found in literature. With beguiling felicity, teacher Hill transmitted her fondness for Shakespeare. Somehow the woman's instructional gifts so excited Ted's pleasure for British authors such as Milton, Swift, Dickens, and Kipling that she saved him from yet another well-earned D.

South Pas' preeminent American History teacher and tennis coach combined many of the qualities Ted so much admired in McKinley's Renner and Bishop. Stocky Harry A. Swart was not only a combative athlete—his battered boxer's face testified to that—and a Navy veteran of the First World War, but a teacher who delighted in disputation. A great admirer of President Franklin D. Roosevelt, Swart nonetheless encouraged those holding opinions contrary to his to sound off. Ted did. Eventually so did most of the class. Vigorous argumentation never became disorderly; one-time Navy prize fighter Swart ran a taut ship. Ted enjoyed every minute of it, even Swart's demanding examinations.

For the Hinckleys' scholarly sluggard to have confessed affection for a disciplined classroom, even one featuring his cherished American history, remained difficult. Instead of appreciating that hard, pain-producing hours of work-study were indispensable constraints for achieving excellence, Ted perceived them as shackles preventing him from finding himself. School's bondage was reprehensible. He craved the bond of military camaraderie. Reading, talking, and even writing about American history was pleasant enough but no substitute for actually making American history.

By the summer of 1942, and apprehensive that her son's testiness was approaching a crisis—his father's refusal to let him have a driver's license didn't ease the rising tension at 1211 Avoca—Eunice anxiously sought a summer job for her son, the further away from Pasadena the better. A family friend arranged for Ted's employment at a camp of migrant cotton pickers outside Button Willow, an almost treeless village located in California's hot, water-short Great Central Valley.

Button Willow's old-fashioned general store, single gas station, and seedy movie theater welcomed Ted as he stepped off the bus. Evening fell before the camp manager drove up. Shown his scabrous, single-room shack, presented with a broom and brusquely informed of the camp's food arrangements, the camp manager departed, but not before warning the Hinckleys' innocent, "Tomorrow you'll be out in that cotton field with Will at half past seven. Oh, yes, if you're smart, sonny boy, you'll never get caught with one of these Okies' daughters in your cabin."

The windowless cabin lacked electricity and inside running water, but then that was true of Y camp. Nighttime had fallen over the pickers' community by the time Ted finished vigorously sweeping his shack's four walls, its dirt-covered rafters, and plank floor. Fortunately he had brought along some food. A call of nature made him realize he really didn't know where the men's toilet was located; no matter, he relieved himself behind his cabin.

At dawn his wind-up alarm failed him. Having missed breakfast, he relieved himself as the night before and hurried off to find Will. Will greeted him warmly and set about instructing the novice field hand how to shovel dirt from one irrigation ditch to another in order to facilitate watering the endless rows of cotton. An hour transpired under a burning summer sun. Observing the energetic Pasadena youth, Will urged him to slow down and use his canteen, casually commenting, "There's no rush. That sun'll git you if you're not careful." A bit tired but determined to demonstrate he was worth the promised twenty-five cents an hour, Ted smiled and ignored Will's counsel. A half-hour passed and Will repeated his gentle warning. The apprentice heard him, but not really. Five minutes later Ted collapsed; his lips, nose, and eyes touched the well-warmed loam of the San Joaquin Valley.

"Damn it! I tried to tell you." Staggering to his feet the sun stroke victim listened. Instructed to go over to the men's john clean the mud off his face and lie down, the woozy youth thanked his fellow picker and headed for the common toilet. Nothing he had ever seen prepared him for what met his senses within that purgatory. Flies blackened its walls. The stench was overpowering. Two of the three flush toilets were packed with human excrement and inoperable; the third, also filled, did flush when Ted activated it. Y camp had stinking three-holers but here where flush toilets existed, the pickers, or somebody, was not sufficiently revolted to flush the damned bowls.

An hour later driving the big city boy into town, the camp manager couldn't restrain a dig. "Too much sweat for you?" Chagrined not in the slightest Ted snapped, "I think I could handle your sweat, but your filthy toilets—never!"

Ted's abrupt retreat met with a distinct coolness from the Major. Hearing of his misadventure, Caltech's Professor S. J. Bates, father of Ted's old McKinley friend Stuart Bates, phoned and suggested Eunice's lad join his son at the just-forming Pacific Southwest Area YMCA Emergency Harvest Camp at Santa Paula. Twelve hours later Ted was again on his way north with Professor Bates. After Button Willows' god-forsaken Okie camp, Santa Paula's slick new high school gym—the makeshift dormitory for the one hundred and fifty high school age orange and lemon pickers—above all its spic-and-span washroom facilities, seemed like a commutation from a Devil's Island sentence. It was a grand experience greatly enriched by stimulating male associations from all over Southern California.

After Stuart nominated Ted for camp president, and the Pasadena contingent beat out both the Santa Monica and Glendale candidates, President Hinckley's mud-splattered ego swelled happily. Two months of climbing Santa Paula's smudge pot-sooted citrus trees required energy but how satisfying for body, mind, and spirit the end of each work day. Steaming showers, generous suppers, followed by letter writing, volleyball, or, best of all, reading—whatta life! Santa Paula's Public Library, its movie theater, and even a town social, welcomed the Y harvesters; easy-to-read novels by John Steinbeck, Pearl S. Buck, and Ernest Hemingway hurried Ted's 1942 summer to a contented close.

Returning home, proud of his contribution to the war effort, and rejoicing that only one year of high school servitude remained, President Hinckley confidently assumed his father would finally let him wear that badge validating adolescent virility. "No, I'll not let you get a driver's license." A stunned silence followed by an explosive protest achieved nothing. Fortunately Ted telegraphed his punch. His father deftly blocked it, locking him in a viselike embrace. A weeping mother separated the two men, but her tears failed to abate either her son's burning hostility or the Major's intransigence. A month later Ted passed his seventeenth birthday and his mother signed the paper signifying Teddy's manhood; her trustfulness ran into a stone wall. The Major absolutely refused his son any use of the family car.

Claude E. Lashbrook quite lacked Paul Somers' charisma. As Executive Secretary of the South Pasadena YMCA, Lashbrook didn't even enjoy a private office, merely a desk and some filing cabinets in the rear of an insurance office. Nevertheless Lashbrook quickly won the respect of those with whom he worked; strengthened by an unswerving Christian commitment, "Speed" Lashbrook got a lot done with very little.

In November 1941, Speed invited Ted to join a group of South Pas youths attending the Pacific Southwest Hi-Y Congress at Yosemite. There in the Camp Curry auditorium he and his fellows huzzahed Johnny Rait's rendition of "Stout-Hearted Men." Decades later, Yosemite delegate Thornton Hamlin recalled for Ted how deeply moving was Rait's singing of the "Lord's Prayer." During the summer of 1943 it doubtlessly gratified Eunice Hinckley when Speed appointed her son a tent counselor and then director's assistant at Camp Ta Ta Pochen. William Danforth's moralistic injunctions in his widely-distributed *I Dare You* hit Ted just right; around each of Danforth's Christian maxims he fashioned both campfire and tent vespers.

Only a few weeks remained at South Pasadena-San Marino High School when Ted was asked to deliver one of the three ten-minute student statements at the June 1943 commencement. Certainly his mediocre grades didn't justify his presence on the platform with academic stars Lois Lee Knight and Doris Eldred. Admired history teacher Swart had rejoined the Navy. Ted, therefore, turned to Miss Foote, his drama coach. She urged him to give the speech, "say what you believe." Perhaps he did. But then perhaps his statement was little more than the half-muddled platitudes of an insecure youth trying to please his betters. According to the 18 June 1943 *Pasadena Post*, "Theodore C. Hinckley Jr., predicted that if each boy and girl tries to create an example in themselves of what mankind should strive to become, man will triumph over the besetting trials of the future. To achieve this, qualities of honesty, humility, tolerance and willingness to serve must be cultivated."

Hurrying off the field, mortarboard and diploma in hand, and anticipating a happy evening's celebration with his pals, Ted was stopped by two well-wishers, Richard Hudson and Warren Stilson, congenial classmates whose company he had only recently come to enjoy. A three-year honor student, Dick Hudson was marked for future success; he should have spoken instead of Ted. Dark-eyed Warren was on his way to the Army. Ted wished each of them well. Fate dictated otherwise. A year later a German 88 mm shell blew away Stilson's handsome head. Outliving war's madness, Hudson would become a one-man peace crusader.

By June 1943 Ted decided God had best fitted him for the Navy; glorious hallucinations of himself slaying either Japanese or Germans had almost vanished.

CHAPTER IV
"Anchors Aweigh, My Boys, Anchors Aweigh!"

What had Shakespeare said? "All the world's a stage and we are all players on it." In September 1943, San Diego's spacious Navy boot camp certainly provided Ted a well-equipped stage. Attired in spanking new, if ill-fitting uniforms, his fellow players, like himself, were either draftees or volunteers. Whether officers or enlisted men, too many still fumbled their lines. Occasionally one did encounter a salty stage manager, a seasoned Navy Regular who frowningly emphasized "the Navy way."

Ted chuckled to himself at how "Sir," and it was unfailingly "Sir," acted his part. Months ago this scowling Navy chief petty officer now commanding a company of raw recruits had been a kindly teacher-coach in a public high school. Sir's feeble grasp of Navy life and lore had been hurriedly acquired in a "ninety-day wonder program." Assigned to this Navy recruit training station, the Navy Reservist had transformed himself into a stern-visaged company commander. His charge: transform a scrambled bunch of Americans ranging in age from seventeen to forty, most of whom were not Regulars, into homogeneous "fighting men"— another inward chuckle.

Body, mind, and spirit? Ted's tired body hurt. No surprise, a Navy boot's regimen was expected to be tough. And while his mind remained a clutter of anxieties, all were immediate concerns; yesterday's had evaporated. His spirit? His feelings about himself, his shipmates, and life had never been more harmonious. He had survived the first two weeks of boot camp despite its repeated immunizations, 0530 reveilles, rigorous calisthenics, and sleep-stealing guard duties. The four weeks left should be a pushover. But after that? Like waiting for the curtain to go up on South Pas High's stage, the half-thrill, half-fear anticipating Navy adventures produced a most agreeable tingle. How immensely satisfying to finally be a minute part of that prodigious machine, what the press called "the Allied war effort."

For the Allied cause, 1943 became the hinge year. From January through March, German submarines threatened to win the Battle of the Atlantic. On land the "invincible Wehrmacht" prepared for its spring campaign and the "inevitable collapse" of Russian defenses at Leningrad and Moscow. But it didn't turn out that way. Notwithstanding ghastly expenditures of life, both Leningrad and Moscow stood firm.

Stalingrad's foot-by-foot climactic defense recalled the First World War's Verdun. Midyear found Hitler's massed legions fighting furiously to pinch off the Kursk salient; after suffering terrible losses in history's epic tank and infantry battle, the German Army began what became a perpetual if ratcheted retreat. At sea, small U.S. Navy carriers (CVEs), ungainly-looking flattops built on merchant ship hulls, at last extended air protection all across the Atlantic. The Nazi wolf pack U-boat offensive had peaked.

Nor was Germany itself spared. Operating from England's "unsinkable aircraft carrier," Allied bombers commenced round-the-clock, and then thousand-plane air raids pounding German military and civilian targets. In September 1943, the weakest of the Axis powers surrendered, but war within the Italian peninsula was far from over.

Halfway around the world along the northern coast of New Guinea, General Douglas MacArthur demonstrated how to win by leapfrogging the enemy. Concurrently the Japanese-occupied Dutch East Indies were outflanked. The rollback of death-before-surrender Japanese defenders begun in the bloody Guadalcanal campaign continued. Was America's South Pacific momentum, like the Russian push westward, immutable?

Of course in the fall of 1943 no one, excepting possibly the most visionary of Allied war leaders, could discern how irreversible was the door closing on the Axis nations. "To win this war," Margaret Mead wrote, "we must feel we are on the side of the Right." Ted's generation not only believed they were on the right side but thanks to an astounding wartime prosperity found themselves smilingly solvent. By 1943 nearly twice as many Americans were working in military or civilian jobs as had been employed in 1933. In truth, the home front was awash with money. Without the wartime price controls, inflation could have become severe.

Apprentice Seaman Hinckley recalled his own affluence during the previous summer. Following his June high school commencement, he had endured a long, impatient wait until his swearing in to Uncle Sam's Navy on 15 September 1943. Ruminating about his departing friends provided a pleasant pastime. In June, with a "I'll be seeing you in Tokyo" post card, Larry had railed east to begin college and officers' training. In a couple of years would the Hinckleys' swabby be saluting old pal Ensign Lawrence E. Hoyt? Uncomfortable with such inferiority, the boot's thoughts shifted to Jim. A year younger than himself, it was he who had finally convinced the Major's son to go Navy; "the Army doesn't need your lousy knees and sinusitis." Currently Jim was preparing himself in Pasadena Junior College's ROTC. Smart idea. Ted wished he had mastered the manual of arms before arriving at San Diego. But then the Hinckleys' son had not sat idle as he waited for his Navy call-up.

Jobs at Pasadena's Union Ice Company—quickly converted to the rapid packaging of the new Birdseye frozen foods—and the White House Laundry had taught him he didn't want postwar employment bent over some damn machine where one's hands either froze or steamed. Of that summer's experiences, the middle-aged, sheet-snapping women at the White House Laundry may have been his best teachers. Tired of stuffing heavy wet sheets into an extractor all day long, Ted asked the laundry manager if he might not try out the sheet mangle. Spreading out damp sheets looked to be a breeze. Those scrawny old women with broomstick arms merely snapped each sheet and placed it on the flat canvas moving toward the mangle. What could be simpler? Ted got his chance, and within less than ten minutes he knew his seemingly robust arms were going to fall off. Everyone else at the laundry had a good laugh; Ted's already high respect for the opposite gender ascended several notches.

Stimmy's letters from Army Air bases also had plenty to report on the ladies, first from Utah and then from Arkansas. Lordy! Two women in one bed! Ted recalled his last wild adventure with his devil-may-care friend. Both of them could have been killed in the Alhambra hills. By a double miracle the bottom of Stimmy's 1934 Ford didn't get ripped apart when his car screeched to a halt and balanced precariously on an excavated hillside garage foundation. What were his buddy's odds of becoming an Army Air Corps second lieutenant? If he didn't crack up, Stimmy should wear the prized pilot's silver wings. Except for Jim, who like himself would before long also be sporting a sailor's hat and bell-bottom trousers, virtually all of Ted's neighborhood and school pals were in uniform. He knew of none who had been drafted. A considerable number faced years of college culminating with an officer's commission. Seventeen-year-old Seaman Hinckley envied them those shiny officer's bars but definitely not their academic addresses.

"Fall in." Ted gladly did so. This was the afternoon when each of the approximately one hundred fifty men in his barracks would discover if they got a specialty school to earn their rating as petty officers third class. Those who didn't faced prompt sea duty.

Recruit Company 389 reflected America's broad age and ethnic heterogeneity—except there is not a single African-American face in the company photograph. Men from west of the Rockies predominated with but a sprinkled geographic representation from east of the Mississippi River.

The previous evening Ted had enjoyed arguing with Huddleston, a coal miner's son from Kentucky. Huddleston—in the Navy one generally addressed enlisted men by their last names—insisted "niggers ain't the same as white people," humans, yes, but equals, no. When it was pointed out that even if that were true, "they were equal in the sight of God," Huddleston's reaction bordered on apoplexy. His eyes rolled, he had trouble speaking, and indeed, Ted wondered if he had suffered some kind of seizure. Clearly to discuss race with anyone with a southern accent was hazardous.

"Single file, fill up those chairs, and go down that hall when your name and room number is called."

Like everyone of the tens of thousands of men being processed through the San Diego Naval Training Station, Ted had been subjected to two full days of diagnostic examinations to determine what he could and could not do. Except for the sound and light tests, most of the time had been taken up turning dozens of pages filled with hundreds of illustrated questions dealing with every imaginable technical vocation. The experience dazed Theo's son. One section exhibited a multitude of tools; seaman Hinckley could identify almost none of them. There were no warmhearted laundry ladies to laugh at his ignorance, nor did any Pasadena pal offer sympathetic encouragement. All he could hear was the rustle of paper by the hundreds of men, who like himself were awakening to an authoritarian truth: although valued persons among family and friends at home, here in basic training, boots were dog-tagged, discretely-numbered nobodies.

"Hinckley, room number sixteen."

Rising from his chair, freshly-minted number 565-52-17 walked down the corridor. He had no idea what fate had in store for him. Barracks' scuttlebutt had convinced him his chances for admission to a Navy photographers' school were nil. Ted's enthusiasm for photography went back to 1939 when savings from odd jobs had enabled him to purchase a used eight millimeter movie camera. Later he assembled a darkroom. Before leaving for V-12, Larry had generously brought over his expensive enlarging equipment. That trust had been matched by Stimmy's giveaway sale of his 1934 Ford. If only for five weekends, Eunice Hinckley had the pleasure of watching her beaming son drive off to the beach accompanied by friends not yet in uniform.

When August arrived and the Navy still had yet to call him up, Ted's parents, seconded by Jim, had urged him to enroll in a secretarial skills class at Pasadena's Sawyers Business School. "Ted, you'll make a good yeoman," urged Jim, "and the advancement is fast in that rating." His friend's advice, coupled with that of a few other uninformed teenage experts, seemed to make sense. Arriving at San Diego, Ted checked off yeoman, photographer, and quartermaster as desirable petty officer specializations.

"At ease, Hinckley. Have a seat." Like Sir, the second-class petty officer facing him from behind a very narrow desk wore a technical classification; day in and day out, he took square pegs like the present party and inserted them into if not square holes, holes that might vaguely fit each boot's peculiar capacities with the Navy's "current needs."

"Looking over your light and code responses it appears to me that you should do well with code. How about it? Do you think you would be interested in radio communications?"

Ted enjoyed listening to the radio, and deciphering code sounded like fun. Perhaps he recalled the five Little Orphan Annie decoder pins earned years earlier for drinking an appropriate amount of Ovaltine.

"Yes, Sir, that sounds interesting."

"How about an aviation radioman?"

"Yes, Sir, that sounds fine."

Only after returning to his barracks and its excited babel comparing interviews did Apprentice Seaman Hinckley awaken to what lay in store for him. No, he was not destined for naval intelligence; the code he would be working with was the Morse code. And if he didn't wash out, he might someday be operating a radio in a Navy airplane. Then it hit him. Walter Mitty Hinckley might actually fly into battle against an enemy! Stimmy had roared with laughter at Ted's terror on Long Beach's roller coaster. What would he say now? And all those other friends and family members? It took a day or so for his euphoria to pass, for the blueprint of his future training to reveal itself. Although sympathetic with company comrades who must soon report for sea duty, Seaman Hinckley had avoided being stuck at the bottom of the Navy's ladder. Months of shore duty lay ahead, but one day, God willing, he too might wear some silver wings.

So far Ted found Navy life almost entirely to his liking. The fixed routine, the trim, well-ordered environment, and the elementary classes explaining the Navy way—"not the right way nor the wrong way but the NAVY way"—supplied lots of diversion. At moments it was hard to suppress his laughter when a pompous officer dished out raw propaganda, or Sir growled menacingly. Who were they kidding? No doubt many members of this recruit company realized, as Ted certainly did, that the repeated, multi-company passing in review on the station's huge parade ground, with the band blaring and the guidons snapping to attention, was intended, as was so much of boot training, to submerge the individual into the regimented mass. San Diego's gentle ocean breeze and its obliging October sun made the hours of marching about relatively untaxing. Indeed, the hardest working men at these colorful functions were the oompah-pah, oompah-pah bandsmen whose "Anchors Aweigh" and John Phillips Sousa marches echoed across the base.

There was an afternoon, however, when Sir's fledglings discovered exactly how hot "the grinder" could become. Angry that absolute silence had not prevailed after the preceding evening's "lights out," Sir ordered the men to fall in and double time to the drill field. Instead of halting there, the entire company continued jogging with Sir's shouts sustaining a rapid pace. Around and around and around that asphalt area circled the men of Company 389. Larger and larger and larger it got each time the motley collection of sweating swabbies circled it. An hour passed. Spreading spots of perspiration united to soak their well-washed whites. Another hour approached. They found themselves jogging on a red-hot waffle iron. Swelling murmurs arose from protesting lungs, aching muscles, and burning feet. San Diego's kindly sun had taken on a Death Valley radiance.

Abruptly Ted realized his knees, his lousy knees were not killing him. Of course his whole body protested, but his mind laughed at the company's ordeal. The Navy had cured his Osgood-Schlatter disease! The first of his peers to give out was a large, badly overweight recruit. His face was crimson; gasping for air, his body, like a crippled B-17, slipped out of formation, and instead of turning at the corner of the tarmac, just kept stumbling on until he crashed into some bushes lining a nearby road. Three or four others collapsed, although none met such a dramatic demise.

Nor was this the last time that the sins of two or three brought down the wrath of Sir on the whole. Tediously enunciated by wartime Hollywood movie makers, and a coach's locker room cliché, boot camp echoed the mandatory tribal morality: Win or lose, we fight collectively, but the failure of a single individual to do his duty jeopardizes all. Childhood nursery rhymes had first familiarized Ted with this survival verity—the little Dutch lad with his hand in the dike—the loss of the horseshoe nail that resulted in the kingdom's loss—he accepted the military concatenation as he accepted its authoritarian corollaries. As for the absurdities of military life, indeed, existence in any vast regimented organization, years of reading shielded him with philosophical resignation. Gigantism's stupidities and petty asininities, could be highly amusing.

To prepare sailors for the unlikely circumstances where they might be required to serve ashore with rifles, a day was set aside to familiarize them with the M-1 rifle. Company 389 boarded busses and drove out to nearby Camp Pendleton, the furnace in which U.S. Marines were hardened for Guadalcanals to come. Enjoyable in every way, the experience also enlightened Ted on how lucky was his service selection.

Pendleton's inhabitants slept on dirt, crawled in dirt, and not infrequently ate various diluted forms of dirt. Most of the Marine grunts looked exhausted; none smiled. Afterward, the Navy's spic-and-span asphalt, even its flat, overcooked food, tasted better. Posted around Camp Pendleton were large, ridiculous caricatures of the "Jap." Buck teeth, horn-rimmed glasses, sinister eyes, Ted and his fellow bus riders thought it all very funny. Was this intended to inflame Marine hatred, ridicule an enemy who anyone with any brains knew was exceptionally tough, or what?

Hate. Few words struck such a sharp, discordant note. How was it that the word hate had chiseled such an ugly, negative impression? Was it a campfire talk by Speed Lashbrook, a Sunday School lesson, or something Ted had read? Christians might hate an individual's evil acts, but truly hating a human being was absolutely unchristian. Hate was synonymous with violence, and perhaps it did facilitate organized murder. But hate was a two-edged sword. Hate weakened the mind. Hate could destroy its practitioners. Distaste, dislike, disgust, but hate? Ted's upbringing had left him incapable of hating people. Had he witnessed his mother's murder, the rape of his sister, or the destruction of sociopolitical structures that gave meaning to his life then, yes, he could have hated.

Family, friends, school, church, YMCA, Pasadena, California, the United States of America, thanks be to a merciful God, all of these precious institutions were alive and well. Ted knew of the atrocities practiced by the Japanese. But he had also read about the exchange of cruelties which bloodied America's Western frontier. Even before high school his dad had recounted how in 1905 he had actually interviewed white American soldiers who had witnessed bamboo being driven under

Filipino fingernails to elicit information. No, attorney Hinckley's son was not cut out to be a "blood and guts Marine."

Navy life seemed less a theatrical production and more of a living reality with each passing day. Boyhood experiences greatly facilitated his accommodation to military life. The Naval Training Station's Sunday church services—required of boots—delivered generic moral messages he had often heard. Seamanship classes and slide shows requiring instant ship and plane identification—Allied as well as enemy—he and Jim had already mastered them. Scullery duty was little different than cleaning up the large greasy pots and trays at Camp Orizaba. Evening retreat also recalled Y-camp. Across the Navy station everyone within hearing distance of the bugler halted what they were doing and stood at attention facing the descending flag. Like a prayerful Moslem facing Mecca, Ted felt uplifted. Ah, the sweet elation of being united with these officers and men expressing respect; among some of his fellow adolescents this rite may have awakened a deference stronger than possibly anything that had heretofore claimed their loyalty.

Rather quickly, disfiguring cracks marred Seaman Hinckley's beautiful image of collective pride. Profanity was a minor one, considerably more disturbing was the vulgar, ongoing commentary on women.

Like every other boy reaching out for manhood, Ted's exposure to colorful language had expanded since elementary school. Pasadena WASP antecedents forbade the common use of much more than "damn," "hell," and "bastard," and then only among male associates. To call someone a "son-of-a-bitch" without smiling invited a fight. At the outset the swabbies frequent use of "fuck" had proved disconcerting. Notwithstanding its versatility as verb, adverb, noun, and adjective, the word's harshness, and after awhile its dreary ubiquity, irked him. Like the constant shining of shoes, polishing the deck, and scrubbing urinals, "fuck" appeared indispensable to military life. By the time Ted departed from boot camp, he found himself occasionally if uncomfortably uttering the ugly-sounding word. "Shit" did seem more euphonious. Certainly within the enlisted man's world its scatological nuances never ceased to amaze him.

The limitations of male swagger had first dawned on Ted in the sixth grade when the girls' baseball team soundly defeated the boys' nine. Somehow, and for all their strange pleasures with dolls and dress-up antics, girls seemed to excel in anything they put their minds to. By high school, the brains and beauty of the opposite gender had effectively demolished any childish notions of female helplessness. The Chinese mother in *The Good Earth*, her counterpart in *Mrs. Miniver*, the sacrifices of Fantine in *Les Miserables*, above all the trials of his own industrious mother with her two errant males, left no doubt which of the genders was more Christian. Modernity had about removed the Victorian female from her pedestal. Nevertheless, Ted, like Lindbergh, Lincoln, and so many of the notables he venerated, rather idealized women. Understandably then, barracks talk referring to them as so much meat at a butcher shop distressed him. For all his prudishness, Ted had always relished a dirty joke. Whenever shipmates recounted capers ashore, he was all ears. But the debased characterizations of women by a vocal minority saddened him. Time and time again he asked himself, "Don't they have mothers? Don't they have sisters? Isn't he married?" Conversational bestiality in Company 389 was voiced by WASPs and non-WASPs alike; nor did those mouthing barnyard values represent any particular ethnic or age group.

Along with other barracks' scuttlebutt was the rumor that their mess hall food was liberally spiced with saltpeter. The thought of impotency among such a sexually active age group sparked considerable comment. Company 389's apprehension climaxed one night about 0200. Exuberantly shouting, "It's not true, it's not true. I had a wet dream," a Greek-American awakened most of the men asleep on the lower deck. Jubilant cheers arose from neighboring bunks. Before returning to their slumbers, the laughing revelers congratulated one another on their virility. Ted thought the entire matter hilarious. Such horseplay, along with other humorous episodes, undoubtedly helped him cope with his comrades' sorry denigration of women.

Sailor society had plenty of flaws. Of supreme importance, the Navy was revealing to Ted Hinckley, sometimes kindly, sometimes uncomfortably, his own flaws, his own abundant inadequacies.

Shortly before the end of their boot training in October 1943, the apprentice seamen-soon-to-become-seamen second class got their first San Diego weekend liberty. Ted took his with five men who, like himself, were about to head east to Memphis, Tennessee for training as aviation radiomen. A delicious meal of scallops at the Golden Lion restaurant, a movie off the Plaza, followed by a happy reunion with his mother at San Diego's Broadway YMCA capped a perfect liberty. Certainly the reports from the home front were positive. Sister Jane had plenty of boy friends, his dog missed him, as did "Stimmy's car," and his room and books were ready for "Admiral Hinckley's inspection." The Major? Recalling his painful departure from his father, Ted dodged that question. His mother's warm greeting and their mutually satisfying conversation, echoed none of the family tension that had pervaded his last two years at home.

Millington, Tennessee's Naval Air Technical Training Center lay approximately twenty miles north of Memphis. In 1942 it had consisted of little more than barren earth stacked with piles of lumber. By the time Seaman Second Class Hinckley arrived there in early November 1943, the sprawling government tract boasted neat rows of wooden two-story barracks, classroom buildings, machine shops, chow halls, gyms, a firing range, and chapel. For a tyro sailor to become an aviation radioman, machinist, or ordnanceman required approximately twenty weeks. Situated across the highway bordering NATTC was an airfield, a cadet aviators' training station operating dozens of the Navy's famed open-cockpit, two-wing Yellow Perils. The continual buzz from the biplanes' radial engines reminded Ted and his fellow strikers (Navy term for apprentices seeking a specific rating) that someday they too would be airborne.

"*Vaya con Dios.*" And with that warm good-bye, his Mexican-American friend, along with a half-dozen other San Diego acquaintances departed Millington for New Orleans. Even before commencing their technical training at NATTC, a fresh new round of interviews and written and physical exams had shot down their dreams of flying. NATTC reaffirmed what boot camp had begun: Ted, his classmates, in fact everyone in the entire Navy was in constant competition. Competition advanced one from grade to grade, rank to rank. Failure to compete, to measure up meant being passed up. Competition for some duty assignments, special schools, even certain ships and air squadrons could be surprisingly difficult. Competition crafted and then honed the end product of this vast killing machine. Wartime competition dictated death or survival for a nation and its way of life. Marines tasted its Darwinian essence in their brutal training; fun-loving sailors didn't really appreciate that "battle is the pay off" until their first combat.

Ted's swelling determination not to wash out may have surprised him more than it did his parents. Following wake-up calisthenics and excellent breakfasts, week days were devoted to class work, skeet shooting, and physical conditioning. Running the obstacle course and its parallel tests for tempering the flesh posed no serious difficulty. To perfect their deflection shooting, the trainees blasted away with shotguns at clay pigeons—hundreds and hundreds of them. Ted loved it—a succession of Fourth of Julys! Disgusted at his careless novices, an instructor placed a bottle of catsup in an empty wooden apple box. He then ordered a heretofore loudmouth to fire a round at the box and bottle standing five feet away. No Independence Day romp, skeet shooting could obliterate someone.

For aviation radiomen strikers, a majority of their classroom time was spent learning to send and receive the Morse code. Like a typing class or language lab, the process demanded endless stimulus responses, in this case responses to "dit-dah recordings." Commencing at a slow pace, the rapidity of the signals steadily increased week by week. Twenty words a minute after twenty weeks was the goal; a majority never quite reached that speed. Ted didn't, but as his scores in radio theory, radio operation, semaphore and blinker signaling, and most everything else were in the top third, he slipped by.

While his mind cooperated, his body didn't. Appointed a section leader and hardly settled into the NATTC routine, he came down with measles. Two months later he contracted a dizzying case of scarlet fever. Of course he lost his section leadership. Worse, each sickness necessitated being set back and joining another class, thus extending his training at NATTC. Letters to his parents never fully revealed his angry frustration, nor the haunting dread of never flying. "Whenever I feel low or discouraged I just think of the car, the dog, and a pal on the way to the beach."

Unlike so many of the men with whom he served, Hinckley's pre-Navy youth had wanted for nothing; indeed, his parents had given him a nurture rich with educational and recreational experiences. It, therefore, reveals something about the quality of Navy life in 1943-44 when the lad who had had it all never stopped being delighted by the diverse resources available in Uncle Sam's Navy. Ted took full advantage of the first-run movies, as he did the base's low-priced pogey bait (candy). Although he never signed up for any of the numerous night classes leading to advanced civilian certifications, he did get a prime seat when NATTC imported a road show performance of *The Male Animal.* Ted had earlier benefited from the James Thurber-Elliott Nugent quasi-comedy at the Pasadena Playhouse. Walking back to his barracks, he pondered why some officer—surely he couldn't have been a Regular—brought aboard a stage production with a theme so cross-grained to Navy authoritarianism. Why the Navy went to such trouble to nourish minds puzzled him.

Evenings not devoted to writing letters or attending the current flick found his nose in a book. A few classmates called him "the professor." Some raised the quite normal question, "Why don't you ever go ashore?" Not long after arriving at NATTC, Ted did take a weekend liberty in Memphis. Accompanied by other sailors, he bused around the city to see the sights and, hopefully, some pretty girls. He ate genuine southern cooking and enjoyed a movie. With five swabbies he shared a so-so night's sleep in the city's popular Peabody Hotel. On two counts the occasion spelled the end to such excursions. First, at least until he got promoted, he couldn't afford liberties. At San Diego in a fit of patriotism he had signed up for the maximum defense bond withholding; he now had scarcely enough money to take care of his everyday sundry expenses. And while his NATTC bunk was no substitute for a bed in the Peabody Hotel, it was free. Ditto for that delicious Memphis cuisine. To ask his parents for recreation money was unthinkable. Furthermore, Memphis' crush of fun-seeking strikers and aviation cadets had skewed the male supply-and-demand curve. If going to town meant merely looking at pretty girls, why leave NATTC?

Attractive, snappily dressed WAVES had been in evidence at San Diego, but only at a distance. At Millington they mixed with the men right in the classes; a few were teachers, even administrative officers. Their abilities quickly eliminated Ted's misgivings about women in the military; feminine charm couldn't mask their seriousness of purpose. And given the random snickers they smilingly suffered, he had to conclude their patriotic sacrifice matched, if not exceeded, his own. On a number of occasions he really wanted to ask one of them to attend a Training Center movie with him. Reason checked his heart. To get involved when he really had no sure idea what lay ahead seemed most foolish. Heaven knows why Ted felt it necessary to write his sister of a mythical lovely. "Had a swell date a couple of nights ago. Beautiful black hair, brown eyes, tan complexion, and what a figure. We went to a dance at the Methodist Church, and dinner at her house afterward. She has two brothers in the Navy . . ." Perhaps Jane may have believed this harmless bit of fantasy. However, if she didn't, kindness restrained her

from ever inquiring about older brother's "beautiful black-haired" creation.

Off base or on, healthy gender
relationships were befogged by steamy
sexcapades of which sailors never
seemed to tire. One morning before
marching off to class, jocular impru-
dence suddenly took on hushed, grim
overtones. Ordered to line up at one
end of their barracks with two stern-
faced officers in attendance—a most
unusual occurrence—a personable
classmate was commanded to step
forth and stand at attention. The lieutenant then read the deck court find-
ings which forthwith terminated the
accused's duty at NATTC. In essence,
this married bluejacket had trifled
with the affections of a Memphis belle.

*Sister Jane, whose lengthy wartime
letters proved to be marvelous morale
boosters.*

Furious that he had tired of her, and informed that he had a wife back
home, the scorned woman insisted that charges of adultery be brought
against him. They were. And before the day ended, the adulterer was
on his way to New Orleans and sea duty.

Only a half-wit, an impossibly naive person could have believed that
NATTC had purged itself of adultery. Lonely, sex-starved, predatory
married men and officers alike played that game. The incident stunned
the barracks. Going ashore was not only a waste of money, it could be
positively dangerous—momentarily Millington's cause célèbre proved it.

Swimming at the Center's large pool calmed Ted's body, usually
spent by the time a weekend arrived. For his mind there was NATTC's
wonderful oasis, its library. How differently the *New York Times* and the
Chicago Tribune viewed America. In 1940, and to his parents extreme
displeasure, Franklin D. Roosevelt had won an unparalleled third term.
Now in early 1944 there was speculation that America's commander in
chief was preparing to run for a fourth term. Domestic politics might be
off limits in the military during wartime, but in that library's Sunday
newspapers, man's greatest game was snarlingly alive. Ted loved it.
Library subscriptions to *Life* and the *Saturday Evening Post*—when
someone else hadn't beaten him to them—updated him on a world at
war. *Yank*, the armed forces weekly, did likewise. *Yank* featured Milton
Caniff's "Male Call" with sexy Miss Lace; indisputably the cartoonist's
black-haired creation advanced the war effort.

Unmotivated to sign up for an Armed Forces Institute course, Ted did
cherish his own reading course. A friend's recommendation of *Oliver
Wiswell*—thereafter he read every Kenneth Roberts novel he could get
his hands on—along with Fletcher Pratt's *Fighting Ships of the U.S. Navy*
helped hurry up his two hospital stays. He stalled out with his mother's
gift of *The Robe*. However, a *Mercury* magazine condensation of *Love at*

First Flight, detailing the adventures of Navy aviation cadet life, tickled his fancy. Why not apply for pilot training? No, sitting up front and actually flying a plane was premature. He had yet to master his responsibilities as a rear seat radioman-gunner.

Body, mind, and spirit, yes, the Navy had generously provided for the religious life of its charges. With some simple interior changes, Jewish, Catholic, and Protestant chaplains utilized the same religious sanctuary at NATTC. Indeed, while Ted was there, men belonging to the Church of Jesus Christ of Latter Day Saints requested that they be supplied a meeting place. The Mormons were promptly accommodated. Reading about this in the base newspaper, the *Bluejacket*, he may have had a little better idea why he was willing to risk his life for amalgam America.

One evening Ted joined a group of barracks buddies to see *The Sullivans*. The five Sullivans had gained national prominence in America after their cruiser, the USS *Juneau*, had been sunk in a battle off Guadalcanal. Unlike Mrs. Lydia Bixby to whom President Lincoln wrote his famous condolence after being erroneously informed of her loss of five sons, Mrs. Alleta Sullivan actually had lost five sons: Joseph, Francis, Albert, Madison, and George. Hollywood's treatment of the deceased Sullivans exhibited none of the vaingloriousness of *Bataan* and too many other war films. *The Sullivans* footage dealt almost entirely with their prewar Iowa roots. A tear-jerker, Ted was not spared. Once again he was compelled to reconsider why he had enlisted and what the war was about. The film tended to confirm a stereotype being formed by his naval service: unlike the recruits from the East and West Coasts, military service for men from middle America's heartland was less a lark than a commitment. Word that a new destroyer had been christened *The Sullivans* pleased him, as did a news photo of their sister, Genevieve, in a WAVE uniform.

Unintentionally the simple nobility of the Sullivans tacitly ridiculed those seeking to transform "the war effort" into a crusade. If there were WASPs itching to evangelize the Japanese, Ted never encountered any. Certainly he never envisioned himself a gallant warrior in some global Christian crusade. A brain snap of himself acting as a squire to some knightly pilot was agreeable but silly. Like millions of Americans, he had been repeatedly affected by the sobering "Four Freedoms" credo so eloquently embodied in Norman Rockwell's paintings. And undeniably each passing day left him more impressed by his embattled country's majesty and might. Nevertheless, and notwithstanding all his patriotic pride, Seaman Second Class Hinckley and his shipmates desired little more than "to get the damn war over and go home." But having blasted "the Nazis and Nips to smithereens," what then? And what were millions of "fighting men and women" going to do when they went home to "a peacetime America?"

No one could fully answer the ethical as well as the social implications raised by such enigmatic projections. Periodically NATTC's chaplains struggled with them. Ted generally attended the Sunday morning Protestant service. Both the music and the message appealed to him. A believer, the prayers to an Almighty God comforted him. The size of the Training Center justified several Protestant chaplains; however, for most sailors to turn to one of them for guidance—all chaplains were officers—confessed weakness. With their superior education, officers had fewer compunctions about seeking out a chaplain. At Millington, Ted never took it upon himself to shoot the breeze with a padre, nevertheless he greatly benefited from their thoughtful sermons. Reluctant to wrestle with the morality of war, the chaplains didn't hesitate to examine how the war was changing men in uniform. Capturing his special attention were pulpit reflections on what Christian men and women should be doing to prepare themselves once victory was won.

On 29 April 1944, and at last a seaman first class, Aviation Radioman Hinckley had won a victory for himself. NATTC's band enlivened that happy graduation day with "America the Beautiful"—it was becoming more beautiful every day—"Anchors Aweigh," and the "Marine Hymn"—the latter in honor of the "Seagoing Bellhops" who had also completed their training in either radio, mechanics, or ordnance. A third class aviation radioman's rating had eluded him. Albeit, he had learned a great deal about Navy communications and the fundamentals of aerial gunnery. Recalling all this was the officer presiding over the graduation ceremony. Ceremonial protocol, as Ted was also learning, held a high priority in the Navy.

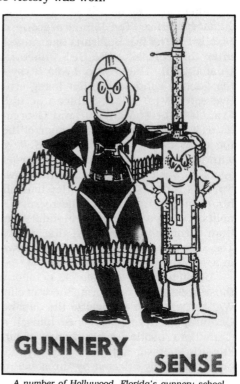

GUNNERY SENSE

A number of Hollywood, Florida's gunnery school publications were entertainingly illustrated by the cartoonist Robert Osborn.

Revealingly, every participating officer listed in the graduation program, Navy or Marine Corps, was a Reservist. Supplying the invocation was Chaplain M. R. Costanzo, whose sermons had repeatedly boosted Ted's morale. Costanzo gave him a reassuring smile as the certifications were presented.

Immensely relieved that he would soon be on his way to Hollywood, Florida for full-time gunnery training, Ted joined his three closest training school buddies for an evening of celebration.

Warren Hageman and Ray Gumm formed a Mutt and Jeff duo. Well over six feet in height, laconic Gumm hailed from London, Kentucky.

His mature judgment considerably exceeded his eighteen years. Possibly Hageman's short stature had early on driven him to excel; an engaging quipster, his uniform was the only one that sported a brand new third class radioman's rate. The third of the three men to whom Ted had been closely drawn, all of whom would accompany him through the remainder of his Florida training, was J. Harold Smith. An Oregon farm boy, Hal was a Mormon. He had already presented Ted with a copy of *The Book of Mormon*. In his good-natured yet earnest fashion, Hal explained "America's greatest homegrown religion." Ted was proud of his three friends and looked forward to introducing them to his family.

Had these four happy-go-lucky sailors known the flaming ferocity awaiting each of them aboard their respective flattops, would they still have rejoiced at the prospect of becoming Navy flyers? Like the millions of other American servicemen and women, their tomorrows were lived today.

CHAPTER V

"Set gear for bombing runs, we are approaching target."

Gazing at his fellow sailors playing cards, reading, writing letters, and drowsing in their troop train bunks—triple level, no less—Ted conjectured on what lay ahead. Could he cut the mustard at Hollywood, Florida's Naval Air Gunnery School? Would he find the place as agreeable as the NATTC scuttlebutt had described it? In about a month's time, if all went well, his right shoulder would display a machine gun with wings on it, the patch of a certified aerial gunner.

Thus far the train ride down Florida's eastern coast was pleasant enough. But "where are the mountains," his West Coast associates humorously asked? And "when are we going to get to the end of this swamp-covered peninsula?" Ted was struck by the state's long stretches of tropical coastline, seemingly unbroken except for small towns and military bases. Recalling that it was along this coast that American history had begun, he wondered if he would ever fly over St. Augustine's historic Castillo de San Marcos. Centuries ago French, Spanish, and British arms had clashed here. Thoughts of those desperate men struggling for empire awakened reflection on his own century's titanic global-wide contest.

By mid-1944, for a Japanese war leader to believe the Americans could be defeated required remarkable optimism. As the Nipponese historian Saburo Ienaga afterward summarized: the "vast differences between Japanese and American military industrial production capacity was manifested in air power, naval tonnage replacement, battlefield equipment, [and] front-line supply capability." Ienaga believed it was "mainly due to overwhelmingly superior American air power that the Japanese Navy lost control of the seas. The Pacific island front collapsed: Tarawa and Makin [in the Gilbert Islands] fell in November 1943 and Kwajalein [in the Marshall Islands] in February 1944." Nipponese "defenders were wiped out almost to the last man." Admiral Isoroku Yamamoto's dread of awakening "a sleeping giant" had been realized. Luckily for him, he did not survive to endure the entire catastrophe befalling Japan's Pacific Empire. The Japanese code having been decrypted, Yamamoto's plane flew into an ambush. On 18 April 1943, sixteen dual-tailed Army P-38 Lightnings knocked him out of the sky.

But rolling back the Japanese was extracting a terrible cost in American ships and lives. Indeed, during October 1942, with the carrier

Hornet sunk and the *Enterprise* heavily damaged, there was a suspenseful moment with not a single fully operational U. S. carrier in the whole Pacific.

Supplying the critical difference between defeat and victory was America's overpowering military industrial production. As 1943 began, Americans celebrated the commissioning of the 27,000 ton USS *Essex*, (CV-9). Her arrival marked a new class of carriers. Over 880 feet in length, the *Essex* class flattops would become the workhorses for winning the Pacific War. Joining the *Essex* during 1943 were her sisters, *Intrepid*, *Bunker Hill*, and four more "fast carriers" honoring those which the Japanese had previously sunk: *Lexington*, *Yorktown*, *Hornet*, and *Wasp*. But the bad news for Tokyo war-planners did not stop there. Throughout that fateful year nine more flattops called light carriers (CVLs) were commissioned. Constructed on cruiser hulls, they handled about half as many warplanes as the larger *Essex* class. Nevertheless these 11,000 ton *Independence* class light carriers were quite capable of keeping up with the big, fast-moving fleet CVs. As for the ungainly-looking escort carriers that had checked the German submarine menace, they also played expanding roles in the Pacific War. In 1943 alone, thirty-five of them slid down the ways!

Despite their lack of armor and reinforced bulkheads, as well as an inability to charge along with their larger sisters, these "baby flattops" displayed a praiseworthy versatility. In addition to their antisubmarine work, escort carriers, sometimes referred to as "Jeep" carriers, assisted with aircraft transport, fleet logistical supply, and as bases from which amphibious landings could receive offshore air support. The November 1943 battle for Tarawa Atoll is rightly recalled for the frightful casualties among the Marine amphibious forces. Not so well known is the fate of the escort carrier *Liscome Bay* backing up the landings on Makin Atoll to the north. Hit by a torpedo launched from a Japanese submarine, her bomb storage ignited. With none of the stout construction of the *Essex* class, or even the *Independence* CVLs, the *Liscome Bay* quite literally blew up. Pieces from her pelted an American battleship a mile away. Over six hundred men aboard the baby flattop either went down with her or were burned to death by flaming oil.

Housing their deadly swarms of airplanes and accompanied by an expanding panoply of battleships, both heavy and light cruisers, and dozens of destroyers, America's carrier behemoths savaged the far-flung Japanese-held islands. All too slowly the Japanese admiralty awoke to their mortal danger. One of the reasons Nippon had lost the 1942 battle of Guadalcanal had been her fumbled effort to reinforce not only her forces there but to block an American seizure of Rabaul in the Bismarck Archipelago to the northwest. Reinforcements of soldiers and planes (many taken from Japanese carriers) were poured into Rabaul. Having pounded it, "rubble" as Admiral Halsey called it, Rabaul and its 100,000 defenders were thereafter ignored except for periodic "neutralizing attacks" by Army and Navy aircraft. With the Gilbert and then Marshall islands victories, Nimitz's island hopping strategy proved unstoppable.

Must the Pacific War end before Seaman First Class Hinckley and his fellow NAGS trainees fulfilled their great adventure? Eunice Hinckley prayed it would. Acutely aware of youth's folly, and struggling to prevent the sole male heir of the family from getting himself killed, both his mother and his Aunt Louise (Pat Chopin's widow) admonished him to weigh the advantages of a naval officer's life. Blandishments describing college joys were dangled before him. Before answering his aunt, who insisted on believing he was in the Army, Ted cooled off. But his mother's loving concern must be addressed. On June 11, weary of her well-intentioned epistles, Ted tried to explain why he sought sea duty with Navy Air.

> Mother, and I guess this might be an open letter to all mothers—I want a part of this war and not . . . at this time [to pursue] a college education. I am not brilliant, college is for the brilliant under present circumstances. My sons will someday ask me my status in the great war. I must and shall if humanly possible be able to tell them of a great sea, a wind swept carrier deck and roaring planes and a defeated enemy. . . . I look forward to death with fear of pain but a belief of everlasting peace . . . death for a man who has tried to be good should be celebrated.

Perhaps this may have comforted his mother.

As in hundreds of other American communities, large and small, Hollywood, Florida's merchants and tavern keepers had hailed the conversion of the old Riverside Military Academy into living quarters for the hurriedly constructed Navy Air Gunnery School. By the time Ted's class arrived in mid-May 1944, it presented a surprising degree of permanence. Tennessee's NATTC had proved sufficiently accommodating, but the living facilities at NAGS Hollywood bespoke fraternity house life: four men to a room with a private bath. Most rooms boasted a scenic view of palm trees, ocean, and tropical verdure. Outdoor athletic facilities built for the military academy—tennis, badminton, basketball, and volleyball courts—had been substantially improved, and the food was as attractive as the milieu.

WAVEs were everywhere. A cheerful lot, they were the "pistol-packing mamas" handling much of the actual firing range gunnery instruction. No less obliging were NAGS classroom instructors, some of whom were civilians. Indeed, the warm cordiality of the entire gunnery school staff smacked more of a prep school or hotel than a military installation. Given Florida's famous year-round sunshine and Miami a mere half-hour drive, it was no wonder some of Ted's classmates began scheming to join NAGS ship's company.

Pleasantly surprised at such conviviality, Ted was awakening to the happy fact that Navy airmen, officers and enlisted men alike, received treatment and benefits extended to very few uniformed Americans. Were these sailors so naive as not to discern why this was so or why they would soon be drawing flight pay once they entered actual flight operations at nearby NAS Miami (Opa-Locka)?

For all the anticipated glamour attached to those coveted aircrew-man's wings, Ted noted that at each stage in his training a few associates found some means for transferring out. A nightmare sequence of falling helplessly through space is well nigh universal. And even the most reckless of teenage drivers has suffered a panic flash at the fleeting possibility of cremation in an automobile crash. At NATTC Ted had read of a Flying Fortress crewman trapped inside a crash-landed, blazing B-17. Blocked from reaching the desperate flyer and unequipped to smother his imprisoning inferno, dozens of men helplessly endured the doomed gunner's screams for succor. Trainee Hinckley had not slept so well that night.

Peer competition, among other factors, quashed any notions about remaining safely on the ground. From Arkansas, Stimmy wrote he had completed ground school and was airborne. Word from another Pasadena pal, Louis Blatterman, indicated he too might take wing.

Facilitating Ted's surfeit of flashbacks was a daydreamer's directory of winged prewar barnstormers. Of course Lindbergh predominated. Word from his mother indicated Lucky Lindy was currently testing airplanes for the Navy. One-eyed Wiley Post had been less lucky. Spotting profit in aviator Post's streamlined *Winnie Mae*, toy manufacturers turned out a balsa kit replica for kids. Ted's *Winnie Mae* model had stalled out, meeting the same abrupt fate that befell airman Post. Then there was Jimmy Doolittle with his "unflyable" 1930s Gee-Bee. Somehow the risk-hunting Doolittle had survived those roaring air races. Could anyone forget his 1942 "bolt-out-of-the-blue" Mitchell (B-25) bomber strike against Tokyo or how those flyers had elevated their dispirited countrymen? And then there was aviator Frank Hawks who had urged American youngsters to eat Post Bran Flakes for a healthy breakfast. Ted had devoured so much of the stuff that the cereal company not only honored him with five tin-stamped wings, the last painted gold, but had advanced him to "flight commander." All that seemed so long ago, a source of reflective bemusement in 1944.

Not many flyers passed up that year's *A Guy Named Joe*, a movie tracing an American youth from flight school to combat. At one point in the aviation film, Spencer Tracy, the veteran airman, was asked by an admiring boy, "What's it like up there?" At the actor's reply, the poet in Ted's soul took off.

When you're up there . . . everything's kinda still, and you've got a feeling you're halfway to heaven. You don't even seem to hear your own motors—just a kind of buzz far off . . . like the sky was calling you . . . like the sky was singing you a song. . . .

The earth's so far below you don't care about it any more. It's the sky that's important. The sky is your pal. You feel like nudging the sky and saying, "Hello sky—how are you today, sky—and how was the moon last time you saw him?" . . . . the clouds float toward you like old friends you never want to say good-bye to. . . . And you say to yourself, "Boy, oh boy—this is the only time a man's ever alive—it's the only time he's really free!" And

the old sky, he smiles back and says, "You're right, brother—
you're right!"

Post Bran Flakes for the mind? At Hollywood, Florida, with his feet firmly planted in an inviting sandy beach, how nice to romanticize about the
beauty of being an airman.

The first week of training at NAGS concentrated on the principles of
gun-sighting, gun maintenance, and the technical aspects of both the
.30- and .50-caliber Browning machine guns. Because Ted's class was
designated to take their operational training at NAS Miami and would be
flying in the Avenger, all of the trainees were required to become profi-
cient in the torpedo plane's .50-caliber dorsal turret gun as well as the
.30-caliber stinger protruding below. NATTC had already acquainted the
fledgling airmen with these weapons whose scrambled parts must now
be assembled in just minutes. Each student was supplied with a ruled
notebook for diagramming and taking careful notes. A General Motors'
Spark Plug and Frigidaire Division, now converted to manufacturing
Browning machine guns, provided each trainee with a copy of *How the
Gun Works*. Rather like the manual given a new car owner, the illustrated booklet neatly fitted in the pocket of a sailor's dungarees.

Instead of waking up at night with the drumming dah-dit, dit-dit-dah
of the Morse Code, Ted's somnolence soon vibrated to bursts of machine
gun fire. However, first he must memorize the mechanics of these deadly instruments: butterfly handgrips, trigger, trigger pin, trigger bar pin,
sear, firing pin extension, firing pin spring, firing pin, etc.; and the
recitation of such indispensable information as: "The ammunition belt
is pulled into the gun by the belt feed pawl which is attached to the belt
feed slide. When the bolt is forward, the belt feed pawl has positioned a
cartridge directly above the chamber. The belt holding pawl is in a
raised position to prevent the ammunition belt from falling out of the
gun." A far cry from his usual reading. But, like his mother's spoonful
of castor oil, if he wanted to go out and play with his cap guns, it had to
be taken.

Four cardinal rules directed "How To Be the Oldest Living
Gunner."

1. Learn to recognize instantly *all* types of aircraft, and be able to
   judge their speed, direction, angle, and distance.
2. Know your guns and turret thoroughly—how they work and
   how to keep them working.
3. Know all about how to use tracers.
4. Practice and keep on practicing. Then *practice* some more.

If there were some sailors who tired of injunction number four, Ted
never heard of them. But the simplistic notion that a machine gun
could be employed like a garden hose was forthwith abandoned. An
attacking enemy plane knew just when to begin firing. Furthermore, it
had far more fire power mounted in its wings. To hit an incoming Zero,
a gunner must have "the GUTS AND CONFIDENCE TO WAIT until he
closes to decisive range." Not quite "Don't shoot until you see the whites
of their eyes," but it seemed so.

Before actually applying their classroom knowledge on the NAGS range, hours were spent in a simulator. This elaborate training contraption proved far more humiliating than any pinball machine. Seated in a darkened room behind a light firing machine gun, the trainee faced a movie screen on which appeared various war planes, enemies and friends alike. Every time the gunner blasted away with his light gun, an audio system barked out an appropriate rat-tat-tat. Sighting was done through a circular light sight. (On an actual, warplane two fixed metal sights sat atop the .30-caliber weapon; the larger turret gun utilized an enclosed illuminated sight.) When the filmed attacker was in the proper position to be shot at, that is located correctly on the simulator's circular light sight, the trainee blasted away. The instructor also had a guidance light which enabled him to intervene once the mock firing began. The Navy's Bureau of Aeronautics' *Gunnery Sense* rhapsodized how each pupil had the potential "to handle his weapon with all the precision and skill of a great musician."

Comments by simulator instructors were less florid.

"You're wasting precious ammunition. He's not even in range."

"Lower your fire, damn it. I said lower your fire!"

"Lead him half a rad, not a whole one."

"Damn it to hell, you're leading too far. The target, Hinckley, the lousy target—are you blind?"

"Sailor, that was a British Spitfire you just shot down."

The aerial battle station for aviation radiomen was the .30-caliber belly or tunnel gun. Pointing down and rearward from the radio-radar-bombardier compartment, Ted's weapon did not emit the large slug of the .50-caliber turret gun mounted topside. But the radioman's machine gun did erupt with an ear-gratifying rate of fire, eleven hundred rounds per minute, as opposed to five hundred for the .50-caliber.

Among other transition apparatuses were shotguns that looked and tracked like machine guns. Clay pigeons supplied the targets. Following the first week, the trainees spent every other day at the range located out in barren wetlands. Navy educators had formulated a step-by-step program which demanded maximum safety. Congeniality braced by absolute do's and don'ts may perhaps describe the atmosphere of that deafening place. For Marines, it was a familiar, deadly cacophony; for sailors, a diverting oversized shooting gallery.

Nothing quite prepared one for actually shooting a .30-caliber automatic weapon. For all the fun of muscling the vibrating, roaring instrument, keeping one's eyes open while his chin rested on his hands clasping the butterfly hand-grips—critical for sighting along its barrel—posed something of a problem. Ted consistently shot in the top half of his class; indeed, his shooting scores steadily improved. Unfortunately his code sending and receiving scores stubbornly refused to.

Midway during NAGS, he received a phone message from an Ensign Bob Sands, attached to the nearby Navy Navigation School. "Come over Sunday and have dinner with us. Ted, you don't remember us but I graduated from South Pas High a couple of years ahead of you." "Us" turned out to be Bob and his mother, who had come out from California to assist him with housekeeping chores. Ted had never before eaten pecan pie; in Mrs. Sand's dessert, the profusion of pecans went right on through to the bottom crust. Far richer than all of Mother Sands' delicious cooking was her son's lively mind. A recent Princeton graduate and ebullient about almost everything, Bob provided a stimulating companion during Ted's Florida training tours. The first class seaman had a hearty laugh when Ensign Sands urged him "to apply to Princeton when the war's over." Certainly the flattery was an anodyne for teenage insecurity.

In truth, this youth's particular insecurities were being eradicated in a hundred ways. Sigmund Freud might have accounted for the WASP's swelling masculine confidence by citing a machine gun-induced catharsis. Seaman Hinckley knew nothing about Dr. Freud's aggression theories, but he sure did enjoy ripping away at the large white sheet whenever it came careening down the gunnery range track. A May 31st letter to his parents spelled out Ted's continuing anxieties. "If I ever get wings you may well be proud—but sometimes I have my doubts." According to his letters home, among his continuing weaknesses were "math of all types—ouch" and "nervousness I still spring and jump—too impulsive." But he did "have many assets. . . . Don't drink. Don't smoke. Don't gamble. Don't touch cheap women." And then in case his father thought less of him for such monasticism, "P.S. Don't worry I am no lily, and the fellows openly respect me." Respect for himself was rapidly rising. In a Father's Day letter to his dad, Ted confided he wished to become either a lawyer, historian, or YMCA worker. Ted Jr. also expressed his desire to get married as quickly as possible after the war. Patently, Navy life had notably accelerated much more than professional goals.

Prior to graduation, Ted's class boarded a Navy bus for their introduction to NAS Miami. Located at Opa-Locka on Miami's outskirts, the airfield was roost for the flock of Avengers which each week zoomed about in the skies above Hollywood's shore front. It proved to be a most memorable day. Memorable because the junior birdmen ascended to 30,000 feet without ever leaving the ground. Memorable because they talked with aircrewmen who had actually been in combat. And especially memorable because they at last inspected first hand the largest single-engine warplane in the Pacific War, Grumman's redoubtable Avenger.

Before being locked in Opa-Locka's steel pressure chamber, Ted, along with his six-man group, had their blood pressure measured by a Navy medic. The corpsman-teacher then accompanied them on their mock ascension to 5,000, 10,000, and 15,000 feet. At that point the decreased air pressure required that oxygen masks be firmly in place and functioning. Protected from anoxia and the "kindest death imaginable," the men eventually got up to 30,000 feet. To convince the trainees exactly how treacherous was the intoxication of anoxia, one of them agreed to remove his oxygen mask and react to a set of commands. No different than an inebriated sailor, the guinea pig quickly, smilingly lost control of his senses. Before he completely passed out, his mask was slapped back on. An unforgettable experience, but for most of the trainee flyers, anoxia never posed a threat. Torpedo bombers usually flew to their target well below 15,000 feet.

As at NATTC, periodic guard duty obligated nighttime watches. Standing watch for two or three hours offered abundant opportunity for reflection. Reading was, of course, forbidden. And of course whenever lighting was available, Ted dodged this restriction. Due to the gunnery range's extent, sentries generally floundered around in semi-darkness. In the early morning hours of June 6, and half asleep, Ted found himself momentarily mesmerized by a moon-lighted cloud pageant. The night sky appeared to be filled with giant Rubenesque-like men; the figures seemed tormented and engaged in a deadly struggle.

"Hinckley, your watch is up," came out of the darkness. And then those long awaited words, "We've invaded Europe." At breakfast everyone speculated on how long it would take General Eisenhower's Army to demolish the German defender. But might not the cross-channel invasion be reversed? After all, the colossal amphibious assault could be shattered. It had happened at the Dieppe rehearsal in the summer of 1942. No one voiced such a probability. The crushing momentum of Europe's Allied war machine was irresistible. How wonderful to have perception become reality!

Rejoicing at the historic 6 June 1944, success, Ted wished he could have been present "and helping blast to hell the Huns who still thought they were the master of any Yankee Doodle Boy." Rather carried away with the epic moment, he admitted to his parents, "I get terribly hot inside when I think of the Japs and Huns who caused this damn mess. I feel like I might become a menace in air combat instead of an asset."

Warrior Hinckley's psychological condition was stable enough, but his physiological repair had become one big pain in the crotch. Florida's humidity had cursed him with a disabling case of jock itch. Sickbay salves, three showers a day, and a plenitude of baby powder, nothing could eradicate the bane.

His last day on the range, these were the scores that counted. With an enraging itch, he stumbled out to his assigned turret. Nothing would have given him greater pleasure than to tear off his dungarees and attack his torture.

"What's the matter, sailor?" inquired the cork-helmeted WAVE supervising his .50-caliber station. With a wan smile, he blurted out his agony. "Let's not use this turret," she replied. "I just bore-sighted the gun at the end of the line. Nobody is assigned to it. Let's try it."

Climbing into the turret hurt. Looking at the ammunition belt, Ted noted its bullets were capped with blue paint. He had seen the instructor before, appreciated her twinkle at the mess hall, and now she was telling him exactly what to do to get a maximum score. He followed her coaching precisely. As the target rounded the corner, and with his weeks of training synthesized into microseconds, he sighted and slammed away. A few hours later the day's scores were posted. Blue-rimmed holes perforated the sheet—Hinckley was top man!

The hours-long examination, designed to prevent anyone from achieving a perfect score, was tough. Ted knew he had flunked it. Twenty mistakes were permitted on the radio code phase; Ted had nineteen. As at Millington, only those who scored highest in their class were promoted. To his great astonishment, and euphoria, he not only passed but was rated a third-class petty officer. For the first time in his adult life, in stiff competition with his peers, he had attained excellence. Only weeks afterward did the self-styled "cock-of-the-walk" dare admit that it was not himself but the caring generosity of that WAVE gunnery instructor that probably made the critical difference.

In June of 1944 NAS Miami couldn't boast Hollywood's four-to-a-room living quarters, but it possessed everything else. Above all, Opa-Locka had aircraft, lots of them. Finally the trainee aircrewmen could enjoy uninterrupted sleep—no more sleep-stealing guard duty. Shotgun-armed "gyrenes" supervised airfield security. "Marine sentries shoot to kill," warned the base information officer. "Stay away from the perimeter fence after dark." But within, rank had its privileges; apprentice seamen swept the aircrewman's living quarters, cleaned the toilets, and handled scullery chores.

Ted's lingering personal doubts had vanished, notwithstanding the periodic pain from his infernal jock itch. In eight weeks the third-class radioman-gunner could claim those coveted wings and be headed home for a twenty-day leave. That is, unless he screwed up. Surviving classmates from NATTC and NAGs reassured one another all would be well.

In truth, flying was going to require a quite different form of confidence building. A month or so earlier, an Avenger's faulty engine had cut out on takeoff. Impulsively the pilot attempted the impossible—a 180-degree turn on a dead engine. The plane dropped like a stone. All three men aboard were killed. The officer who described this "cockpit failure as well as engine failure" cannot have been surprised when a member of Ted's class opted out. Flying behind an inexperienced pilot required a faith the dropout could not muster. Nobody condemned him. Everyone else wished very much to live.

Following a day or so of base orientation, more physical examinations, psychological interviews, and interminable paper shuffling, Training Flight 335 took shape. Pilots and crews melded. Pasadena's enthusiastic third class radioman met an embryo Avenger pilot from Carlinville, Illinois, as well as a turret gunner from the Pacific Northwest. Not so long ago twenty-one-year-old Ensign William P. Witt had "plowed a mean furrow"; unreservedly the tyro birdman was eager to return to Lincoln Land "just as soon as this damn war is over." Witt would remain Ted's pilot until war's end. The third member of the Witt-Hinckley Avenger team, Ellsworth P. Shaffer, was a butcher's son. Al had already become a highly-qualified aviation-machinist. With a broad pumpkin grin and an eye for the ladies, he soon vowed to educate his Puritan tunnel gunner on the joys of libidinous living. Ted got the last laugh. Two

The Nit-Witts at NAS Hilo, Hawaii
(Left to right: Ellsworth P. Shaffer, William P. Witt and author)

years later Hinckley would serve as best man at Aviation Machinist Mate Shaffer's wedding. As for the two aircrewmen's relationship with their relaxed farm boy pilot, it always remained "Mr. Witt." All three preferred it that way.

The CO of their operational class, Marine Captain LaBat, had acquired Avenger combat experience in the Solomon Islands fighting. Tall in carriage and trim in appearance, LaBat turned out to be a pilot's pilot. But what about the airplane that Ted henceforth described ad nauseam to old California friends, his parents, and anyone else who mistakenly inquired, "And what do you fly?"

In the opinion of the 1943 Navy Bureau of Aeronautics "the TBF 'Avenger' . . . is probably the best carrier-based torpedo plane so far seen in action." Throughout that year and 1944, both its hardiness and versatility tended to confirm the Bureau's praise. Actually the forty-one-foot-long aircraft, with its broad, fifty-four-foot wing span had not done so well in its initial encounter with the Japanese.

At the June 1942 Battle of Midway, six TBF-ls had taken off from Midway Island. Ironically, they had been rushed across the Pacific and just missed their fleet destination with doomed VT-8 on the *Hornet*. Only one Avenger returned to Midway from their battle baptism. None apparently had inflicted any damage on the enemy. However, that lone survivor confirmed what Navy aviators generally affirmed: Grumman Aircraft Engineering Corporation of Bethpage, Long Island, New York "builds one helluva plane." Midway's solitary survivor had staggered home with "only the trim tab for longitudinal control, with one wheel and the torpedo bay doors hanging open." One of its gunners was wounded, the other dead.

Not an auspicious launch into Naval Air history. Nonetheless, the Avenger's 1700 horsepower (later increased) engine gave it a maximum speed of over 275 mph, while its ability to carry four 500-lb. bombs or a ship-stabbing torpedo, plus .50-caliber wing guns (one in each wing) for frontal defense or strafing, made it a much more deadly aircraft than its 206 mph TBD predecessor. By the time NAS Miami's Flight 335 was in training, TBFs had been joined by TBMs, the same warplane, with minor modifications, but built by General Motors Corporation, Eastern Aircraft Division, Trenton, New Jersey. Ultimately over 9,800 Avengers, a majority of which were TBMs, came off the production lines to serve aboard CVEs, CVLs, and CVs.

On July 1, radioman Hinckley had yet to fly. But already he was extolling the Avenger's virtues and his pilot's competence. Undoubtedly he desired to reassure his parents—and himself.

All the pilots swear by them. According to ACI (Air Combat Intelligence) . . . the TBF is the finest plane in the air for its size, speed, strength, job and defense. The fellows all act like a bunch of kids when it comes to their pilots. They lie awake far into the night arguing why their skipper is by far the finest torpedo plane pilot in the world.

And his fellow crewman: "a genius when it comes to mechanics." Such hyperbole when his son had not flown can only have amused his father. One must guess the Major's reaction when a few weeks earlier the family's Florida correspondent wrote him he would rather "die a million times before missing this grand finale." For all the youth's foolish bravura, the Pacific War was indeed moving toward its inexorable finale.

During June, concurrent with the Allied assault on Germany's European fortress, Admiral Marc Mitscher's Task Force 58 opened a new front in the Pacific War. Equipped with nine fleet and six light carriers, Mitscher's fighter sweeps hit Saipan and Tinian in the Marianas. It was a daring cross-Pacific leap from the Marshall Islands seized earlier in the year. To assure that the invasion of the Marianas would be successful, "Japan's Gibraltar," Truk Atoll to the south, had been neutralized in February by smashing aerial and surface bombardment. During Truk's pummeling, and rejoicing after three kills, an F6F Hellcat ace remarked, "These Grummans are beautiful planes. If they could cook, I'd marry one."

Counting on support from Japanese warplanes flying from airfields in the Marianas and Guam, Admiral Jisaburo Ozawa determined to challenge Mitscher's fleet. Unaware of how badly American carrier aircraft had battered these islands, Ozawa's outnumbered ships and flyers encountered a veritable cyclone of destruction. The "Marianas Turkey Shoot" witnessed the sacrifice of hundreds of Japanese aircraft. At the conclusion of the mid-June Battle of the Philippine Sea, Japan had lost three flattops: two had been sunk by U.S. submarines, the third by Avengers. Due in part to faulty U.S. torpedoes, six of Ozawa's carriers had escaped. But the American invasion of the Marianas was successfully launched. And although the Japanese defense proved as formidable as ever, the relative cost in American lives was fewer than at Guadalcanal or Tarawa.

The following month, American amphibious forces landed on Guam. Outnumbered, out-gunned, and desperate, Nippon suffered one bitter defeat after another. Honoring their Bushido code, they had no other alternative.

On July 5, in an effervescent letter to his parents, Ted celebrated his first flight—his first since 1928.

Excited? You bet your boots. . . . I got a quick glimpse of a lad on his pop's shoulders waving futilely at us and thought of how Larry Hoyt and I used to wave at the Navy planes at Del Mar [sixteen miles north of NAS San Diego] . . . . Oh how beautiful it was. . . . Our plane made a sharp bank to the port and came up not fifteen feet apart from another plane—and then another plane formed on our starboard until all six planes were flying in formation. Until then it had all been a dream, a beautiful thrilling new experience. Now I looked out and could see six Avengers, Jap hating and glorying in their prestige as the deadliest Navy plane in the world.

So much for the home front; no Navy public relations officer could have puffed any better.

As the three flyers, Witt, Hinckley, and Shaffer, had walked out to their inaugural flight together, Ensign Witt had remarked, "Men, we are going to be together a long time. We shall learn to work as machines with a brain. . . we will be companions and as a team. . . we will fly in some battle zone." Minutes into their first flight, Witt's radioman was in a battle zone. His entire sensory system began shouting out all kinds of distress signals. His eustachian tubes complained at the erratic bobbing up and down. His nose and lungs gagged on the mixed smells of engine fumes, greased metal, hydraulic fluid, and overheated plastic. The small, oval windows port and starboard offered but slight relief, blurring eyes confronted fuzzy knobs and meaningless switches. His stomach was somersaulting.

Lucky Lindy in his open cockpit with the clean air caressing him, "a guy named Joe" with those stirring words about "the only time a man is ever really free"—what in the hell was Ted Hinckley doing imprisoned in this foul-smelling, madly vibrating death trap?

Witt's voice: "Radioman, we're out over water. You can put the guts in your gun." This safety regulation had been instituted to assure that Miami's citizens didn't get a deadly shower from an errant machine gun or gunner.

At that Shaffer inverted his turret and the housing for his gun pointed straight up. Below him a very sick radioman struggled to shove the .50-caliber upward into its casing. Somehow he did so. Turning around, he tried to fold up his metal bench seat so he could check his own belly gun. But Ted's belly had had enough. Reaching for the waxed paper sack which the Navy had provided, he just made it. Shaffer had meanwhile returned the turret to its proper position. His hand waved wildly. Handed a waxed sack, he too relieved himself. The Avenger's tunnel smelled like a sewer. Hinckley kept adding to the stink; not all of his vomit reached its paper target. Trying to wipe up the mess only added to his air sickness.

Fortunately fledglings had been properly forewarned about this particular rite of passage. Ted gained a modicum of comfort in knowing that his buddies, old and new were doubtlessly suffering the same agony.

Flight 335's inaugural operation had been posted as a bombing and gunnery exercise. TBM glide bombing differed from dive bombing primarily in the dive angle. The technique had first been developed in July 1942 after the Battle of Midway aboard the *Enterprise* by the reorganized Torpedo Squadron Six. Instead of going straight down on a target, Avengers glide-bombed at approximately forty-five degrees.

"Pilot to radioman. Set gear for bombing runs we are approaching target . . ."
"All set, sir . . ."
The first plane pulled over and went into its run! I could see his bomb drop beyond the target [dye marker]. Then we dropped and so did my stomach.
Their Avenger could not possibly avoid crashing into the Atlantic Ocean. More vomiting by both crewmen.
I felt a little relieved but forgot my duties. It was not two minutes when the pilot yelled over the ICS.
"Radioman, Radioman where did I hit, let's get on the ball," in a most angry tone.
"Sorry, sir, did not see it."
"Next run don't fail to see it!"
"Roger sir, out."
For six runs after that I gave him his results. All the time I was giving him the results of the hits scored by the flight leader up in front. . . . The gunnery hop was called off . . . [due to approximately a dozen puking crewmen].

On landing, Hinckley "caught hell" from Witt; "none of our practice bombs had been released." But the pilots, too, were green, although none as green as Shaffer's ghostly face. Familiar with the bonding accompanying group pain and punishment, Ted awoke to how group distress could overcome the heretofore rigid separation between enlisted men and officers.

The heck I received from my pilot was light compared to what another pilot in our flight received from the Skipper for landing incorrectly. He simply cussed him out, gave him hell, degraded him. . . . All the pilot could do was just what I did. Take it, profit by it, and never make the same mistake again.
But of course some did. One pilot whose father must have operated a jackhammer handled his stick so crudely that whenever he swung into the formation, a midair collision seemed imminent. Three sloppy join-ups and he was out.

By July 8, Ted could write his parents that although still plagued by air sickness, "Think I have conquered fear." Such prayerful speculation might reduce air sickness but not his uneasiness encased in the bowels of a malodorous TBM. Manifestly this sailor was no budding Lindbergh. On their third hop, convinced his plane was tearing apart, he snapped on his chute pack and prepared to jump. Only Witt's startled intervention stopped him. Nor was he alone. Another terrified fledgling in a different class did jump! On yet another flight, Hinckley succeeded in losing the formation's sleeve target housed in their bomb bay. Watching his sparkling new watch—a gift from sister Jane—joining the improperly deployed sleeve fluttering down into the Gulf Stream, he thanked God it was not his left hand. Fortunately, whenever he and Shaffer had an opportunity to hammer away at a sleeve target, they did well. Witt was right, "Don't think about anything but your task, otherwise you'll get sick." Their pilot should have added, "and scared."

Halfway through his training, Florida's gift to his "private parts"—his mother's term—had become almost unbearable. Every time he put on his parachute harness the spreading scabs cracked. Some were bleeding and the infection had spread fore and aft. He looked like something out of Dr. Newcomb's rogues gallery. Angrily demanding relief from a rather wide-eyed nurse, the crippled flyer was informed, "You're going to sick bay if this medicine doesn't do the job." It didn't. And he didn't report to sick bay. In four weeks a Pasadena heaven and Eunice's home remedies should alleviate his pain in the ass.

Interwoven with their numerous group flights were ground school classes. Henceforth "friend or foe" recognition slide sessions required a more discriminating eye. Minor differences in ship and plane silhouettes might spell the difference in future sea battles. In fact, both Japanese and American aviators continued making erroneous damage assessments of enemy vessels. Comic on occasion, mistaken identification too often proved tragic. Attacked by American planes, U.S. submarines grew wary of rescuing downed naval aviators.

At NATTC, Ted and his classmates had been introduced to aerial radar. Two weeks of hush-hush instruction had demonstrated how the black box with its green-lighted screen and dancing blips could be used in navigation and sighting ships at sea. Ted was struck by the horizontal radar antennas attached beneath each wing, not because he controlled their search movement but due to the intriguing name "Yagi." Named after its inventor Hidetsugu Yagi, the directional antenna once again reminded Ted how fatuous was the old prewar canard, "All the Japs can do is copy others." Twice at NAS Miami he boarded a two-engined Beechcraft SNB for inflight radar training off the coast of Key West. As with most of his equipment, Hinckley's self-confidence remained only so-so.

Classes in bombing, photography, sea survival, and particularly on how to deploy a parachute won attentive audiences. For Avenger crews, the TBM radioman's hatch was the sole means of airborne escape. Therefore each man's chest-pack parachute was stowed directly over that solitary starboard hatch. Unlike the pilot who sat on his conventional, always attached parachute, the turret gunner had no room for a parachute. Radiomen generally chose not to wear a chest chute because it encumbered their tunnel mobility. However, all TBM crews wore their parachute harnesses.

Parachutes promised deliverance. Ted was all ears. Standard Operating Procedure dictated "four convenient phases": the decision to bail out; the act of leaving the plane; the procedure during descent; and the landing. Judging from Opa-Locka's instructor, the landing, which should have been the easiest phase, had recently caused the most difficulty. For starters, men descending in parachutes too often slipped out of their harness hundreds of feet above the open sea. A fatal optical illusion had convinced them they were but a few feet from salt water, thus the warning to absolutely never free themselves from their chutes until their feet were actually in the water. Once that had been successfully accomplished, the life jacket was to be inflated. "The Dilbert who reverses these steps will be incapable of releasing himself from his harness." The likely result of doing so was being wind-dragged across the surface until drowned.

Attached to every life jacket was a small flashlight and packet containing sea-marking dye. "Don't release the chemical dye-marker prematurely." Until ocean waves dissipated the powder, its yellow-green splotch was "visible for up to eight miles at 5,000 feet altitude."

Nearing the conclusion of their operational training, Flight 335 learned something about the TBM's bomb bay, its shackles which carried the bombs, and the 2000-lb. aerial torpedo. Aircrew ordnancemen already knew a great deal about these features, but just as they should grasp the elementary essentials of voice-wave radio communications, so were radiomen and aviation mechanics expected to understand how bombs were loaded and armed. Within the tunnel at Ted's feet, a bulletproof glass window enabled him to peer directly into the TBM's bomb bay. Because their over-water bombing exercises had devoted so much time to glide bombing, he correctly assumed that there was less likelihood they would one day carry a "fish" into combat.

Confident that his Avenger flock had mastered the tricks of formation flying, Flight 335's teacher led them on a night flight. Since this was Ted's first, he had to regale his parents about his "fantastically beautiful" August 1 experience.

You fasten your safety belt . . . the plane in front of you and behind you is a big black shadow which every now and then spits forth a flaming backfire from its exhaust system. . . . The plane vibrates violently . . . in a few short words [you] ask the greatest pilot of them all to make the flight a success. The Signal Officer drops his signal light and the ship makes one terrific roar and leaps forward like the sudden charge of a maddened lion. The tower lights go by, the runway lights flash by like tracers and then you feel the plane cast off the power of gravity and fly. . . . You don't have the bounce accompanying daylight flying. . . . [The engine] fumes are consumed in the moist night air.

August 17, 1944 and the Opa-Locka graduates celebrate their wings and impending leave. (Extreme right: author and behind him gunner "Al" Shaffer.)

No future Antoine de St. Exupery this flyer, but perhaps his prose does indicate pleasure was eclipsing pain.

Rejoicing at the news that his post-leave duty station would be somewhere on the West Coast—this meant the Navy would pay for his transportation home—Ted reviewed what the Navy had thus far taught him. "If I live through this I sure should come out a winner as it really has made me see so many things I never saw before, appreciation of an education, religion, *life*, a home, friends, oh so much." With little more than a week of training remaining, he cautioned his mother, "Don't go to any terrific extremes because of my homecoming. Really all I want to do is rake leaves in the front yard, run Beau, go out with Jane, talk with Dad, help with dishes, see some old friends and look at my books and dream." A day or so later he admitted, "I have been too fortunate. Keep on praying Mom it's working wonders."

On 17 August 1944, eight pilots and eighteen crewmen cheered the completion of Flight 335's operational training. Following the aircrewmen's joyful, long-anticipated twenty-day leaves—fate cooperating—some would get squadron assignments, more training, and combat. Regrettably, Ted's three comrades, Gumm, Hageman, and Hal Smith, due to different Opa-Locka flight sections, appeared to be permanently separating from him. Perhaps they might be reunited at San Diego. Or would they end up at Norfolk and Atlantic CVE duty? Good-humored Hal had given up trying to convert him to Mormonism; he surely would be missed. Ditto for the "tall and short of it" Gumm-Hageman duo; over the last six months their Ohio Valley drollery had repeatedly boosted the Californian's morale.

En route on his railroad trip home, Ted hoped he could visit Stimmy and Larry. Army Air Cadet Stimson had just left Arkansas. But V-12 Cadet Hoyt remained digging into his books at the University of New Mexico. It was a happy reunion. Larry had recently seen *Two Girls and a Sailor* and, like a good portion of America's military, had fallen head-over-heels for June Allyson in her debut starring role. A fan letter he had written her had won a printed post card reply—a source of jest to everyone but himself.

Aware that old friend Ted itched to boast about his freshly-minted wings, Larry inquired, "Why the holes in your wings?" Never modest, Ted's ego took off. One wonders if the same Ovaltine employee who designed Little Orphan Annie's decoder pins came up with the Navy aircrewman's wings. Scuttlebutt had it that originally the three holes running along the top-center of the wings were to be implanted with stars for aerial combat, air-to-ground attack, and air-to-sea attack. By mid-1944, the ballooning preponderance of protective fighter planes assured that few if any Avengers would be attacked by a Japanese pursuit plane. About the same time the aircrewman's wings, which initially had been awarded only after actual fleet flying assignment, were presented at the end of operational training; the three stars to be inserted following either three months in combat or fifteen strikes against the enemy. As it transpired, only those raised on a heavy breakfast diet of Post Bran Flakes really worried much about all this.

CHAPTER VI

"You've joined the Navy's finest Torpedo Squadron."

Relaxed and happy, his body restored by Pasadena salubrity, Ted shifted into high gear as he drove his father's 1940 Plymouth away from the Chrysler plant. "Pick me up at five, and remember," his father gently admonished him, "you are driving the family car, not flying an airplane." The war was indeed changing everything. For too much of the world, the autumn of 1944 continued to be a period of harsh sacrifices, ruin, and death. Yet, within the Hinckley household, wartime had aroused constructive energies. Celebrating his sixty-fourth birthday, the Major had taken on a stimulating middle management job with the Chrysler Corporation. Wife Eunice busied herself at church with mercy-related activities, while daughter Jane zestfully prepared for her junior year of high school. To her brother, his sister's maturing loveliness was a source of repeated surprises.

Their scattered relatives seemed comfortable. To be sure, Julius Kleffel remained incarcerated in a Japanese prison at Shanghai, but the businessman's wife and children had been repatriated to the West Coast aboard the SS *Gripsholm.* Ted's two aunts were playing their parts to win the war. Aunt Louise was working part-time in a hospital; hopefully she knew the difference between cyanide and castor oil. Hazel Upthegrove had become a "Rosie the Riveter" at one of Michigan's B-24 Liberator assembly lines. Apparently her oldest son was doing splendidly at Annapolis. Ted wondered if Nelson's path might cross his own; very unlikely, given the extent of the Pacific War.

The eighteen-year-old airman could but faintly discern the vast social reorganization taking place in American life. Was it true that women presently comprised almost a third of the nation's civilian labor force? With friends old and new circulating all around the country, indeed, crisscrossing oceans, he was keenly conscious of his homeland's accelerated geographic mobility. As for the armed forces' juggling of socio-ethnic classes—blacks too often excepted—the new diversity seemed normal enough, particularly to a youth who had for four years attended a Pasadena secondary school which mixed the city's poorest youngsters with those from the wealthiest families.

About life, the Navy had taught him a great deal. If anything, the hedonism so often articulated by sailors had reinforced his inherent Calvinism. Of John Calvin's theological teachings, he knew virtually nothing. Ted remained a parochial and complacent WASP, his Judeo-Christian beliefs as normal to him as his identity with his Pasadena home.

Quite abnormal was the rental of 1211 Avoca's empty maid's room. Who germinated this "war effort" idea was never clear. When the occupant, a pretty, blonde defense worker, invited a male coworker to spend the night with her, the wartime sacrifice of the maid's room abruptly terminated. The Major might visit his "Los Angeles lady fair"—Eunice's euphemism—but sexual liberality stopped at 1211's doorstep. Emphatically this was the rule governing Jane's participation in the Pasadena Presbyterian Church's war-born canteen. "You can smile and talk with those lonely men, Jane, even dance with some but never leave the church's confines with any of them." Nor did Ted object to his parents' injunction. He was not unfamiliar with wild horses. Experience had taught him that some who wore the uniform, despite its patriotic allure, were themselves worse than wild horses.

Forty-eight hours was all he had left of his leave. He had visited with most everyone. Before leaving he just wanted to drive around by himself and touch his special Pasadena. Notwithstanding occasional nettles of melancholy, that meandering morning drive yielded a bouquet of memories. Cruising down Orange Grove Avenue, he spotted the Valley Hunt Club, recalling the times he had gone swimming there with Stimmy. Swims at the beautifully sited Annandale Country Club had been possible thanks to the Hoyts' membership. Then a final visit to 202 Madeline Drive to cheer Mom Hoyt in her snappy Red Cross Auxiliary uniform. How justifiably proud she was of her oldest son Bill. Promoted over two senior fellow officers, Bill would soon skipper his own LCI (Landing Craft Infantry). He had been in the thick of it, probably at Saipan and Guam. Would his LCI participate in the pending Philippine invasion? But then Formosa might be next on the march to Tokyo.

Motoring down Del Mar Boulevard, Ted noted the spot where he used to wait for his second heavy stack of Los Angeles *Sunday Examiner* newspapers; mighty generous of his McKinley chum Harrison Baker to share that newspaper route. Various movie theaters and stores along Colorado Boulevard drew precious savings from his memory bank. Passing Sears recalled his parents' perennial teasing about his clothes and shoes acquisitions: "When are you going to stop growing?" A sudden urge to park his dad's car and go into Vroman's Bookstore seized him. Acutely aware of his limited funds, he kept his foot on the pedal.

Driving up Lake Avenue had always enlivened him; the street's wide, straight ascent toward looming Mount Wilson conveyed a sense of flying. Judging the Plymouth had climbed sufficiently to view Catalina Island way off out there in the Pacific Ocean, he pulled over and parked. Sure enough, the island was still there. Innumerable recollections of Catalina Y camps floated before him.

Hungry for a bit more nostalgia before returning to 1211, Ted descended down Altadena's Christmas Tree Lane. During this upcoming Christmas would the Lane's lights come on again? Would Altadena's

Boy Scouts facilitate the flow of sightseers as in prewar days? Gas rationing, as around Miami, didn't seem to be much of a problem about greater Los Angeles. Before driving down Oak Knoll to visit good old McKinley, Ted stopped the car to stroll within the courtyard of the Pasadena Playhouse. Smiling inwardly, he recalled the evening he and Jim had applauded Victor Jory's performance in Lillian Hellman's *Watch on the Rhine*. Damn, he regretted Jim's absence with the Navy. Once again Ted realized how solitary was his military leave. Everyone, just everyone had gone to war. Yes, high school friend Kenny Wright had a few evenings before arranged a blind date for him at an Occidental College dance. But then Kenny, like Larry, Stu Bates, and other old friends, was preoccupied with his V-12 college labors.

What he wouldn't have given to round up Jim, Larry, Stimmy, Louie, Stu, and all his old pals, and with their dogs and sleeping bags, spend a night on Raymond Hill. What a pity that apartments were going up there—cheap wartime construction. But the migration of people into Southern California must be housed somewhere. The Major mistakenly predicted that at war's end, "California will suffer an economic blow when all these Midwesterners return home."

His son could hardly condemn the new affluence when it had so kindly embraced his own family. On one hand he thanked God that America had been spared. On the other, the free spending, high living atmosphere in certain quarters troubled him. His father reported a local merchant had been involved in black market dealings. Found guilty and fined, he resumed his unlawful practices; to the culprit, the fine was merely a cost of doing business. Most Pasadenans didn't need to engage in black market dealings. So dynamic was the California economy that a family's requirements could be obtained legitimately, or so it seemed to Ted. Certainly the news magazines left no doubt that as compared with the other major powers involved in the global conflict, the United States was extraordinarily well off. Rationing and shortages had become little more than petty annoyances. Indicative of the burgeoning American cornucopia was the mushrooming proliferation of supermarkets. Approximately 4900 existed in 1939; just five years later 16,000 supermarkets were operating. Blessed by full employment, the nation's vaunted middle class was doubling.

America's quadrennial presidential contest had warmed up. Of course Ted's loyal Republican parents backed challenger Thomas Dewey. It did seem a foregone conclusion in September 1944, that President Roosevelt would be reelected for an astounding fourth term. This shocked a lot of Pasadena WASPs. But wartime had made shocks commonplace. Resignedly, the Major reminded his family of President Lincoln in 1864. And a war-weary Eunice actually muttered something about, "Maybe it's just as well not to change horses in the middle of the stream." Ineligible to vote for Republican aspirant Dewey, Ted anticipated four years hence. Come 1948, he could emulate his parents and vote Republican. Admittedly most of what he read about America's commander in chief won his approval. The President had flown aboard a Pan

American Clipper to his historic Casablanca Conference; the youth could not but be impressed by the trip—the first time an American President had left the United States in wartime. Then came the meeting of F.D.R., Churchill, and Chiang Kai-shek at Cairo—the world was shrinking. Maybe there really might be a lasting peace when Germany and Japan surrendered.

The author, foolishly eager to acquire some glory bars, on his last Pasadena liberty, September 1944.

Thanks to wartime prosperity and a serviceman's star hanging in their front window, reconciliation permeated the Hinckley household. Only upon slumbering did his dog, Beau Geste's tail cease wagging. The Major was just as proud of his son. Desirous of showing off the sailor-airman to his long-standing Panama Canal days crony, Los Angeles attorney James P. Kelleher, Theo invited the lawyer to join the Hinckley men for lunch at Hollywood's Musso Frank's Restaurant. Ted had always warmed to the company of the big, blustery Irishman, a delightful raconteur. The three men had a jabbering good time of it. Gifted with an abundance of Irish blarney, Kelleher kept focusing their conversation on "after the war." Later, petty officer Hinckley recalled something about "your parents provided you a good roundhouse" and "now you're in the switching yard" and "from what I gather, you're on the right track heading out." Blarney? Subsequently, the Major's son wished he had listened more intently.

His leave over, Ted reported to San Diego's North Island NAS. To his great relief, he was notified that instead of being stuck in a CASU (Carrier Aircraft Service Unit) pool he was slated for squadron assignment. Then he ran into his trio of comrades, Warren, Ray, and Hal. Overjoyed, he heard they too would soon be headed north to the San Francisco Bay Area. Like himself, they were apparently assigned to an air group at Naval Auxiliary Air Station Santa Rosa. In the hurried weekend liberty left, Ted made certain they shared his pride in Pasadena and tasted his mother's delicious home cooking.

Aboard the same Southern Pacific Pullman car carrying them to San Francisco was the University of California Los Angeles football team and their popular coach, Babe Horrell. Eunice Hinckley had known Horrell's Midwest family, so Ted introduced himself; an agreeable conversation ensued about the upcoming September 30 U.C. vs. U.C.L.A. contest. The star of the team, quarterback Bob Waterfield, impressed the eight aircrewmen, less because of the ballplayer's gridiron accomplishments than due to his relationship with the dazzling pinup beauty Jane Russell. A few years before, the restlessly unhappy South Pasadena High School senior might have surrendered his soul to exchange roles with the sports page celebrity. But now the anticipated glamour of flying off a flight deck midst multi-costumed plane handlers tending dozens of roaring aircraft easily surpassed the approving din of a dozen Pasadena Rose bowls—even with an adoring Jane Russell in the bleachers!

Bused over to NAS Alameda, the Opa-Locka airmen were briefly housed within odd-looking "quonset huts." Already occupying several bunks in the metal barracks were some aircrew veterans of the Pacific War awaiting reassignment. Attired in flight jackets emblazoned with various squadron insignia, Ted itched to hear their "sea stories." Somehow he restrained himself. Minutes after settling down in his bunk with Kenneth Roberts' historical novel *Northwest Passage*, Paul Valenti, one of the Opa-Locka gang came running in. The short, muscular Valenti, always breathing an enthusiasm for life, yelled, "Tomorrow we'll be joining Air Group Six at Santa Rosa." Hoots of derision burst from the old salts. For a second Ted thought their ridicule was serious; then he realized it was part envy, part male competitiveness spiced with sailor jocularity. No air group or squadron could be as good as the one these salts had just been to war with. After the hubbub quieted down, Ted returned to eighteenth century Indian-fighting alongside Major Robert Rogers.

This time his absorption was broken by one of the old hands who strolled over to him. "Sailor, you've joined the Navy's finest Torpedo Squadron." Questioned as to whether he had ever read the best-selling *The Raft*, Ted replied he had. In fact, a 1942 "Dell War Book" paperback copy was in his home library. "Those men were Torpedo Six flyers." The book revealed neither their carrier nor squadron. Adrift in a rubber raft without food or fresh water, the three Devastator airmen had fought the sea for thirty-four days and survived. A few minutes later, better informed and pleased to be identified with the famed Torpedo Squadron, aircrewman Hinckley put down *Northwest Passage* and joined the Pacific War veterans. It was not déjà vu. He had yet

The original VT-6 emblem featured a great white albatross whose wings formed a "V." The seabird's bill held a "fish" (Navy lingo for torpedo) shaped into a six. Presciently, the artist placed a deadly waterspout in the distance.

to fly into combat. Nonetheless, in his mind that night he kept imagining VT-6's solitary albatross winging toward a towering waterspout.

At the war's outset, elements of what in 1942 became Air Group Six had been attached to CV-6, the USS *Enterprise*. On 7 December 1941

Torpedo Squadron Six formed one of the ship's four squadrons. Luckily at sea, their flattop had just missed getting caught in the Pearl Harbor destruction. Three days later, *Enterprise* aircraft sank a large Japanese submarine—the first such kill of the war. Throughout the Pacific War and despite all her severe battle wounds, the *Enterprise* repeatedly hosted various air groups. On V-J Day, the Big E was still afloat and by then the nation's most famous carrier.

For the newer flattops, the *Essex* class carriers, a carrier air group usually consisted of about ninety to one hundred aircraft, divided into four distinct squadrons. Approximately fifteen Avengers made up a torpedo squadron. About the same number of SB2C Helldivers composed the typical carrier bombing squadron. The remaining aircraft were fighters and fighter-bombers. Fighting Six (VF-6) boasted Grumman's F6F Hellcats, the illustrious successor to the tough little F4F Grumman Wildcat with which Navy Air had begun the war. Chance Vought's Corsair fighter-bomber was a relatively recent addition to carrier decks. None other than Charles Lindbergh had checked out the Navy/Marine Corps pilots first assigned to them. With their unmistakable gull-wings, the F4Us had earlier won wide respect as land-based Marine fighter-bombers in the South Pacific campaigns. By the time Ted joined Air Group Six, the Corsair's 417 mph ranked it the fastest shipboard aircraft. Understandably, Air Group Six's commanding officer, Commander Henry L. Miller, opted to fly one of these "Whistling Death" machines.

An Annapolis graduate, class of 1934, Miller had been born for battle. He personified what John Keegan has described as a man who probably would have been unhappy doing anything else but soldiering. Not for an instant did Ted consider introducing himself to Six's CO. With his slate-cold eyes and firm mouth and jaw, Miller's ramrod carriage signaled, "Follow, or get out of my way." He had taught Jimmy Doolittle's Tokyo raiders the subtleties of carrier takeoffs; afterward, from November 1942 until May 1944, Miller commanded an air group aboard the USS *Princeton* (CVL-23). With an abundance of combat hours and well-deserved decorations, he could have secured a beach assignment. But Miller was Regular Navy, a professional who genuinely did seek the cannon's mouth. At Naval Auxiliary Air Station Santa Rosa, he prepared Air Group Six for its third war cruise.

In the interim between Opa-Locka and their Santa Rosa assignments, Ensign Witt with the three other Flight 335 pilots destined for Torpedo Squadron Six, had been qualified for carrier landings. Far removed from the Pacific War, on Lake Michigan in fact, the four aviators had completed over a dozen landings aboard the training flattop *Wolverine*. She was yet another wartime brainchild that worked. A converted Great Lakes excursion liner, the *Wolverine*, along with her sister ship *Sable*, eventually qualified hundreds of pilots. Hinckley, Shaffer, and indeed, all the recent Opa-Locka gang, rejoiced to see their pilots, flyers who had repeatedly proved they actually could land on a heaving, wind-swept carrier deck.

NAAS Santa Rosa lay approximately fifty miles north of San Francisco. Surrounded by dairies, fruit, vegetable, and garden seed farms, containing a population of 12,000 and an inviting main street, Santa Rosa reminded Ted of Santa Paula. However, now instead of climbing smudge-encrusted orange trees and sleeping in a high school gym, airman Hinckley would be housed in a trim Navy barracks and fly over the orchards. Quite a change in two years. Full of himself, he toted his freshly-issued flight costume, including his superfluous goggles, into town; like his peers, the beaming aviator got himself properly recorded by Santa Rosa's photographer. Bursting with pride

Bugs Bunny levity replaced albatross reality in the revised Torpedo Squadron Six insignia.

at his flight jacket—one had to be a bona fide airman to be issued that brown leather garment—he didn't reveal his disappointment at its Walt Disney squadron insignia. Was it the decimation of Torpedo Squadron Six in the epic 1942 Midway sea battle? Why had someone supplanted the gallant bird with this carrot-munching, torpedo-riding Bugs Bunny? Perhaps an officer had read Samuel Coleridge's "Rime of the Ancient Mariner," and then maybe public relations had reflected on what the albatross too often symbolized.

Word that Warren Hageman had been transferred really was disappointing. Pals Hal and Ray had arrived at NAAS Santa Rosa and begun training with Air Group Five, but wag Hageman had been spun off to another base. Life seemed less a passing parade than a giant railroad station.

Throughout October, Torpedo Squadron Six pressed its membership with a variety of combat-simulating flight activities. Adapting the four new pilots and crews to the habits and personalities of the battle-seasoned squadron was especially critical. With but a month remaining before VT-6 was scheduled to ship out, why had the four Avenger teams they replaced been dumped? Ted never did get the entire story. Apparently one pilot had been tossed out for flat-hatting over a women's dormitory at U.C. Berkeley. Another confessed "his nerves were shot." Worried that Witt's shenanigans might get all three of them decked, his tunnel gunner fretted at the likelihood of spending the rest of the war in some damn CASU. Then Eunice Hinckley came up to Santa Rosa to see her son actually fly. Not only did Ensign Witt graciously sashay her around the town, but smartly dressed in his flight greens, he escorted both Hinckleys out to dinner. Thereafter, in his radioman's eyes, the short Illinoisan stood seven feet tall.

Because the Avengers were being prepared for rocket-firing, Eunice never did get a chance to see her son fly. By way of compensation, he took her to see Dana Andrews and Don Ameche in *A Wing and a Prayer*. Featuring a fictional Navy torpedo squadron, the film turned out to be a fairly good representation of what preoccupied her aviator. Regrettably, the radio gunner in the movie was killed. To Ted's surprise this seemed in no way to upset his mother.

Rocket training required that the squadron fly to a naval auxiliary station located by California's Salton Sea. Four mounts on each wing permitted a TBM to carry a total of eight 5-inch high velocity rockets. Fired in a volley, their destructive wallop could shatter a tank or peel back the stoutest kind of infantry blockhouse. For three days, "the Torpeckers"—the aircrewmen's affectionate name, and far more commonly used than Avenger—erupted with aerial rocket firing.

"We all work and play together," Ted reported to his parents. "The Chiefs are all part of the gang." The Chief ARM (aviation radioman) bothered him, however. "He is an old timer and does not believe in giving out rate advancements unless you have served two years under the same (rank). I have hopes he will be transferred out at the last moment." His estimate of his fellow enlisted men: "fine, clean men everyone. I had often heard it said that a squadron could not tolerate a misfit. This is true . . . not a lad in the outfit who is not exceedingly polite and cheerful with a squadron member."

Aircrewmen John McCormack and Mark Hardisty had been among the first to welcome the Opa-Locka recruits. Hardisty bubbled with affable hospitality; McCormack's suave, self-assured manner reminded Ted of Larry. Beneath the squadron's gregariousness, the cordial swabby banter, Ted sensed something much deeper, a fellowship he must earn. How others judged him remained extremely important. "When you are a member of a squadron your position in the Navy in matters of prestige . . . is doubled," he informed his father. "If questioned to son's position . . . , be sure to mention the fact that he is in Torpedo Squadron Six, one of the oldest VT squadrons in U.S.N. which has been in everything from Midway and Guadalcanal to Tarawa and Truk."

Commanding Torpedo Squadron Six was twenty-nine-year-old Lieutenant Commander William Garland Privette. Ted's admiration placed him in his forties. Privette knew a great deal about airplanes both in the air and on the ground. This was his second tour leading VT-6. Should one of his charges flout flight procedures, a harsh edge affixed itself to the North Carolinian's soft southern accent. He demanded the best from himself, and his pilots sought to reciprocate.

Among the squadron's aircrewmen, Privette's radioman, James Katke, unquestionably stood out as the most popular personality. Katke was a born clown. Never happier than when he was spoofing his peers, the Wisconsin-raised youth even dared poke fun at their air group CO, "Happy Hank" Miller. Katke delighted in pinning nicknames on people. To receive one of his monikers was an honor, a sign of affection. One member with a huge, melon-shaped head became "Egghead"; another

Left to right: James B. Katke, VT-6's comedian; W. G. Privette, squadron CO; and TV celebrity to be, Richard A. Boone.

with a prominent proboscis was christened the "Nose." An unassuming Christian gentleman won the appellation "Righteous Richard." "Pruneface" turned out to be a prankster who with Katke had "borrowed a jeep" and then fallen out of same into a cactus bush. Months passed before Hinckley was honored with "the Vibrator."

During one of Commander Miller's October 1944 Santa Rosa pep talks to the entire air group—what Katke labeled "Happy Hank's Happy Hour"—VT-6's jester stuck his neck way out. Struggling to describe how grim it was going to be "out there," a dour-faced Miller urged each officer and enlisted man to prepare himself physically and psychologically. Katke, seated well in the rear of the auditorium, and in a heavy German accented monotone, began mimicking Miller: "Now men, vee iss headed out soon for zee big time. It vill be tuf, but at least ve vill be vell fed; mit plenty of sauerkrauten, mit de cabbage zoup, and for dessert, ve vill haf monkey vomit." Despite their best efforts, some of those within hearing distance of Katke could not suppress their laughter. Thinking the snickers were aimed at him, Happy Hank was anything but happy. To Pasadena's rank-conscious WASP, Miller was a paragon of power. But for VT-6's devil-may-care comedian, the frowning air group CO was merely another martinet to be satirized.

It did amuse Ted that a couple of shipmates called "dad" and "pop" hardly tipped thirty years of age. One of them, First Class Ordnanceman Marcell I. Varner, a sterling individual who was indeed the squadron's "Pop Varner," would become a comforting confidant for Ted. Another senior personality commonly addressed as "Daniel" was in fact Richard Boone, also an AOM 1st class. Boone flew as Privette's gunner. In

1944, who would have dared predict that in the next decade the extro-verted petty officer with the wonderful, reverberating laugh, large nose, and pitted face would become TV's megabucks Paladin.

For the aircrewmen one last mainland exercise remained: Lake Chabot Gunnery School. Here at a machine gun range located in the hills southeast of Oakland, Ted and his squadron mates spent a few days honing their shooting skills, puzzling over machine gun malfunc-tions, and playing the never-ending recognition games. It was good news that the number of Japanese ship silhouettes was diminishing but bad news that the Zero was being replaced by superior aircraft. According to ACI, these hot enemy fighters were capable of matching the newest American pursuit planes. But could the Japanese get them into mass production, and, most dubious of all, did they have the time left to train fresh pilots for such hot aircraft?

At Lake Chabot, Ted was once again acquainted with the unpre-dictable vagaries of Uncle Sam's wartime personnel procurement. "In the best interests of America's military needs" sometimes shredded an entire class of officer trainees. Old friend Austin Woodward, a McKinley "golden boy," an outstanding figure in the classroom and on the playing field, and presumably the recipient of an Army commission in its A-12 program, had met such a fate. Joining VT-6 at Lake Chabot was a brand new chief petty officer, George W. Chapman; recently in the Navy Aviation Cadet program, he had fallen victim to "in the best interests of . . . " Earlier, following the Battle of Midway, Chapman had served aboard the old *Hornet* (CV-8) with surviving VT-6 elements. During the 1942 Battle of Santa Cruz, when the order to abandon the mortally bat-tered *Hornet* was at last given, Chapman's pilot had been ordered to land on another carrier. Although a pre-Pearl Harbor enlistee, no hash marks ladder climbed up his sleeve like those embellishing the coats of VT-6's two superannuated CPOs. However, where they carried around flabby bodies with faces to match, the youthful Chief Chapman exuded an invigorating Jimmy Stewart charm. To get him back into "the Navy's finest torpedo squadron" had required wheeling and dealing. Everyone welcomed Chappy's return.

In late October, the entire squadron boarded the USS *Ranger* (CV-4) docked at Naval Air Station Alameda. Launched in 1933, she was the first United States flattop to be designed and built from the keel up as an aircraft carrier. Displacing but 14,500 tons, the old lady had never-theless distinguished herself during the first two years of the war. *Ranger* aircraft had supported the 1942 landings in North Africa as well as pounded German shipping along Norway's coast. By mid 1944, and equipped with the latest in catapult and radar, she had been assigned training duty on the Pacific Coast. Among the air groups that polished their skills aboard her that fall was Air Group Six. Warned to curtail his correspondence—"From now on it may be censored"—Ted forewent the pleasure of writing about the thrills of his initial carrier takeoff and land-ing.

In one of his final stateside letters to his father, Ted rejoiced at the headlines heralding the coming liberation of the Philippines. "Things are really moving over there in your old stomping grounds. I guess when they finally do occupy Manila there will be very little left of it." At October's end, there was in truth very little left of the Japanese Navy. The savage, far-flung, three-day Battle for Leyte Gulf (the Second Battle of the Philippine Sea) actually comprised four distinct naval actions. It should have marked the end of the Pacific War.

Although badly outnumbered on the sea and in the air, Nippon had made a brave show of it. Closing in on the American landing force at Leyte Gulf was the Japanese super-battleship *Yamato* (68,000 tons; 18.1 inch guns); each of her giant turrets weighed as much as a destroyer. Quite literally within sight of a fleet of luckless baby flattops and frantic U.S. destroyers desperately laying down smokescreens, there was a moment when a smashing triumph could have been theirs. But it was not to be. Japan's losses due to both air attack and surface action were four carriers, three battleships, six cruisers, four light cruisers, and eleven destroyers. The Japanese fleet, in Admiral Samuel E. Morison's words, was destroyed "as an effective fighting force."

Carrier historian Clark Reynolds has wisely qualified the Admiral/historian's conclusion. Following the Battle for Leyte Gulf, "Japan had one last hope of using its carrier force. She still had five carriers. . . . But these had no planes for want of pilots, and little fuel for operations." Then came the submarine sinkings of the immense 68,059-ton super-carrier *Shinano* and the carrier *Unryu*. Thereafter Tokyo sequestered her remnant "fleet-in-being" in her Inland Sea.

At Thanksgiving 1944, the enlisted men of VT-6 could but vaguely foresee that the fate of America's Pacific adversary had been sealed. What they did sense, as the wise men in Washington and Tokyo so well understood, was the intransigent refusal of Japan's military to concede defeat.

America's conquest of the Marianas mightily expedited the land-based aerial bombardment of Japan. In Europe the concurrent decimation of German cities foreshadowed what awaited the Japanese. Doubly foreboding was the new American weapon, Boeing's giant B-29 built specifically for transporting bomb loads to Nippon's metropolises. Superfortresses had commenced their brutal work in June 1944. Utilizing bases in India and China, their first raids achieved only mild success. Rushed into production, the aircraft's malfunctions created troublesome headaches, but nothing like the logistical nightmare of getting aviation fuel to Chinese airfields. By November, the fuel replenishment problem was licked when the B-29s began their bombing missions directly from the Marianas' easily-supplied Saipan. The terrible fate in store for Japan's beautiful island nation seemed inescapable.

Japan's military was not blind, but reason could not overcome ideological passion. In 1944, Japan's civilian-military leaders, the *Jushin*, "were preoccupied with placating military and civilian fanatics and ensuring domestic stability in the event of a surrender," writes historian

Akira Iriye. The tragic hubris of the samurai state must be played out. "Too abrupt a halt in fighting, followed by a humiliating defeat, would not serve [the *Jushin's*] purpose." By their "hesitation and indecisiveness, the Japanese leaders prolonged the war by one year."

Shortly before Air Group Six's departure from San Francisco, Ted received a letter from old friend Jim Downs. He had won his rate as a third class quartermaster. Exuberant with sea duty aboard the USS *Munda*, a baby flattop, Quartermaster Downs wondered why Ted had not acquired "a smaller type plane so he could have gotten on the *Munda*." Continuing his foolishness, Jim opined that the two sailors "could make the Navy cower before our crazy plans." Utterly unaware that each would one day become an absent-minded professor, Ted admitted to his parents, "Jim is the only guy I could be put on a desert island and live peacefully with. All my other pals are swell chaps but Jim was the only one who ever really understood my peculiarities."

Dated November 8, and the first of many, Ted's envelope was stamped "PASSED BY NAVAL CENSOR." To soften the news of his San Francisco departure, he consoled his mother, "Your visit did me real good and I think it did you good too." This was followed by solace regarding his dangerous duty. "More and more as time goes by do I realize how very fortunate I was to get in VT-6." He also wanted to tell her how God had spoken to him aboard the troopship *General E.T. Collins* (AP-147). If officialdom's prying eyes had dampened her son's epistolary verve, censorship's restrictions fortunately failed to extinguish his pen.

Reacting to a submarine report, the *Collins*, instead of heading west to Hawaii, went south to San Diego. After a brief stay, she turned around and crossed back under the Golden Gate. Less than a year old, the Navy troopship was jam-packed with Marines. As in his previous contacts with "seagoing bellhops," Ted was struck by their grim—not glum—purposeful, subdued qualities. At San Francisco all of the over two thousand Marines were restricted to the cramped *Collins* anchored offshore in the Bay. Air Group Commander Henry Miller took quite a gamble. Somehow he wangled permission for his command to relish one last night ashore. Ted enjoyed some excellent seafood, Gene Tierney's *Laura*, and made himself a bed on a carpet in the San Francisco Y. Fearful that he might miss the liberty boat, he arrived at the Embarcadero a half an hour early. To his great astonishment, every man in the squadron got to the dock on time. Their state of repair left much to be desired. Booze and bimbos, not bullets, had wounded a number of them. Somehow, despite their disabilities, they all tumbled into the ship-to-shore boats. Oh, for his movie camera. But then that would hardly have been fair.

With "Up anchor," the *Collins* headed west. Meals were eaten standing up. She had no room for a ship's library. And lacking a ship's service, passengers could purchase neither pogey bait (candy) nor gedunks (ice cream). All too soon the crush of bodies induced claustrophobia. To stay below, indefinitely cooped up reading, was impossible. Like warrior ants, the gyrenes covered the troopship; their perpetual knife-sharpening got on one's nerves. Even the usually sanguine Pasadena WASP became depressed. Conscious that large numbers of his fellow passengers would soon be spilling their guts charging up some enemy-held beach, Ted thought a lot more about war's inherent madness than he was wont to. Four days passed mulling over mankind's barbarities. He hadn't had a bowel movement for almost a week. Just when his body, mind, and spirit hit bottom, to his happy surprise, who should he encounter but Lieutenant Costanzo, the chaplain whose sermons at NATTC he had so much admired. Invited to come to Costanzo's cabin and talk, Ted, of course, did so. Theirs was not a protracted conversation—Costanzo's seagoing ministry was to the multitude of Marines—but it accomplished wonders for Ted's malaise. The Chaplain's "Hang in there, lad, God has a ministry for you," provided the sailor a refreshment no PX ever could.

Lovely Hilo, Hawaii was never intended for anything but Polynesian pleasures. Although swamped by military personnel, Hawaii's "Big Island" did its best to live up to its legendary hospitality. In less than a week, some of VT-6's officers established very friendly relations with nurses at the local hospital. This was the first time, but definitely not the last, that Ted awoke to the inherently unfair gender supply-and-demand realities. Invariably the limited supply of uniformed women, whatever their rank, were monopolized by the men with the shiny bars and fatter wallets.

NAS Hilo (until 1943 the Army's General Lyman Field) possessed an adequate library, a spacious swimming pool, tennis courts, and delicious "Seabee chow." Indicative of how serious was the Japanese threat to Hawaii, Hilo's Seabees (Navy Construction Battalion) were rushing construction of a recreational building. Ted laid back. VT-6 ground personnel, pilots, and especially their skipper, Lieutenant Commander Privette, prepared for war.

Aware of Hawaii's listless lifestyle, Privette ordered the six pilots comprising Witt's section to test themselves, their aircraft, and their crewmen's stomachs. For three hours the six Torpeckers zoomed and flathatted all over the mottled green-brown landscape of Maui and Hawaii. Despite the engine's racket, Ted thrilled at the serene beauty racing by below. At one point, playing follow the leader, the six screaming machines taunted Pele, the volcano goddess. Roaring down into Maui's vast Halelakala crater, empty but for the terrified wild goats, the TBMs skimmed across the volcano's floor. Long since, Ted had ceased resigning himself to the Pearly Gates; in truth, he now found a degree of pleasure in the aerial gymnastics. As Witt touched down at NAS Hilo, his radioman looked up to see how Shaffer had handled the gut-twisting ride. That was a mistake. Ted's face met a shower of vomit. For all the stinking cascade, he congratulated himself. His stomach felt fine; his fear of flying had almost disappeared.

A few weeks later during practice low-level bombing runs, Pele got her revenge. An Avenger engine caught fire. Flying at approximately 800 feet, the pilot, Lieutenant (j.g.) A. F. W. Kresse, struggled to keep his plane stable so his crewmen might hit the silk. Seconds later, with flame engulfing him, Kresse bailed out. Neither crewman escaped. Regrettably the turret gunner had recently joked how his chute harness was "so much damn trouble" he didn't wear it. Whether his radioman, none other than the courtly McCormack, died gallantly trying to assist his gunner with his harness no one would ever know. Whatever, wearing harnesses became absolutely de rigueur.

For quite a few aircrewmen the almost three months spent at NAS Hilo turned out to be too slack. When not in the air, the lower grade petty officers, particularly the ARMs, had virtually no responsibilities. Aviation ordnancemen serviced guns and explosives, while mechanics fretted with aircraft engines, wheels, hydraulic systems, and much else. But radio technicians, not ARMs, maintained the air group's communication gear. While ARMs swam, played tennis and mahjong—a few even golfed—their pilots attended classes and struggled about in Hamakawa's deep undergrowth testing their survival skills. Killing a farmer's pig, some ate quite well. Others who gorged themselves on a rich-tasting tropical nut realized all too late they had devoured Hawaii's indigenous substitute for Exlax.

Reflecting the aircrewmen's ennui was the rise in liquor consumption. NAS Hilo, like every Navy base larger than a telephone booth, had its enlisted men's beer garden, the counterpart to the officers' club. To his loss, Eunice's well-indoctrinated son never entered a Navy beer garden; a WASP upbringing had instilled "liquor promotes the Devil's handiwork." Empirical proof aplenty was provided by the social eruptions that an excess of beer randomly exploded in the barracks. Returning from the library one evening, Ted discovered two good friends bloodying each others' faces. Three sheets to the wind, the airmen slugged it out until they collapsed. Doubly distressing, no one acted to break up the barracks broil. Another chap who had attended Cornell for a semester or two and whose alcoholism was well advanced, repeatedly broke out with an Ithaca fight song, but only after puking up his recent beer garden swill.

Certainly the besotted, crazed antics of a jack-leg Mormon should have intimidated his fellows. Each VT-6 member had by this time been issued his own .38 Smith-Wesson revolver. On one occasion, thoroughly lubricated and yelling insanely, he vainly tried to bury himself within a pile of building materials stowed near the barracks. Then there was the evening when his inebriation erupted in an unearthly delirium tremens howl. When sober the man was a bundle of pleasantries. What could shut up this drunken werewolf? To calm him down, the wild-eyed creature was confined to the shower room—all the nozzles turned on. The sight of the naked, intoxicated wretch screaming for his wife, of all things, proved highly entertaining to some. For Ted the twisting, jerking muscular frame capped by the man's terrified countenance was a searing sight. Its hellishness recalled one of Uncle Pat's Gustav Dore engravings depicting the Inferno's damned.

Such riotous scenes were not the rule. Regrettably, however, they caused Ted to withdraw from some off-base opportunities that would have made him not only better informed but a better man. When several of VT-6's Opa-Locka gang invited him to join them on a round-the-island taxi tour, he begged off, fearful of John Barleycorn's presence.

Kicking himself for failing to date more lovelies on his August leave and seeking to fill up his time, Ted expanded his correspondence to include two Pasadena girls, Barbara Leh and Doris Eldred. One evening as he departed from the base library, he noted a bulletin board announcement encouraging sailors to take an upcoming Navy Aviation Cadet entrance examination. VT-6's Chief Chapman seconded the idea; so did the base chaplain Lieutenant G. Weldon Gatlin. After talking the matter over with Mr. Witt and Lieutenant William H. Fitzpatrick, VT-6's personnel officer, Ted did so. Both assured him he need not worry, "Hinckley, you'll taste combat. It will be awhile before you hear whether you passed and then six months or so before you actually enter pilots' training." In truth, the youth had no great burning desire to pilot an airplane; what he now wanted was those shiny bars.

Ted's affection remained his reading. He shared his pleasure with Hendrik Willem Van Loon's *The Story of Mankind* with his parents. It's been "acclaimed an amazing account of World History for both young and old. I certainly propose to study it. . . . It gives you the answer[s] to the rise and fall of great empires and Kingdoms not with . . . aggressive leaders but in the actions of the people." Paperbacks published by the Editions for the Armed Services, Inc. circulated throughout the squadron until they fell apart. Among the hardback novels enjoyed by aircrewmen at Hilo were *Leave Her to Heaven, Forever Amber, Moon Tide,* and *Shore Leave.* Ted surprised himself at the pleasure he found in two books forwarded by his mother: Harry Emerson Fosdick's *As I See Religion* and C. S. Lewis' *Screwtape Letters. Screwtape's* subtle snares rather startled him. That he had so far eluded a sailor's sins of the flesh meant little; Ted Hinckley's badly flawed character provided a veritable studio for the designs of Screwtape and Wormwood.

Ensnarement of a more immediate sort was discussed by VT-6's Air Intelligence Officer, Lieutenant R. M. Sandidge. Equipped with a Harvard L.L.B. and a Kentuckian's whimsy, it was "Sandy's" job to inform flyers on what they could expect within the strike zone. His lectures never fell on deaf ears. An obligatory bail out over enemy territory dictated imprisonment at best, torture at worst. Ted could dismiss torture when in Tennessee. But by the time Witt's belly gunner looked down on Oahu's historic Pearl Harbor, the prospect of being shot down had become real. Sandy's Hilo lecture on what to do was right out of *Prisoner Sense*: "Don't carry papers or any other written material near the enemy;" "Don't try to be clever and give false information." "Need to know" was axiomatic. "If you don't need to know secret information for accomplishing your mission, DON'T know it." "Remember the rules of war require only that you give your name, rank, and service number."

In 1944 Air Group Six's personnel could not know about the fate of Dauntless pilot Ensign Frank W. O'Flaherty and his rear seat gunner Bruno Gaido. Plucked from the sea by a Japanese destroyer after the Midway battle, the two prisoners were held for a week. Satisfied they had squeezed out any useful information, their captors weighted them down and threw them overboard. Ted and his fellow flyers expected little mercy if they had the bad luck to be captured, especially at the hands of infuriated civilians. "Try by all means," Sandy warned them, "if you can't escape, attempt to get yourself taken by men in uniform." For three reasons Ted kept his shoulder revolver well oiled: as a signaling device; to warn away enraged civilians; and to shoot himself. Mrs. Hinckley's son might be a WASP but his faith in his body's capacity to endure torture was nil. Could he really kill himself? Maybe he should go out like the First World War ace Frank Luke and, Custer-like, die with his boots on.

Back in Pasadena, friends and family were also awakening to the fact that the Major's son actually was about to thrust himself in harm's way. One family friend took it upon herself to inquire exactly how dangerous an aircrewman's job really was. That an official actually took time to reply reveals something about the good old U.S.A. Addressed to Mrs. Marc Leh, it came from the Executive Office of the Secretary of the Navy and was signed by Lieutenant Leon W. Shloss, Public Relations.

It appears that you have been given misinformation about the danger of being a radioman-gunner in Navy Torpedo Bombers. Of course, to begin with, we must realize that war by reason of its purpose is dangerous.

Nevertheless, I can inform you that fewer aircrewmen (radio gunners and others) are lost than pilots. Further, it is a matter of record that many of our Torpedo and Dive Bomber Squadrons have gone through months of combat operation without ever being attacked by enemy planes due to the efficiency of our Fighter Squadrons in escorting and protecting them.

There is this one other point to consider: If the airplane in which you are flying is hit by enemy fire, it makes very little difference whether you are sitting in the front or pilot's seat, or in the back or gunner's seat.

Attorney Hinckley completed the forms for collecting the government's $10,000 life insurance policy on his son. Then he began pondering how he might console the Hinckley women.

Throughout the closing days of 1944, Bing Crosby's "White Christmas" supplied sweet sentiment for NAS Hilo's aircrew ready room. Disturbing for Ted was a letter from Mrs. Hoyt. Her beloved Pasadena home in which he had spent so many happy hours had suddenly been sold out from under her. What must sons Bill and Larry think when they heard the melody "I'll Be Home for Christmas"? Also distressing: home front "strikes and shut downs in the big cities." Ted angrily equated "any strike organizer" with "the Japs."

Certainly Eunice bent her best efforts for him and his fellow flyers. So much candy, and especially fig jam—Ted's favorite—arrived, he had to airmail her a polite cease and desist. Two Christmas presents really counted: a fine wristwatch from a relative he hardly knew, Robert Platt, a Navy pilot in the First World War, and a New Testament from his mother. One side of the Testament had a steel cover, ostensibly to ward off an enemy bullet. A stateside skeptic later demonstrated a .22 short could pierce the metal jacket. Albeit, the Testament neatly fit her son's chambray shirt pocket, and lacking a good luck charm, the talisman thereafter flew next to his heart.

CHAPTER VII

"All hands man your battle stations."

Looking about NAS Hilo's chapel, Ted was pleased to see a healthy representation from Air Group Six scattered among the worshipers. Thanks to Chaplain Gatlin and his sailor assistants, 1945's first Sunday service radiated both comfort and challenge. A selection from Alfred Lord Tennyson graced the worship bulletin.

> Ring out the want, the care, the sin,
> The faithless coldness of the times;
> Ring out, ring out my mournful rhymes,
> But ring the fuller minstrel in.
>
> Ring out false pride in place and blood,
> The civic slander and the spite;
> Ring in the love of truth and right,
> Ring in the common love of good.
>
> Ring in the valiant man and free,
> The larger heart, the kindlier hand;
> Ring out the darkness of the land
> Ring in the Christ that is to be.

Particularly gratifying were three old standbys: "Faith of Our Fathers," "Holy, Holy, Holy," and "The Navy Hymn." Each hymn awakened a lusty congregational participation. For Ted, Gatlin's sermon, "Begin with God," evoked other rudimentary messages delivered over the years by California's Christian spokesmen.

Despite a few moments of dragging melancholy, the holiday season had passed swiftly. In typical Navy fashion, Hilo's cooks prepared some superb meals. To reassure his parents, Ted forwarded them a copy of the attractively printed Christmas Day menu. Among the commissary's delectables were cream of mushroom soup with saltines, stuffed celery, fruit cocktail, roast turkey, baked ham, oyster dressing, sweet potatoes, buttered asparagus, giblet gravy, Waldorf salad, parker house rolls, apple pie a la mode, fruit cake, coffee, and cigarettes. There were those who bitched that the sweet potatoes were canned and the oyster dressing "didn't match mom's." But then what did they expect?

Quite unexpected was Nazi Germany's surprise Christmas offensive. Perhaps General von Rundstedt's initial success in the Battle of the Bulge (Ardennes Offensive) briefly quieted the more chronic of Hilo's complainers. "The Germans are really going to town with their remaining forces," Ted wrote his father, "as much as I wish his death, old [von] Rundstedt is a great field commander." Before long, Eisenhower's massive ground forces and Allied air superiority stalled the Germans and then paralleled what MacArthur's air-land dominance was accomplishing in the Philippines. Everywhere America was winning a global war, driving back enemies in Europe and Asia as well as on the high seas.

Commander Miller never bothered to convene an all-squadrons pep talk at NAS Hilo. By early 1945 he may have reflected a facile American assumption: the Pacific War, like some titanic engineering project, had become a matter of numbers. Just as during the preceding decade American dam builders had conquered the mighty Columbia, the Colorado, and even the destructive Tennessee, so would the nation's prodigious armaments tame Nippon.

Afterward Ted recalled how agreeable were the final six weeks at Hilo. Evenings were spent in the library prepping himself for flight school. He received night radar instruction, enjoyed rocket-firing off Hawaii's south coast, gunnery hops, and deep sea fishing from an air-sea rescue boat. In conjunction with Marines there were ground-air support flights. The former, no doubt, were the same men the air group had mingled with aboard the *Gen. E. T. Collins*. One part of the exercise required that Air Group Six aircraft, primarily fighters and fighter-bombers, simulate precision bombing. Elaborate lime markers on the ground traced out what were supposed to be enemy trenches and artillery positions. Various aircraft buzzed about hazardously; per usual, strict air silence was to be observed. Witt's plane was elsewhere, therefore Ted never heard the following dialogue. Afterward, everyone heard about it.

A fighter pilot, no doubt completely confounded by the maze of chalk lines: "This gawd damned exercise is all fucked up. The Navy is all fucked up, and I am all fucked up."

Instantly Commander Miller snapped his mike and demanded, "Who said that! Identify yourself!"

For a brief interval, silence. Then an obviously disguised voice replied, "I ain't that fucked up, Commander."

At that, another half dozen Hellcat and/or Corsair pilots popped their mikes and gave their respected CO a horselaugh.

Hank Miller's aerial maneuvers may have been ruined, but apparently not his common sense. With only a few weeks ashore remaining, he granted his squadrons a sequence of three-day leaves. Some of the Opa-Locka gang, men and officers, had never visited Oahu's Honolulu. Accordingly, Lieutenant Commander Privette arranged for pilots Witt and Ensign N. B. Bitzegaio—old friends since cadet days—to fly to Ford Island. Ted was not about to let an opportunity to inspect Pearl Harbor slip by. For a full day, like some prewar rubbernecker, he reveled in Waikiki's historic sights from Barber's Point to Diamond Head.

By midnight, stuffed with a steak dinner and still chuckling over Hollywood's latest contribution to the war effort, he waited for the channel liberty boat to carry him across to Ford Island. But for an officer and an enlisted WAVE, he was alone. Ted tried to ignore their amorous entanglement at one end of the dock. Both were intoxicated. Obviously they had not fully satisfied their carnality. Ted damned an environment in which an officer caste could corner the market. Back in his Ford Island bunk, his raging wild horses granted him no rest. He had yet to read Melville's all-male maritime classic. Nonetheless Ted gained a degree of comfort realizing that once at sea, he would be in an all-male world. There, sex could be shucked. Foolish boy.

To sustain high morale, CO Miller momentarily stretched Navy regs and promoted a number of VT-6 personnel. The squadron rejoiced as four first-class petty officers won the much coveted CPO rank. Among those who joined the popular Chief Chapman were Richard Boone and Ray Crow. The latter should have won a Katke sobriquet, "Happy Man" for his forever upbeat personality. As for the squadron's three Regular CPOs, individuals Ted now secretly labeled "the gruesome threesome," the promotion of the four uniformed civilians may have produced less jubilation.

One-time Navy nurse Eunice Hinckley was quite familiar with the old salt genre. Having labored on their well-tattooed anatomies, she begged her son to forego such art. Ted could not forego kidding her. "Mom, I hate to tell you this but I had a huge clipper ship tattooed on my chest. . . . My breasts are the tops of both the foremast and the mainmast." Perhaps it comforted his mother when she was informed that he had talked about becoming a clergyman with Chaplain Gatlin.

No doubt intended as a cinematic pep talk prior to their departure, a recently-released Navy Technicolor film, *The Fighting Lady* (the new *Yorktown* CV-10) was shown to each of Air Group Six's squadrons. Much of its live-action footage was devoted to the 16 February 1944 attack on Truk. At that time Air Group Six was on its second war cruise. Operating from the *Intrepid* (CV-11), Torpedo Six had also participated in the smashing strikes on the Truk bastion. Audience commentary and not a few cheers erupted from those who a year earlier had actually flown in its two-day trashing. Never before had the Opa-Locka gang witnessed this form of noisy camaraderie; within the room, the vicarious thrill of battle proved contagious.

All the old hands agreed, the Japanese fortress in the Caroline Islands had been less formidable than expected. Truk's flak had been heavy, and some fighter opposition was encountered. However, most of the larger Japanese warships had recently slipped away. Aircrewman Dick Gentzkow recalled how he and his gunner, Mark Hardisty, watched in disbelief as their Avenger's torpedo ran straight and true right into a Japanese cruiser, and then failed to explode. Not until that moment did Ted realize the U.S. Navy had been plagued by bad torpedoes. Could malfunctioning "fish" explain why neither VT-6 nor VT-8 had scored a single hit at Midway in 1942, or why later in the year while flying TBFs off the old *Hornet* during the Battle of Santa Cruz, Torpedo Six again scored zero?

While the Japanese began the Pacific War with their superb Long Lance torpedo, the American Navy's Mark 14 torpedo proved to be grossly unreliable. Outraged sub skippers were the first to awaken to this suicidal threat. Only reluctantly did the Bureau of Ordnance seriously investigate the string of malfunctions; after all, the Mark 14 was their creation. Not until Lieutenant Commander Lawrence R. Daspit took his sub *Tinosa* on patrol in midsummer 1943 did America's U-boat skippers at last obtain the vital proof so infuriatingly confirmed by their periscopes. Encountering a mammoth 19,000 ton Japanese tanker, Daspit put four of his torpedoes into her. They exploded, but the tanker didn't sink. He then fired nine more individually into the dead-in-the-water tanker watching in disbelief as not a single one exploded. Despite his rage, Daspit carried his last torpedo home, insisting Navy ordnance experts eat their steel crow. They stubbornly refused to do so, even after Hawaiian tests repeatedly confirmed that the Mark 14 didn't explode when fired straight into Kahoolawe and Oahu cliffs. Luckily Admiral Chester Nimitz got wind of the stonewalling. By 1944 the U.S. Navy possessed torpedoes that worked, at least most of the time.

Mid-February operations off Hawaii aboard the USS *Shangri-La* (CV-38) smoothed out Air Group Six's night-flying capabilities. None other than President Franklin D. Roosevelt himself had given CV-38 her exotic name. In 1942, asked where Doolittle's bombers had flown from, Roosevelt had replied, "Shangri-La" (a mythical utopia created by novelist James Hilton). Although generally unappreciated, the air group and the new fleet carrier possessed a historic affinity. Riding shotgun for the *Hornet* and Doolittle's famous raiders had been the *Enterprise* with Air Group Six.

The *Shangri-La* was on her shakedown cruise. Its "airedales" (flight deck and hangar deck personnel) gladly shared their valuable insights on the peculiarities of Hellcats, Avengers, Helldivers, and Corsairs. Everyone was enjoying themselves until it came over the radio that Tokyo area airfields had been attacked by carrier aircraft, sites that had not felt America's sting since bombs had fallen from Doolittle's B-25s. VF-6 and VBF-6 had hoped to be in on that February 16 Tokyo scalping; hundreds of Japanese aircraft were destroyed on the ground and in the air. After two days, Task Force 58 withdrew; three dozen American planes had gone down before the guns of Japan's dwindling aces.

Ted's developing friendships were understandably with Torpedo Six enlisted men. They shared the same living quarters and, when they weren't flying together, shared a common ready room. However, there was one member of the four hand-picked enlisted men attached to the air group staff with whom he developed a deeply rewarding friendship. Recipient of a college degree and benefiting from years of outdoor labor in the verdant Pacific Northwest, Jack Streeter, AOM 1st class, could have obtained a commission. Why had Streeter, unlike the vast majority of those who possessed a college education, rejected the shiny bars and all the perks they guaranteed? Why would anyone choose the crowded crews quarters over the pleasantries of the officers' wardroom? A cross-grained individualist, but in a relaxed, totally unassuming way, Jack, like many a Reservist, disliked ordering people about. All man, he showed a motherly concern for the entire air group's membership. Sensing this, his shipmates, instead of voicing the usual surname salutation, addressed him as "Jack." Personally responsible for not only Commander Miller's wing guns but much of the air group's deadly ordnance, Jack personified trust. Ted had first become acquainted with him at NAAS Santa Rosa; it was aboard the *Shangri-La* that the association began to blossom into a friendship.

Savoring the colorful pageantry of *Shangri-La*'s flight deck, a deafening three-ring circus whose technological teamwork eclipsed Indy's 500, Ted was joined by AOM Streeter. Although thrilled by the sputtering, snarling Hellcats being herded into take-off position, the two men were defeated in their attempts at conversation. Observing their dilemma, a red-shirted ship's company ordnanceman motioned to them to step down from the port catwalk and join him for some coffee. Flattered at the invitation from an airedale whose nimble bravery they had just been admiring, Jack and Ted ducked down and entered the hatch. "You flyboys get the glamour," Jack kindly chided Ted, reminding him that the men juggling the aircraft immediately over them drew no flight pay. Yet midst that crowded deck of flashing propellers, a single miscalculation spelled instant death. Four other tyro members of VT-6 crouched down and joined them. Perhaps that may explain why the usually reserved Streeter seized the moment to describe the labors of the indispensable plane-handlers whose coffee they were drinking.

Hardly back from their training-cruise on the *Shangri-La*, Torpedo Six's enlisted personnel bade Hilo good-bye and boarded an inter-island steamer for passage to Pearl Harbor. Evening's shadows were falling before the *Waialeale* cast off from Hilo's dock. Erelong the bottles were out and a goodly number of the aircrewmen began appreciating Bacchus's best. Unready to retire to their bunks, Ted joined Jack, Chappy, Katke, Pop Varner, and some others shooting the breeze on deck. It was a beautiful night for letting Hawaii's matchless vistas float by. What better time for reliving squadron history.

By no measure could Torpedo Squadron Six be described as venerable. Yet, like any military organization with combat-tested members, VT-6 boasted its heroes. For any of their peers to have ever referred to these aviators as "heroes" would have invited ridicule, curses, laughter, not unlikely all three. Certainly Six's skipper at the Midway battle, Lieutenant Commander Eugene Lindsey, merited the encomium. Shortly before that epic contest, he had been injured in a carrier landing. Hours prior to launching their TBDs against Admiral Yamamoto's approaching fleet, Lindsey's superior asked him if his body could handle the task. His tart reply, "This is what I have been trained to do." Lindsey led the attack against the Japanese carrier *Kaga*. His

Devastator, along with nine others bearing the albatross logo, never returned to the *Enterprise*.

Ensign John McInerny had started out as a fighter pilot in 1942. Not long after Midway, he engaged in a heated airborne navigational altercation with his flight leader; quite deliberately, and doubtlessly justifiably, McInerny *twice* broke formation, trying to convince his superior they were on the wrong heading! Thereafter he piloted one of the early TBFs. Following the *Hornet*'s destruction, this blacksmith's son flew his Avenger off the *Enterprise* and then later the *Intrepid*. Pop Varner delighted in describing "Big Mac's" efforts to turn his Torpecker into a Wildcat. After Tom Lea painted his portrait for *Life* magazine, McInerny won immortality; he laughingly predicted that Lea's illustration would produce a beating from his old man when he got home.

By early 1945, only one of Six's pilots could claim to have served on all three of the squadron's war cruises. Lieutenant Commander Harold J. W. Eppler had twice flown from doomed carriers. At Truk, his bombs had torn apart an enemy destroyer. Returning from one strike, Eppler had exhibited masterful aerial leadership, otherwise infuriated Japanese fighter pilots might have splashed a formation of Avengers. With his punched-in nose and premature balding, VT-6's executive officer seemed much older to Ted than his twenty-seven years. Quite appropriately, the squadron's honored Chief Chapman flew as "Epp's" turret gunner.

Among the famed flyers identified with Torpedo Squadron Six, Edward "Butch" H. O'Hare was preeminent. An Annapolis graduate (class of '37), O'Hare had gone to war in 1942 with Fighting Three aboard the old *Lexington*. Gambling ran in his genes. Butch's father, Edward J. O'Hare, wealthy head of Sportsman's Park race track, had been gunned down in Chicago's gang wars. In early 1942, Lieutenant (j.g.) O'Hare's Wildcat was credited with downing five land-based Japanese Betty bombers. Only the exhaustion of his ammunition had compelled him to break off his interception. But O'Hare had successfully scattered the Japanese attackers. Hungry for heroes, America's adulation of its first Navy ace reached all the way to the White House.

After the war ended, diligent research by John Lundstrom clarified O'Hare's remarkable achievement. His February 28, single-handed attack on that eight-plane formation, only minutes away from the old *Lexington*, had splashed three of the two-engine Betty bombers and severely damaged two others. Less than an hour earlier his equally famous fellow aviator and mentor, Lieutenant John S. Thach, had himself shot down four Bettys. Decades later, Admiral Thach gave Butch credit for splashing "six in as many minutes." Whatever, O'Hare fully deserved the Congressional Medal of Honor a beaming President Roosevelt awarded him. His repeated solitary attacks had somehow survived the defensive fire of over two dozen enemy tail, dorsal, and beam gunners. Furthermore, on his final firing run he had flown through 5-inch antiaircraft bursts from American ships. On that glorious day Butch O'Hare may have exhausted all of an aviator's luck.

Advanced two ranks because of his marksmanship and leadership qualities, Lieutenant Commander O'Hare became Commander of Air Group Six's fighter squadron when it was reformed on 15 March 1943 at NAS San Diego. By October, and following further Pacific combat duty, he was made the air group CO. Outwardly modest, inwardly extremely competitive, his coolness in combat had won him renown. One day, approaching on the final leg of his landing, a trigger-happy flattop gunner opened fire on the ace with a .50 caliber catwalk gun. After parking his Wildcat, O'Hare walked back to the humiliated swabby. Standing on the flight deck and looking down at the gunner, who doubtless wished he were back milking cows, O'Hare calmly chided him, "Son, if you don't stop shooting at me when I've got my wheels down, I'm going to have to report you to the gunnery officer."

Katke, Varner, indeed, all the men who had flown with Six during its second war cruise aboard the *Enterprise* (and later, on the *Intrepid*) never forgot O'Hare's determination to eliminate the menacing Japanese night torpedo attacks. Having been made Six's CO, O'Hare set to work with Lieutenant Commander John C. Phillips, VT-6's skipper, to devise an effective tactic for terminating the Bettys' nocturnal threat. Their plan required a TBF carrying an expert radar operator in its tunnel to coordinate the torpedo bomber's primitive radar gear with the *Enterprise*'s Combat Information Center (CIC—ship's radar plotting center). Given the vector of the incoming bogey (unidentified and presumed to be hostile) by CIC, the Avenger's radar could spot the blacked-out-enemy; two Hellcats flying wing might then destroy the bandit. All three night interceptors must be flown by skilled extroverts. Jeremiahs never tired of warning about the dangers of midair collision, or even the gunning down of a friendly plane in the darkness.

November of 1943 had witnessed the successful assault on the desperate defenders of the Gilbert Islands. Shielded by darkness, Japanese airborne raiders vowed to torpedo the famed *Enterprise* and knock out Air Group Six. As night fell on November 26, there was plenty of radar evidence that the two-engine, "Big Butt Bettys" were on their way. Followed by his wingman, Ensign Warren A. Skon, Air Group Commander O'Hare launched. Then Phillips and his Avenger took off. Manipulating the radar equipment aboard Phillips' plane was Lieutenant (j.g.) Hazen B. Rand, possibly the best qualified aviation radar operator in the Navy. Rand was confident that once the Fighter Director Officer (FDO) aboard the *Enterprise* communicated the direction of the incoming Japanese torpedo bombers he could interpret the crude blips on his rectangular radar scope to reveal the bogeys' location, thereby setting up a kill or kills for O'Hare and Skon. Acting as Phillips' gunner was Aviation Ordnanceman 1st class Alvin Kernan from Saratoga, Wyoming. Like O'Hare, Kernan was one of those rarities, a Navy Regular. No one doubted that this night there should be some glory to pass around.

Aboard the American ships, darkened except for a random Japanese flare, a multitude of "good hunting" prayers ascended for the circling sharpshooters. The previous night, five torpedo wakes had been sighted bubbling through the American fleet. Dusk concluded 1943's Thanksgiving Day; the odds of another such lucky night seemed nil.

Afterward not even CO Phillips could say with certainty what ensued in that ebony sky once O'Hare's team and the twelve or so approaching Japanese aircraft tangled. Speeding off by themselves, the two fighter pilots sought to keep Phillips, as well as the Fighter Direction Officer, informed on what they were about. Occasional bursts of antiaircraft fire from below added to the confusion. FDO left no doubt that Bettys were all around them. Was it to be blind man's bluff in a darkened shooting gallery? Suddenly Rand saw something on his screen. Responding to his radar operator's instructions, Phillips closed in on the bogey. At two hundred yards, he opened fire. His two .50 caliber wing guns kept hammering away until flame erupted from the enemy aircraft. As it crashed into the sea, he yelled out, "Got that one. Any more around?" FDO replied in the affirmative. During his deadly pass, Phillips' turret gunner had also opened up on the doomed Betty. Perhaps it was Kernan's close firing that caused other Bettys in the immediate vicinity to begin shooting at each other.

Over Phillips' intercom a jubilant O'Hare voiced his eagerness to rejoin Phillips' plane killer. Their "dangerous experiment" had succeeded. Before this could be achieved, Rand and Phillips sighted two more Bettys. Using the same right turn approach, Phillips held his fire until he was two hundred yards from his target; he continued firing for almost a minute. As before, the Betty began to burn. A minute or so later Kernan fired way at an unidentified plane that roared past underneath their tail.

Phillips' Avenger had shot down two bombers. The nerves of the three men aboard his plane were as hot as their aircraft's three .50 caliber Brownings. One can imagine the state of the ever-competitive O'Hare; he, too, had just made a kill. Despite the presence of enemy planes, the three pilots agreed to use their wing lights to facilitate a prompt join-up. Skon did so and slipped in off Phillips' port wing. As O'Hare came roaring in, he probably met a burst of fire from Kernan's turret gun. Had he failed to properly use his wing lights on his fatal approach? Had Kernan's nerves misled his eyes, his trigger finger? Or in the dark of night had he shot down yet another disoriented Betty? Kernan's testimony reprinted in the *New York Times* conveys his awful confusion:

> I saw Butch and Skon joining up. . . . Then as I looked to starboard, a fourth plane was closing in on us. It was very dark, but because I could see Skon off our port I knew this was a Jap.
>
> I informed Mr. Phillips and he gave me permission to fire as soon as he was in range. My tracer fire seemed to go into him, but I was blinded by tracers and my gun muzzle, which was white with heat. I don't know whether I shot down the Jap.
>
> While I was firing I saw Commander O'Hare do a wingover across the top of us and he disappeared into the darkness. A few

moments later it seemed that he reappeared and made an outside loop. Then he was gone.

Exactly what occurred must remain forever unknown. O'Hare vanished in that night sky and no trace was ever found of him. Upon landing aboard the Big E and hearing that O'Hare had disappeared, a pathetic Kernan groaned to VT-6's enlisted membership, "My God, I shot down Butch." O'Hare's loss was a tragic turn of events. Acting promptly to cover up a wartime blunder, the Navy awarded both Phillips and his gunner Navy Crosses; Rand received a Purple Heart. In the shoot-out, a bullet had passed through his foot.

Shortly after midnight, and reflecting on Six's aerial warriors, Ted turned in. Despite the liquor-induced clamor aboard the *Waialeale*, he quickly fell asleep. Minutes later he was awakened by one of the Opa-Locka gang. "Ted, wake up. Old Beet Head wants to get his hands on you. He's drunk as a skunk." Also awakened, Shaffer assured him what Ted already knew. Dealing with a staggering, red-faced old fool posed no challenge. However, to kick a ranking air group chief in the balls did. Grabbing a pillow, Ted spent the rest of the night wedged under Katke's bunk. Aware of the derivation of "He's got me over a barrel," Hinckley had no desire whatsoever to experience that bit of prurient history.

At Ford Island the men transferred to the escort carrier *Copahee* (CVE-12) assigned to transport them "to Guam and beyond." By 1945 the Navy possessed numerous baby flattops for performing diverse nautical chores. Launched in 1941 as an AVG (aircraft escort vessel), the *Copahee* was transformed into an ACV (auxiliary aircraft carrier) two years later. By the time VT-6 boarded her in late February, she had repeatedly crossed the Pacific delivering planes and aviation personnel to islands in both the South and Central Pacific. As the fat little ship hoisted aboard factory-slick airplanes and hundreds of tons of cargo, some enlisted men spectators shared a rare moment. Suddenly, without any warning, a large sea chest marked "ACI Files" (Air Combat Intelligence) slipped sideways in a lowering cargo net. Wood plus steel plus gravity equals smash. Forthwith the redolent smell signaled that ACI stood for "alcoholic cool-aid inside." Luckily no permanent impairment of the officers' liquor supply resulted.

Loading the *Copahee* required several days. Accordingly, officers and men were permitted to go ashore. Afraid his libido might be reignited as it had on his recent Honolulu tour, Hinckley stayed safely aboard. When a VT-6 member offered him a generous sum to stand his midnight to 0300 watch, Ted obliged. Guard duty strolling about a flight deck spotted with aircraft half-lighted by the adjacent round-the-clock Navy yard abuzz from welding and hammering shouldn't be too onerous. Putting on his guard belt, Hinckley heeded the Deck Officer's injunctions: "Don't doze off. Walk around the flight deck fore to aft and report anything unusual."

At about 0200, and getting droopy-eyed, the aircrewman heard some sounds emanating up forward from the *Copahee*'s projecting fo'c's'le deck. On investigating, Ted discovered below him two men seated on a

port side storage container, exchanging a large bottle of booze and paw-
ing each other. One of them he did not recognize—perhaps ship's company. The other was an air group chief. Unlike some senior CPOs, this
man was neither elderly not flabby. In his late thirties, big and extremely muscular, there was a certain brutishness about him that gave Ted
the creeps. Possibly it was his weird smile or the cryptic sneers he too
often substituted for speech. Clearly the two imbibers were getting
tanked. They were bothering no one, so Ted continued his stroll.
Sometime later, and almost finished with his watch, he took one last circuit of the flight deck. The two men had disappeared, but strange
grunts emanated from directly below him. Peering down over the end of
the flight deck into the starboard 20 mm gun tub, he saw the chief stark
naked sodomizing the other man. Truly horrified and almost hypno-
tized, Ted jerked away his gaze. What to do? Stunned, he hurried off to
the *Copahee*'s island. His watch over, he turned in his guard belt and
billy club. He reported nothing.

Sleep proved difficult. The following day, and still badly shaken, he
sought out Pop Varner. Varner advised, "Keep your mouth shut. He
outranks you." Sound counsel; Ted should have heeded it. But the
revolting spectacle would not disappear. Seeking relief, he confided in
one other aircrewman. That man's promise of confidentiality proved
worthless. ARM Hinckley would regret his lapse.

A day later, as the *Copahee* was hauling aboard its final freight, who
should come up the gangplank but Hal Smith and Ray Gumm. Yes,
their air group was also getting ready to head out; Air Group Five's designated carrier was the *Franklin* (CV-13). Mulling over memories of their
Memphis and Florida experiences and discussing future aspirations, the
reunion created a cheerful afternoon. Adding to their pleasure was news
that Hageman had also secured a billet with a combat air group—apparently Eighty-four assigned to the *Bunker Hill* (CV-17). With Ted's "*Vaya
con Dios*," the men shook hands and parted.

Dated 21 February 1944, and probably his last letter posted ashore,
Ted's reflections may have occasioned some family tears.

I love you all, you know that but the way I write, and the times I
do not, might lead you to think otherwise. . . . Sis you keep
dreaming and keep sweet and pure, and even though times may
be awfully hard your dark clouds will always have a silver lining.
Dad your son has always caused you trouble and wear. Few are
the times when my actions have gladdened your heart. I guess
my upstreperousness (sic), added to our mutual stubbornness,
has been the cause of a good deal of the conflict. But as you are
my father I know you have forgiven me and I know that I hold no
anger for our old gripes.

And finally for his mother for whom he too often had been a burden, "If I
don't return there will be sorrow at 1211. This is to be expected. . . . [I
will have] won peace and joy in life everlasting. You would be selfish
indeed to take my death [badly]. Other mothers have lost three even five
sons and carried bravely on."

As the *Copahee* pulled away from Ford Island, no Polynesian lovelies swayed to lilting ukuleles. Nothing ashore signaled a salute, not even a feeble wave from a pennant wishing the flyers good hunting and a happy homecoming. The momentum of the Pacific War machine was moving toward its relentless sanguinary climax. Iwo Jima had just fallen, as had many a brave Marine, and B-29s were raining death on Japan's cities. The *Copahee*'s departure merely marked the movement of a tiny part in a colossal clock recording the bloody seconds of a worldwide war. Perhaps this was why on March 1, the vessel's captain overlooked the normal Order of the Golden Dragon festivities when his ship crossed the 180th meridian. Later Ted was handed a membership card certifying his membership in the "Sacred Order."

Americans might substitute paper-shuffling for tradition, but not Japan's military. They embraced it passionately, fatalistically; a kamikaze would once again save their beloved homeland. After a rather hush-hush meeting—for officers only—aboard the *Copahee*, Ted first heard the word discussed. In the thirteenth century, the Japanese David had beheld a Chinese Goliath. A Divine Wind (kamikaze)—no doubt a typhoon—and Japan's bushido spirit had repelled Kubla Khan's massive amphibious assault.

The Pacific War had hardly begun before the suicidal heroism of Japan's military evidenced itself. Whether it was in their miniature submarines below the seas or their pilots in the skies, to die for their Emperor, their beautiful islands, and family was a noble, crowning act. *Taiatari* (body-crashing), in one form or another, did indeed have an ancient and hallowed history. In 1944, and agonizing over the loss of their oceanic empire, the military employed a radical new pebble for David's sling.

Japan's Special Attack Corps first appeared during her bitter defense of the Philippines. On 25 October 1944, led by Lieutenant Yukio Seki, five planes of the Special Attack Corps attacked American vessels. Henceforth, from the Japanese perspective, these sacrifices were fully justified. Even after the war was over, Nippon's preeminent ace declared, "The kamikazes gave us tremendous new strength. Their effectiveness was obvious in the number of enemy warships and transports, once inviolate from our attacks, safe behind their withering firepower, which now responded with the roar of flaming gasoline, exploding bombs, the shrieks of men." With sixty-four confirmed air kills, the last four after he was seriously wounded, Saburo Sakai's opinions must be taken seriously. "Perhaps it will never be fully understood by Americans, or anyone in the Western world, that our men did not consider that they were throwing away their lives. On the contrary, the kamikaze pilots volunteered en masse for the one-way missions." The tragic idealism of these young men is especially moving when one reflects on Sakai's belief that many of those who flew kamikazes recognized "the hopelessness of Japan's position in the war. They did not flinch, they did not hesitate. They flew their bomb-laden planes, and died for their country."

Those directing America's Pacific War were shaken by the kamikaze weapon. While few ships were sunk, too many, large and small, were being knocked out of action. The cost in human life was appalling. To confuse Tokyo, as well as head-off media alarmists, the scale of ship damage was not always fully revealed to the public. The Navy conceded that the *St. Lo*, "merely a small escort carrier," had been sunk at Leyte Gulf. However, limited information was released on the giant, multi-wounded *Saratoga* which had been forced to withdraw from the February 1945 assault on Iwo Jima. Understandably, carriers were prime targets for what Americans labeled Japan's "suicide pilots."

In March 1945, it was just as well that the men of Air Group Six could not know that like the *Lexington*, the *Franklin*, the *Intrepid*, and other fast fleet carriers already hit by Japan's Special Attack Corps, the flattop for which they were destined also had an inescapable rendezvous with kamikaze fury.

Not fury but fun was the mood of Ted and his friends as they spilled into the *Copahee*'s ship-to-shore boats and headed for Guam's inviting "enlisted men's beach." Here, midst the charred battlefield litter remaining from the recent American-Japanese fighting, they splashed away an afternoon drinking and surfing. The *Copahee* required only a few days to transfer her cargo to the immense build-up of war materiel being stockpiled at Guam for future invasions. And then, once again, it was anchors aweigh, their destination: Ulithi Atoll in the Western Carolines.

Ulithi was an astonishing wartime windfall. On 22 September 1944, just a month after America's military had paid so dearly in human lives to wrest Guam and the Marianas, a small invasion force discovered that Ulithi Atoll was utterly undefended. Twenty miles long and ten wide, the fringing coral reef and islets surrounding Ulithi's lagoon provided a magnificent natural anchorage. Quite literally it could accommodate hundreds of ships. Best of all, Ulithi lay but twelve hundred miles from Okinawa, after Iwo Jima the final island steppingstone leading to Japan itself.

Seabee hustle had quickly transformed the atoll's palm dotted islands. Roads, piers, landing strips, barracks, and of course, a beer garden and officers' club rapidly took shape. Within the vast sanctuary a "floating tank farm" of obsolete tankers provided a ready reserve of 400,000 barrels of fuel oil. By the time the *Copahee* arrived on 8 March 1945, Admiral Nimitz had labeled Ulithi "the Navy's secret weapon."

The *Copahee* had been an inhospitable transport. Cheers arose from torpedo squadron personnel as they disembarked into the large flat-bottomed barges used for hauling men and material about Ulithi's lagoon. The marvel of that night never left Ted. It seemed as though he had arrived in some magical floating world. Unthreatened by any Japanese raiders, lights blazed everywhere across that shimmering city of ships. Their different silhouettes—heretofore merely images in recognition manuals—shouted, yes, there really were powerful *Iowa* and *North Carolina* class battleships, deadly battle cruisers named after U.S. Territories, fleet carriers, light carriers, cruisers, and destroyers galore. Although glad his stomach would never have to endure duty aboard a *Fletcher* class destroyer, the sight of these moored, swaying, graceful sub killers pleased him. His joy was a mix of delight and awe. Perhaps it may even have matched the Tin Woodman's astonishment at first beholding Oz's sparkling Emerald City.

News that the men of VT-6 were bound for the USS *Hancock*, had initially disappointed Ted. Why couldn't his singularly honored torpedo squadron have been assigned a more romantic, more historically valid carrier like the *Wasp*, *Hornet*, or *Lexington*? Hadn't the *Enterprise*, the legendary Big E, been Six's ship? On second thought, how dumb to fusticate about a mere name while some of his training school buddies still languished in stateside CASUs.

A mighty ship, a gallant crew, and scores of Hancock sea stories—some of them true—for those who served aboard her 1944-45.

"The Fightin' Hannah," as her 3500-member ship's company proudly called CV-19, was the fourth flattop Ted had boarded since the preceding October. Like the 27,000-ton *Shangri-La*, the *Hancock* was another *Essex* class carrier. Why did she appear so much larger than any of them? Perhaps it was because he came aboard at night from a rolling barge and got well christened with saltwater. Clambering up the forward accommodation "ladder" (stairs), the aircrewmen stepped from the darkness onto the *Hancock*'s brightly-lighted hangar deck, a cavernous aircraft parking garage. A waiting boatswain hurried them off to their compartment, but not before each flyer snapped off a smart salute aft.

VT-6's enlisted men could hardly believe their good luck. Their isolated, up forward sleeping quarters were located right next to the *Hancock*'s fo'c's'le. Adjacent to their exclusive quarters, the empty fo'c's'le lay totally open to port and starboard. Beyond that generous space—spacious enough to accommodate Sunday church services—a lateral bulkhead rose to support the end of the flight deck. Should the ship get caught in a typhoon, that steel wall could absorb any waves smashing over the bow. Beyond this bulkhead were situated two large gun tubs, each containing two pairs of grim-looking 40 mm Bofors. Bandits trying to reach the Hannah by zooming in head on at bow level must penetrate their deadly barrage. By the time Ted had inspected this armament and returned to VT-6's quarters, he had to settle for a top berth. Later, he discovered their compartment's unusually high overhead enclosed the carrier's two hydraulic catapults. They functioned directly over his bunk. Despite the climb to his fourth tier, "high rent district" bed, Ted felt snug and safe.

Following breakfast, he commenced exploring the giant engine of destruction that had become his home. But first he had to go top-side and stand on the flight deck. Was what he had passed through last night a dream? Were there really that many-ships in Ulithi's lagoon? Painted dirty blues and grays, anchored warships of diverse description spread out in every direction from the *Hancock*. Chugging and darting about among them were innumerable small service craft. Here and there larger supply ships and tankers transferred food and fuel for men, ships, and airplanes. Midst tropical repose, America's immense Pacific fleet prepared itself for battle.

A friendly ship, the Hannah's crew spoke highly of their skipper, Captain Robert F. Hickey. The opposite held true for the ship's executive officer, Commander William F. Raborn. But as Jack Streeter reminded Ted, "In any big organization someone has to be the SOB; in the Navy it's generally the Exec." Most of ship's company seemed to have been aboard since her Caribbean shakedown cruise in mid-1944. For all their callowness, CV-19's youthful society sensed this ship was writing their great adventure. And by March 1945, each crewman had an exciting tale to tell describing his role during such and such attack.

The *Hancock* had first struck the Japanese during the preceding October, a twenty-five-day series of raids on the Nanseii Shoto Islands, (one of which was Okinawa), Formosa, and Luzon. The Japanese struck back and lost two aircraft to the ship's gunners. Luckily a bomb which pierced a catwalk merely left a hole and exploded harmlessly alongside. After each operation as part of Halsey's Third Fleet, the *Hancock* took brief replenishment rests at Ulithi. Her airmen had given a good account of themselves in the far-flung Battle for Leyte Gulf, including fatal hits on *Musashi*, a *Yamato* class behemoth, as well as on various cruisers. Further operations against the Philippines followed. On one of them, a kamikaze was blasted out of the air directly over her flight deck, its bomb exploding harmlessly off the port side.

To cripple an *Essex* class carrier, a Japanese pilot or kamikaze—they were not necessarily the same—must penetrate the ship's twelve 5-inch antiaircraft guns as well as the dozens of Bofors and 20 mm Oerlikons bristling from her hull. And, of course, this presumed the attacker had survived AA fire from the surrounding fleet and evaded the circling CAP (combat air patrol) fighters.

Christmas 1944 at Ulithi had hardly ended before the *Hancock* once again savaged the enemy; this time the strikes hit targets in the South China Sea between the Philippines and China. United States submarines had already turned the region into a graveyard for Japanese vessels. But subs can't operate on land nor in narrow, protected harbors. *Hancock* aircraft could. To no one's surprise and everyone's regret, a raid on Hong Kong encountered heavy ground fire; six pilots and five aircrewmen were lost. Then on 21 January 1945, a returning Avenger accomplished what no kamikaze had thus far succeeded in doing.

Standing on the hangar deck, a Hannah airedale pointed upward and told Ted about that terrible day. Although the ghastly flight deck hole had been repaired, the scar so visible from below left no doubt what a horror had been unleashed topside when a taxiing TBM had inadvertently dumped an armed 500-lb. bomb. Exploding next to the ship's island, it killed or maimed dozens of men. Fires erupted on both the flight and hangar decks. Within thirty-six minutes they were under control; rapid, temporary repairs enabled *Hancock* aircraft to continue landing.

On February 10, equipped with a new air group and her wounds healed, the scrappy *Hancock* left Ulithi for her sixth operation against the enemy. On this cruise she participated in the successful strikes on Tokyo's airfields and supplied valuable ground support for the invasion of Iwo Jima. Okinawa and neighboring islands were also pasted. Destroying potential kamikaze aircraft on the ground had become a high priority; due to skillful use of camouflage and dummy planes, this was increasingly difficult. In less than six months, the "Fightin' Hannah" had well earned her name, even suffering minimum damage from a roaring, killer typhoon that had capsized three destroyers.

Except on the forthcoming strike days when they donned their flight gear, Air Group Six's approximately two hundred officers and one hundred thirty-five enlisted men virtually disappeared within their new shipboard community. Ted soon located the ship's library, and on March 10, he witnessed his first on board "smoker" (prize fights). Relaxed socialization with his fellow aircrewmen in their private, air-cooled ready room usually assured round-the-clock coffee, thanks to Righteous Richard, Egghead, or one of the obliging Rover Boys. Situated immediately underneath the flight deck on the gallery deck, VT-6's ready room facilitated rapid egress to their Avengers. With plenty of Torpecker engines to caress, gunner Al Shaffer, seemed content; and as for Mr. Witt, "The wardroom menu is not bad." On the evening of March 11, Ted joined the animated crowd collecting on the hangar deck for a flick.

With the *Hancock's* massive steel hangar deck curtains pulled wide open, the audience could discern other neighboring ships also preoccupied with Hollywood escapism. Irritating not a few enlisted men was the sight of black steward men carrying up special cushioned metal armchairs from the wardroom to accommodate officers' butts. Everyone seated, *One Body Too Many* began. The chattering ceased, and actress Jean Parker walked onto the screen. Abruptly a brilliant light flashed from a nearby ship. In micro seconds the boom from the explosion upstaged Miss Parker. Pandemonium, or so it seemed to Ted, took over.

"All hands man your battle stations!" barked the ship's loudspeakers. For a few moments the deafening racket created by the hundreds of steel chairs being swept this way and that across the armored hangar deck quite unnerved him. Although no one knew precisely what was happening, VT-6's old hands yelled to stand fast. "Let the ship's company get to their guns." Indeed, to ascend or descend any of the ship's ladders was utterly impossible. From below a stream of men surged up. Some raced to man the 40 mms on the sponsons spaced just outside the hangar deck. Others seeking their Oerlikons dashed up the stairs leading to the transom catwalks bordering the flight deck. With all the guns manned, steel hatches crashed shut throughout the ship. In but minutes "Condition Zebra" had assured the *Hancock's* compartmentalized, watertight integrity. Ted had observed his first actual "general quarters." In the months ahead, he would see the drama reenacted many times, but never midst such confusion.

With its personnel sorted out and the ship's ladders empty, the quite useless torpedo squadron men climbed to the flight deck. Across the lagoon, darkness had blotted out the myriad lights; blackness magnified the fire blazing on the stern of the carrier *Randolph* (CV-15). Presently the *Hancock's* loudspeakers explained what had happened. Two or three kamikazes had crashed into the anchorage; only one had scored. At least twenty-five men had been killed and seventeen planes ruined. Either by the use of auxiliary gas tanks or a refueling stop at Yap, the raiders had breached America's maritime sanctuary. Mercifully the kamikaze that had hit the *Randolph* entirely missed her crowd of moviegoers.

Lying in his bunk, Ted retraced the evening's unexpected drama. The sangfroid of squadron veterans like South Carolinian George Patterson, Hardisty, Varner, and Katke had impressed him. But it was the throng of men scrambling from the ship's depths up to their gun stations that lingered in his mind. Until that bedlam, he had simply not visualized black swabbies as gunners. Admittedly, since beginning his aviation training, he had seen extremely few African-Americans, and almost all of those were cooks or "mess boys." Like his white shipmates, Ted vacuously accepted the Navy's historic segregation. Aboard the Hannah, as on other large fighting ships, the primary role of African-Americans was that of food handlers. Their segregated living quarters, like "officers' country," the exclusive ready rooms for air group squadrons, the compartment assigned shipboard Marines, and much else within the ship, reflected the Navy's mini-communities ashore.

If anyone on the *Hancock* ever scorned these diverse, segregated living areas, Ted never heard the critic. Certainly he never heard anyone question why the Hannah had nothing but white male officers. Until the color line first cracked in 1944, Navy tradition had dictated no commissioned Negro Americans. At the beginning of the war, elite services like the Marine Corps and Navy Air totally excluded them. Of this policy, Ted had been ignorant. Comfortable in his WASP status, one doubts that knowledge of this gross inequity would have greatly troubled him. What an irony. Black hands that had frequently fed him, and would soon help protect him, must not fly with him.

CHAPTER VIII
"Eternal Father strong to save. . ."

From the *Hancock*'s communication center, Hinckley heard he had passed the flight school examination. "It'll be July at least," Lieutenant Fitzpatrick guestimated, "before you depart for cadet training." Did Ted really want to exchange his silver aircrew wings for a pilot's gold? Certainly the ready room congratulations were gratifying. Albeit, the likelihood of separating from Torpedo Squadron Six troubled him. It would soon be half a year since he had begun forging the bonds of comradeship with these men; erelong they must be severed. But this was the Navy, and as the complacent Californian was at last recognizing, in uniform or out, to live fully required abrupt changes.

How heady the prospects of someday doing barrel rolls in one of Pensacola's Yellow Peril biplanes. How gratifying to strut before the ladies in those flight greens. War's immediacy swept aside his vanity; Task Force 58 and the Fightin' Hannah were hours away from "the big time." Having been issued a flight log, Ted had decided to let his become more of a diary. Nuts to the Navy prohibition! He must record his once-in-a-lifetime experience.

Okinawa lay approximately three hundred fifty miles south of Kyushu. Of Japan's four major "home islands," Kyushu was the southernmost; its ports and kamikaze nests had to be struck, and struck hard, before risking an amphibious assault on Okinawa. Cracking Iwo Jima's eight square miles of volcanic rock and ash during the preceding month had written a cruel chapter in Marine history. Was the impending April 1945 struggle for 458-square-mile Okinawa really worth another such bloodletting? Must the island's 400,000 noncombatant, non-Japanese Okinawans suffer the torrent of destruction that had swept across the Gilberts, the Marshalls, the Carolines, the Philippines, and the Marianas? Okinawa promised a superb forward base for amassing the vast quantities of war materiel and men to be thrown into the projected invasion of Japan. Furthermore, Okinawa had airfields from which hundreds of American warplanes could check Kyushu's infernal suicide planes. Yes, the island must be conquered.

Approaching Japan was history's greatest battle fleet. Commanding Task Force 58 was Vice Admiral Marc Mitscher. His leathery, wizened face reminded any who needed reminding that "Bald Eagle" had been fighting Japs since Midway. Not water but air had shaped the Admiral's psyche. Mitscher was an airman through and through. When the Pacific War began, battleship sailors had dominated. Now, as America's deadly noose tightened around Japan, Mitscher took comfort that each of his four carrier task groups (CTGs) composing Task Force 58 were commanded by veteran flyers like himself.

The *Hancock* was but one of the flattops assigned to CTG 58.2; its three companion carriers were the *Franklin*, the *San Jacinto* (CVL-30), and the *Bataan* (CVL-29). Commanding these four vessels, their air groups, along with their sprawling parade of escorting battleships, cruisers, and destroyers was Rear Admiral R. E. Davison. Well before leaving Ulithi, and no doubt a relief to the *Hancock*'s Captain Hickey, the Admiral and his accompanying staff had hoisted Davison's flag on the *Franklin*.

Jerked from his sleep by the roaring swoosh of a pre-dawn CAP Hellcat, followed by the clink-clinking of the rewinding catapult, Ted dressed and hurried off to early breakfast. 18 March 1945 marked the first day of combat for many in Air Group Six. For the battle-seasoned ship's company it was yet another dangerous day facilitating the fly boys and dodging kamikazes. To the Hannah's men, the preparation of 100-lb. and 500-lb. bombs was routine. To Ted the proximity of these ugly steel eggs being wheeled across the mess hall signaled that the killing was about to begin. Transported topside to the flight deck, each bomb was armed with a nose fuse. Shortly thereafter the lethal cargo was shackled within the waiting Avengers and Helldivers.

The division to which Witt was attached had not been selected for the initial strike against targets about Kagoshima Sound. With time on his hands, Ted accompanied other aircrewmen watching their shipmates' fueling and bomb-loading labors among the crowded airplanes. Once airborne, Six united with other air groups and disappeared over the horizon. What a beautiful day for flying against the enemy.

Of course the clear skies also meant good hunting for Japanese aircraft searching for American flattops. Now familiar with the normal, relaxed rhythm of shipboard life, Ted was struck by the radically altered atmosphere created by General Quarters (GQ). Steel-helmeted crewmen manning battle stations had food and coffee brought up to them. Below, Condition Zebra dictated a lock-down of each of the massive horizontal hatches spaced across the armored hangar deck. Beneath this immense shield, passing from one compartment to another required the immediate closure of any "broken" hatch. Ted was startled by an ominous silence as he descended from the flight deck via the island and hurried across the spacious hangar deck. Instead of the area's usual activity, no human could be seen. Adding to this eerie absence of life, the entire hangar deck was almost empty of aircraft. Numerous mechanical sensations left no doubt that the Fighting Hannah was angrily alive. Vibrations from her giant engines could be faintly heard as well as felt. Their carrier was surging ahead at battle speed. Off the port side, a wave-spanking destroyer was elegantly framed by an open hangar deck bay. Could that DD be *The Sullivans*? She was in their task group. Eminently better than any Winslow Homer seascape, the feisty vessel's saltwater struggle shouted Neptune's menace. Aboard the extremely stable *Hancock* one forgot he was on a ship, that is, unless perched on one foot to tie a shoe or undress. Like the mighty *Hancock*, the destroyer's guns were fully manned and pointed skyward. Everyone expected a kamikaze assault.

For Bombing Six, "Lucky Day" strike turned out disastrously. It was commonly understood but rarely discussed that the Curtis Helldiver was overrated. Who wants to hear that the military machine they operate is a lemon? An uncooperative plane to handle, the SB2C, although faster than the fabled Douglas Dauntless, was an unpredictable gas guzzler. On their return, six of VB-6's planes had been forced to make water landings. Fortunately all fifteen of the Torpeckers got home after scattering 100-lb. bombs on repair shops and hangars around Kagoshima Airport and hitting various "targets of opportunity."

Lieutenant Forrest Crane, a popular officer, had earlier been reprimanded for being "too friendly with enlisted men." This day the Missourian's Avenger appeared to have been chased by an unfriendly Japanese dragon. Antiaircraft shrapnel had thoroughly chewed up "Frosty's" tail; his elevator was well nigh worthless. Alone after his bombing run, he was forced by his badly crippled bomber to fly westward in an extended, solitary semicircle out over the East China Sea. One miscalculation and his plane would have spun in out of control. Finally arriving back over CTG 58.2 and the *Hancock*, he flew straight in, quite ignoring the landing circle, CAP Hellcats on their final approach, and a frantic wave-off from the Landing Signal Officer (LSO). To no one's surprise, Crane had hardly climbed from his cockpit before being commanded to report to the bridge. Later, VT-6 aircrewmen heard what a royal chewing was administered him by the *Hancock*'s unfriendly dragon.

Having been debriefed, Crane's crewmen came down for a late lunch. Chalk white faces of radioman Henry Reardon and gunner Carl Clatty confirmed that they had seen the Grim Reaper. Terror lingered in Reardon's eyes. Usually loquacious Clatty was nearly speechless. Before Ted could get the details on the morning's strike, he was ordered to don his flight gear and fly with Lieutenant (j.g.) R. A. McCalley in a six-plane search for the ditched VB-6 flyers. It proved to be a futile three hours. Fortunately, of the twelve lost aviators, eight were eventually plucked from their life rafts. Henceforth, Helldivers carried a diminished bomb load; claims for their flying range were also scaled back.

Although a sad day for VB-6, the fighter sweeps had fared better. One Corsair pilot scored the air group's first kill, knocking down a Judy (Japanese torpedo plane). A sobering reminder that Japanese interceptors could still fight back was the loss over the Kagoshima target area of VBF-6's executive officer. Manifestly, the enemy was concentrating their aircraft for kamikaze attacks, not interception. On March 18 so many threw themselves at TF-58 that the *Hancock* could not launch her afternoon strike. Over a dozen were splashed by the circling combat air patrol and the task force's shipboard gunners. Before night fell, kamikazes had inflicted minor damage on the *Intrepid* and the Big E.

The *Enterprise's* unique island profile plus her redoubtable war record may account in part for the relentless pounding she continued to suffer.

"The most thrill packed day of my life," was how Ted recorded 19 March 1945. Following the usual early breakfast, and alerted by the bugle call signaling flight quarters, he and Al scrambled top-side. Parked at the extreme end of the flight deck, their plane with its four 500-lb. bombs would be one of the last launched. A smiling Witt greeted them with last-minute instructions. A prior briefing had explained that TF-58 had moved northward and lay approximately three hundred miles off Japan's southeast coast. Torpedo Six had been assigned a prime target: a surviving Japanese carrier sheltered in Kobe harbor. Assured of Hellcat or Corsair escorts, the likelihood of Jap fighters seemed minimal.

After final preflight checks and mutual backslapping, the three men climbed aboard. Dozens of aircraft engines sputtered and then thundered their power. But Ted's personal wiring was already responding peculiarly. Steaming on the same course directly behind the *Hancock*, and also readying her air group, was the *Franklin*. Were Smitty and Ray as alarmingly tense as he was? Perhaps they had had their first taste of battle yesterday. According to ACI, many of Big Ben's Corsairs were carrying the little-tested "Tiny Tims," huge 11.75-inch rockets; only one could be slung underneath a F4U's fuselage.

Preoccupied checking out his tunnel equipment and surrounded by a herd of bellowing aircraft champing to roar aloft, Ted thought he heard a brief burst of automatic fire. He didn't know it but a Japanese bomber had just zoomed overhead. While almost immediately, the Judy's pilot had accomplished what America's Dauntless dive bomber counterparts had achieved at Midway. The pilot had planted his two bombs right on the *Franklin's* densely-packed aircraft. Like those on the *Hancock's* flight deck, they were fully fueled with high octane gasoline and crammed with explosives.

"Our flight's been canceled," Witt snapped. Enclosed in the TBM's belly, Hinckley had no idea of the catastrophe taking place astern. Following orders, he threw off his flak jacket, disconnected his intercom, and climbed out of his plane's hatch. He therefore never heard the bridge's counter-command, "Get those planes off this deck." Noticing some airedales standing as if struck dumb, Ted followed their gaze. Initially his senses rejected the horrific scene directly abaft. With terrible flames from one end of her flight deck to the other, the *Franklin* was blowing up. Skyrocketing Tiny Tims accompanied the hideous flashes and resounding booms. Turning to port, and obviously doomed, she majestically moved out of formation. Ted was absolutely paralyzed. Just moments ago he had viewed the *Franklin* displayed in her new blue-black paint, and here she was afire from bow to stern. As she swung out on her new course, perpendicular from the *Hancock's*, with her hangar deck curtains folded open, Ted could see directly into her. It was "as if someone had filled in her whole hangar deck with red crayon," he wrote afterward. Good God in heaven! Within that gigantic blazing oven, what had become of Smitty and Ray and the other Air Group Five

Opa-Locka men with whom he had trained? No one could survive such an inferno.

How long Hinckley stood transfixed he never knew. Suddenly something told him to turn around. Another astounding sight. As if by magic the *Hancock's* flight deck, so crowded with expectant wings of destruction, was now absolutely clear except for a single torpedo bomber. It was Witt's plane! And it was taxiing up to the take off position! Fearing a disaster like that tearing apart the *Franklin*, Captain Hickey's team had launched the Hannah's volatile cargo with extraordinary haste.

Shouting, "Hey, wait for me," Hinckley sprinted up the flight deck. Luckily the LSO spotted him. Even before his safety belt was fastened, their plane roared down the deck and sprung into the air. If Curtis Helldivers too often went "over the bow and into the drink," Grumman's birds exhibited a wonderful alacrity when taking off.

Alacrity for 1211 Avoca, Pasadena, had seized Hinckley. Already he found himself suffering the shakes, and they still had a lot of ocean to cross before reaching Kobe. Humiliated, angry at himself, and simply incapable of defeating fear, he tried to occupy himself with the scene below. The listing, smoke-shrouded *Franklin*, assisted by the cruiser *Santa Fe*, and soon after by the *Pittsburgh*, was staggering eastward away from the battle fleet. Until she increased her distance from Japan, the gravely wounded ship presented meat for hungry kamikazes. Ted's eyes spotted Torpedo Six's protective umbrellas of Hellcats and Corsairs moving across the sky. Then a single Corsair with Air Group Five's large white diamond markings passed by. Flying beneath their Avenger, the solitary F4U had apparently jettisoned its Tiny Tim. "Lucky bastard," Ted muttered to himself. Uttering a quiet prayer for those trapped aboard the still blazing *Franklin*—she burned for five hours—he thanked God it had been them, not us. Hardly had his mind formed that craven thought before shame knifed him.

Approaching Kobe harbor, blows less metaphysical crackled within Six's approaching squadrons. Through his partially-opened hatch, Ted could actually smell the cordite from the antiaircraft air bursts. Furiously tossing out metallic paper strips to confuse radar-operated antiaircraft cannon, his hands seemed about the only part of his body reasonably manageable. His body was trembling uncontrollably. To breathe properly proved quite impossible. Fear in flight was not new, but this physical distress approached panic. He desperately wanted to run away. Yet unlike *The Red Badge of Courage's* Henry, he couldn't.

"There she is," Witt commented laconically. Ten thousand feet below, Ted spotted their enemy carrier. He double checked his intervalometer (bomb spacer). And, yes, he had armed the damned bombs. Approaching from the northwest and slipping downward to increase their air speed, Lieutenant Eppler led his spreading formation of Avengers down to an altitude of 6500 feet. Everyone wondered how long they could elude Kobe's thickening flak. Despite the unyielding clutch of fear, Ted prepared to position himself by his .30-caliber machine gun. Their bomb bay doors swung open. Each TBM broke off smartly and began its steep glide bombing run. Ted's stomach was fine, his nervous system a shambles. When would Witt pull out of his dive? Unmistakably their Avenger was relieved to be free of its two thousand pounds of devastation. For an instant Ted looked directly down at their floating target. Giant geysers from 500-lb. near misses confirmed that some of the pilots preceding Witt also suffered the shakes. Terrified as he was, Ted smiled inwardly at the carrier's gunners. Despite the chaos overtaking them, their protective fire slashed upward; streams of incendiary bullets drifted by. And then in seconds it was all over. Witt shut the bomb bay doors. Never had they traveled so fast. They were less than five hundred feet off the water and still alive.

Kobe Harbor, March 19, 1945 and a very scared radioman-gunner at last tastes combat. Perhaps the Avenger is Witt's. Certainly the numerous misses about the anchored Japanese carrier leave no doubt as to the intense anti-aircraft fire.

Speeding toward Kobe's east harbor entrance, Ted belatedly realized he had failed to get off a single shot at the carrier's brave gunners. Suddenly he spotted a surfaced Japanese submarine to their port apparently racing for the open sea. Swinging his belly gun around, Ted's two thumbs closed on his weapon's trigger. What was it that prevented him from shooting? Was it the strings of bullets already splashing around the sub? Was it a generous God? Lieutenant Harvey Odenbrett's furiously-firing Corsair zoomed directly between Witt's belly gunner and the fleeing sub. Had Hinckley fired, his bullets would surely have ripped apart yet another overzealous fighter pilot.

With his gas almost gone, Witt made an emergency landing on the *Essex*. Later that afternoon, and for a second time that long day, Hinckley gave his pilot those welcome words, "Wheels down, landing hook down." Following the slam-dunk of a carrier landing, the three men reported to the *Hancock*'s wardroom for debriefing. Individual flyers described what they had observed; afterwards a wee bottle of spirits was given each of them. At this moment, and its likes thereafter, Ted had plenty of good friends glad to relieve him of his "devil's handiwork." For all of his comrades' post-strike jubilation, Ted Hinckley had little to celebrate.

Witt well merited the credit given him for putting at least one bomb on the target. What about his pusillanimous radioman who forgot to fire his gun? Other flights, other strikes would hear the chatter of Ted's .30 caliber. Yet in his private war against cowardice, total victory proved unwinable. His body exhausted, his mind an unstoppable propeller, he collapsed into his bunk. Whatta day! Once again Bombing Six had suffered losses. Her skipper's tailgunner had been knocked unconscious by ground fire. And two damaged Helldivers ditched in Japanese waters. Thank God, everyone in the torpedo squadron got home.

News the following morning that the *Franklin* had survived honored both her builders and her courageous firefighters. Big Ben's skipper had saved his ship, otherwise the mustang (ex-enlisted man) captain might have confronted a stern-faced hearing board. Weeks later Ted got the great news: both Smitty and Ray, by some miracle, had escaped incineration. He also heard how at the very moment when the Judy had ignited the holocaust, the *Franklin*'s hangar deck hatches lay wide open with men standing there in chow lines waiting to be fed. This unbelievable lapse, when the *Hancock*, and one presumes the other carriers, were locked tight with their crews at GQ. Surely some old hand on the *Franklin* must have asked himself, "Why, if we are in range of Jap targets, isn't our ship at Condition Zebra?" and, "Shouldn't these long chow lines be sheltered beneath our armored deck?" A contorted jumble of twisted steel above that deck, the *Franklin* was out of the war. On the long voyage home surviving crew members eventually exhumed hundreds of corpses from her mangled interior.

No one could doubt that the upcoming struggle for Okinawa would demand a terrible price. The same day that Big Ben was knocked out, the *Wasp* took a bomb hit; some two hundred men were killed. The following day, trigger-happy gunners—"friendly fire" it came to be called—further damaged the Big E. And then on March 21, a flight of sixteen Japanese bombers carrying their new Ohka (cherry blossom) bombs approached TF-58. Actually a rocket-powered, winged bomb, the Ohka was guided by a suicide pilot. Attached to its mother bomber and packed with a ton of explosives, the 600-mph bomb was only released when the target appeared. Sixty miles out from TF-58 all sixteen of the pregnant attackers were shot down by American fighters. Dubbed

"Baka," or fool bomb, no doubt by Navy public relations, Ohkas would prove their deadly punch. But as with everything else in the Japanese arsenal, it was too little, too late.

To accommodate their wounded men and ships, TF-58 was quickly reorganized. A special task group of crippled carriers composed of the *Franklin*, the *Wasp* and the Big E limped away to Ulithi. The *Hancock* now found herself in a newly-constituted five-flattop task group (58.3): *Essex, Bunker Hill, Cabot*, and *Bataan*. The extra carrier meant "a 20% less chance of getting kamikazed," commented one ready room jester. Word that the cruiser *Pasadena* was one of the dozens of warships blasting away at their aerial attackers pleased Ted.

The day following VT-6's Kobe strike, Witt and his crewmen were assigned anti-sub patrol (ASP) duty. By 1945, attacks against U.S. carriers from Japanese submarines were few in number. But given Tokyo's desperation, prudent torpedo watches remained mandatory. Seconds after their Avenger had been catapulted, Shaffer let out a howl. Diving directly down on the *Hancock* was a kamikaze. Looking aft from his turret, Shaffer saw *Hancock* marksmen blow the screaming projectile apart just a few hundred feet above their ship. The plane's bomb and engine continued plummeting right on down. Barely missing the *Hancock*, the flaming wreckage tore through the fantail of the destroyer *Halsey Powell* refueling alongside. Mercifully the bomb didn't explode. During the course of the afternoon while Witt's team vainly searched for a sub's shadow lurking below the ocean surface, kamikazes returned to the skies over their task group. "Enemy types shot down around the task group today," Ted wrote in his flight log, "were Bettys, Zekes, Tojos, and Kates. They can take me home now anytime, anytime. We were at GQ all night—bogeys all over the place." Aware of how expensive their formation assaults, the Japanese reverted to pairs and single-plane approaches on the American task groups.

Seconds after taking off from the Hancock on an ASP search, the Witt team looked back in amazement as pieces of a kamikaze slammed into the DD Halsey Powell fueling alongside.

No longer was the dazzling air-sea pageantry exclusively an American show. With the impending collapse of Hitler's Germany, His Majesty's carriers had reinforced the vast Okinawa operation. Those like Ted who could romanticize over a ship's name must surely have applauded the arrival of the British carriers *Victorious, Illustrious, Indomitable,* and *Indefatigable.* Bespeaking the excessive English respect for tradition, none of their flattops was commanded by an aviator. Forming an independent fleet, they hammered islands south of Okinawa which had facilitated Japanese planes flying between Kyushu and Formosa (Taiwan).

In flight Ted never saw any of the Brits. However, when a Seafire (Navy version of the Spitfire) landed on the *Hancock,* apparently lost, he hurried topside to see the famous plane. The diminutive Seafire was almost tucked under the wing of a Hellcat. Could this Lilliputian creation really be the airplane that had won the Battle of Britain? The gawking Americans shook their heads in amazement. Small, movable parts of its wing and tail were covered by stitched fabric. The plane's numbers had been painted on by hand instead of sprayed through a stencil. Nonetheless, British carriers, unlike the Yanks, had thickly-armored steel flight decks—and what a difference that made whenever a kamikaze hit.

Throughout late March and early April, as the intensity of suicide attacks mounted, VT-6's aircrewmen, accompanied by their counterparts in VB-6, became spectators to these deadly, seemingly daily extravaganzas. Foolishly secure in their ready rooms with nothing but the wooden-surfaced flight deck and its 1-1/2 inches of steel plate to shield them, they would listen with mounting suspense as the *Hancock's* intra-ship radio reported on the incoming bogeys. As soon as the five-inch cannons boomed, everyone grew silent. Would all hell shortly follow? If their ship's 40 and 20 mm antiaircraft guns exploded with their distinctive staccatos, the deafening racket signaled that a kamikaze was probably crash-diving on either the Hannah or a nearby vessel. Somebody, Yank or Jap, was about to die. Well before this, foolhardy aircrewmen not flying had scampered to the large open space on the fo'c's'le forward of their sleeping quarters. Here, just below the thundering deck above, frequently smoking from its bordering crescendo of protective fire, they cheered the sky's riveting carnival. Wild shouts erupted whenever a suicide plane burst into flame and crashed near its intended target. And also like a frenzied Rose Bowl cheering section, groans and curses arose whenever the enemy scored.

The spectacular nature of Ted's hazardous environment, although draining him, magnified his desire to share his Pacific War experiences with California family and friends. Censorship made that impossible. Albeit, he did his best in a letter home postmarked March 22.

Have had the thrill of my life in the last few days. . . . You sure do think a lot out here and I can honestly say I am glad I have seen war. We are all scared and we all pray without any reservation. [Hinckley's capacity for exaggeration had not diminished.] Twice a day the ship observes a period of two minutes of silent

prayer. . . . Aircrewmen are treated very well. We have our own
quarters, private snack galley [shared with VB-6 men], air-cooled
ready room and such.

Letters from Pasadena came in batches. Among the most appreciated
were sister Jane's describing her activities; how heartening to hear she
relished the social whirl.

In 1942 Torpedo Squadron Six had furnished critical air support for
the amphibious landings at Guadalcanal. Three years later, in what
would prove to be the climactic land battle of the Pacific War, VT-6 made
a tiny contribution to the ultimate Okinawa victory.

In certain ways the scale of the late-March invasion preparations,
although not equaling Europe's famous D-Day buildup of the previous
June, may well have formed the largest and most diverse collection of
vessels ever assembled in history. Over fourteen hundred of them participated in the amphibious assault on the paramount Ryukyu Island.
The prodigious fleet boasted more than forty carriers, eighteen battleships, over two hundred destroyers and cruisers, with hundreds of
transports, supply ships, net layers, submarines, mine sweepers, landing craft, repair and salvage ships. To the old salts, perhaps the sweet-
est sight of all was the resurrected battle wagons sunk at Pearl Harbor,
now lying right offshore blasting away at the Japanese. Ultimately over
half a million Allied fighting men would be pitted against the 110,000
defenders. No less staggering was the weight of offshore fire support.
Due to the dreadful losses suffered during the February assault on Iwo
Jima, the bombardment of Okinawa's landing area lasted for seven days,
by far the heaviest in the Pacific War.

Planners had labeled Okinawa's invasion, scheduled to begin on
April 1, "Operation Iceberg." Navy air attacks against the island had
actually begun the previous October; Naha, its capital, had been flat-
tened and airfields and port facilities had been savaged. What, one wonders, did Air Group Six have left to do as it joined the over one thousand
American aircraft participating in the final softening up. Actual support
of the Army and Marine landing forces must wait until the troops were
ashore. Before then, the enemy's airfields, his incoming suicide planes,
as well as diverse targets of opportunity (bridges, supply dumps, personnel, and equipment) were to be repeatedly bombed, rocketed, and
machine-gunned. Adding to the destruction descending on the defenders was a relatively new and heinous munition—napalm. No one in the
torpedo squadron regretted that the chore of transporting this frightful
stuff was assigned to fighter planes. A water landing with napalm too
often meant cremation.

Ted's record of his strike against Okinawa on March 24 rather well
summarized his role in the days leading up to the actual landing:

All in all things clicked beautifully. Took off at 0730 to bomb airfield facilities. . . . Planes were loaded with four five hundred
pounders and the starboard wing was equipped with an auxiliary
fuel tank. After about an hour flying we came to the northern
point and Lieutenant Eppler and Commander Miller decided

upon making this our rendezvous point after we finished attack.
The ceiling was about 2500 feet and after climbing through a
thick overcast we emerged into clear skies. We then circled emptying snow to throw off the enemy radar controlled antiaircraft
guns, dived, and pulled out over the dirt runway. As we pulled
out I strafed the field which was erupting with bomb explosions.
Shaffer and I concentrated our fire on the slit trenches along the
sides of the runway. All planes made it back OK.

In their flights over the island, virtually no antiaircraft fire could be seen.
The heavy guns had apparently either been destroyed by American
bombs or shell fire or hidden away to be used against the landing forces.

What Samuel Hynes has called "invisible fire" (small caliber, non-
tracer ammunition) was a constant threat. Proof of this was the random
Torpeckers that arrived home punctured with bullet holes. One day, flying at about 1000 feet altitude, and passing over the rugged hilly country to the south, with Ted facing downward at his machine gun, he spotted a single burst of enemy fire. It seemed to have originated from heavy
undergrowth along the shore. The only reason he ever saw this invisible
fire was that one of the slugs was a tracer. Like a lonely Roman candle,
it floated up and then sharply sped away from their plane. On another
day, the air group's parachute rigger, Johnie Cone, to whom everyone
was understandably most gracious, came into VT-6's ready room and
presented an armor-piercing slug to its membership. He had discovered
the bullet neatly embedded in one of the tunnel chute packs. Cone's
well-polished gift was greeted with ribald humor as was his complaint
about the squadron's "failure to give him any business." Few doubted
that in time rigger Cone would get some customers.

Seen from the air, Okinawa reminded Ted of Catalina Island, but
utterly absent of human beings. With a subtropical climate, its ground
cover appeared rather like the chaparral blanketing the foothills of
Southern California. Most of the indigenous pines had been logged off.
Enough shrubbery of one sort or another remained for constructing the
islanders' huts and thatching the enemy's clever camouflage. By far the
most distinctive feature seen from above were the large, permanent
horseshoe-shaped tombs which dotted the island. ACI reported they
could shelter a dozen people, but "unless they were being used for military purposes, ignore them." Ted never saw one of them under aerial
attack. Unavoidably many were ultimately blasted open midst the ferocity of the Okinawa ground struggle.

Missions over Okinawa invariably gave Ted the shakes, although in
diminishing intensity. Thanks to the ACI briefings aboard the *Hancock*,
flyers encountered few surprises once in the air. If a rare enemy aircraft
was sighted, it had originated elsewhere and was probably hell bent to
attack TF-58. With Okinawa bombings increasingly redundant, airstrips
in the Ryukyu chain of islands were hit.

On March 29, standing next to their Avenger, Witt's crewman prepared to take off on such a strike. Unexpectedly the ship's bull horn
blared, "A bogey has evaded the patrolling CAP, has slipped past the

picket line of defending destroyers. It's coming in fast." The task group's immediate evasive action scrubbed the impending launch. Before Ted could secure his gear and scramble off the flight deck, the Hannah's guns—every damn one of them, it seemed—opened up all around him. "Oh God was I scared," he wrote afterward, "wow I must have lost twenty pounds and grown sixteen years older in that awful moment." Looking aft where the ship's gunners were directing their firing, Ted saw the Judy. Having just dropped its bomb astern of the *Cabot* (CVL-28) it appeared to be aiming itself directly at the *Hancock's* invitingly volatile flight deck. Paralyzed with fright, surrounded by bullet-belching oerlikons, he could do nothing but hunker down. The Judy might have ignited another *Franklin.* Its pilot was definitely not a member of Japan's Special Attack Corps. As the plane shot past the starboard side only a few hundred feet off the water, Ted noted its dark green color and its tandem occupants. "He was hit by two [of our] twenties," Ted later noted, "but not shot down until he was almost clear of the ships—one of the CAP daring our own fire came in and knocked him over."

Repeated strikes during the closing days of March found Ted and Al "filling up the bilge with brass," that is, emptying their guns. As with so much of modern warfare, distance and speed sanitized their murderous fire. Few airmen suffered nightmares after disemboweling a defending Japanese soldier, nor remorse for crippling a noncombatant Okinawa child. The consequences of their strikes were calculated at ward room debriefings and then shucked. Unlike the foot soldiers immersed in dirt and death, flyers generally were spared the psychological ravages of organized homicide. On March 31, for example: "Milk run today and all aircraft returned in good shape. Every gun in the plane was emptied. Over 500 rounds from [my] inconspicuous thirty caliber. . . . BB's [battleships] and all types of bombarding vessels right off shore firing for all their worth. . . . The area where we are going to land is terribly smeared."

Arriving back, and eager for some fresh air, Ted ambled down the port catwalk to watch a Corsair land. An instant after successfully hooking an arresting cable, the F4U's auxiliary gas tank tore loose. Sliced by one of the still rotating propeller blades, it exploded. Before "Big Sam," Lieutenant (j.g.) Robert Graham, could escape from the cockpit, his entire body had been torched. Hellcat pilot Lieutenant Herschel Pahl had also witnessed the tragedy. "That green nylon flight suit he was wearing melted when it was exposed to the first flash of flame," Pahl recalled. "He was not wearing any cotton clothing under the nylon, so the nylon melted and stuck to his skin." Fire fighters gingerly extracted Big Sam's still living body. Every hue of the rainbow glistened from his bubbling flesh. Like an extravagantly-painted toy, he mechanically walked down off his wing and stumbled into a wire stretcher. Shock, and then, mercifully, death saved him from a hideous nightmare. Over time other ugly images of war faded from Hinckley's mind, however, this one of multicolored, mortally-burned Big Sam stuck.

But even midst the grim, systematic destruction of Okinawa's invisible human inhabitants there were bizarre flickers of comedy. One day Ted was asked to fly with Lieutenant (j.g.) Waddell on a targets-of-opportunity strike against the embattled island. If there existed any immediate threat from enemy fighters, these types of strikes were rarely performed,

When the auxiliary gas tank from "Big Sam's" Corsair tore off the undercarriage and collided with his prop, he never had a chance.

for once over the strike zone, the formation broke up, only rendezvousing later at a designated time and place. Presumably by then each pilot had found suitable targets on which to expend his ordnance. Such attacks usually required flying at an altitude of between 500 and 2000 feet. Ted's pilot was a reputed risk-taker. Just a few days earlier, Waddell had located two docked oilers during a strike against a Kyushu harbor. Having used up his bombs, he dove in with wing guns blazing. Fierce Japanese defensive fire met the Avenger. Afterward, Waddell's gunner, Pop Varner, recalled his pilot "was so fixated on those ships he forgot to stop firing after we completed our run." Waddell was given credit for smoking both vessels.

Skimming along Okinawa's northwest coast, just about the only signs of the enemy were zigzag trenches and periodic clusters of foxholes, what the Marines labeled spider holes, dugouts so narrow that "only a spider could squeeze into one of them." Suddenly Varner spotted what appeared to be a speeding motorcycle. Banking their Avenger around, Waddell dove for a closer look-see. The motorcycle turned out to be a terrified dog leaving a trail of dust as it fled up a dirt road. Satisfied that some nearby structures looked suspicious, they were blasted with machine gun fire and rockets. After pulling out of his run, Waddell snapped on his mike. "Men, I can't believe it, but I think I see someone walking near that small bridge off to our port. Don't fire, we will just give that person a good scare." And with that, another dive almost to tree top level. To get the best view of what actually was happening and to hold himself in place, Ted locked his machine gun, clutched its butterfly handles, and hung on. Zooming up, Ted found himself less than a hundred feet from an old Okinawa woman with long, coiled hair. His machine gun could have torn her apart. With their plane roaring up and away, even warrior Waddell philosophized, "Nothing but a poor old woman."

Easter Sunday, "L-Day"—Okinawa's D-Day—blessed the invaders with favorable weather. From Ted's aerial vantage point, the April 1 panorama looked to be a textbook amphibious assault. In the air swarming over the invasion beachhead, *Hancock* aircraft intermingled with hundreds of other carrier planes. Surely those white-starred planes raised the morale of the soldiers and Marines rapidly advancing below. In truth, everyone rejoiced. On the ground the multi-service operation had been virtually unopposed. For Christians and non-Christians alike, that Easter Sunday proved an unprecedented time for giving thanks. The day following L-Day, a delicious holiday meal, ham and turkey with all the fixings, was served aboard the *Hancock.*

Aware of the futility of defending the landing beach, whose location they had correctly guessed, the Japanese steeled themselves for a remorseless battle of attrition in the hills to the south. With the port of Naha long since reduced to rubble and the island's airfields useless, Tokyo's military leaders were resigned to Okinawa's eventual loss. Such a portentous disaster further dictated extracting the greatest possible price from the invading Americans. Japan could only be next.

In truth Nippon's ruination was already well advanced. On the night of March 9, 334 Superfortresses had rained 1,667 tons of incendiary bombs on Tokyo. Instead of dumping their day time loads at the previous 30,000 feet, the carpet-bombing B-29s had unloaded their nocturnal destruction at 7000 feet. Enemy fighter opposition had thereby been greatly reduced. One quarter of the city's homes were destroyed; some 83,000 people perished; and nearly 100,000 were injured. The conflagration proved to be the most destructive single air raid in history.

Little wonder, then, that those Japanese militarists who had promoted the Special Attack Corps concept succeeded in recruiting fresh volunteers from their armed services. During April, as American troops slowly, steadily, and always bloodily pushed Okinawa's defenders southward, Japan's suicide effort approached its peak. Within Task Force 58 those vessels which suffered most violently from the kamikazes' wrath were the lightly-armored radar pickets (RAPCAP) providing early warning of approaching bogeys.

The Japanese honored their April 6 assault as *kikusui* (floating chrysanthemums). This storm of suicide attackers periodically thundered until mid-May. All too typical was the savage fury that descended on the destroyers *Colhoun* and *Bush.* Disregarding heavy losses inflicted by the destroyers' crack marksmen, one suicide plane after another smashed itself into the two picket ships. Burning, taking water, losing power, and with one gun turret after another knocked out, the *Bush* and *Colhoun* fought on. "Tin cans" they might be, but those of their gallant crews still alive exhibited a die hard toughness. Somehow the surviving sailors would save their shattered ships. Another swarm of *kikusui* arrived and the destruction in the air and on the sea proceeded. One attacker, just missing the *Colhoun*, instantly changed course and crashed between the *Bush's* stacks. The impact nearly sliced her in half. Only her keel remained to connect bow and stern. As evening fell, both vessels slipped under the waves. Also sent to the bottom by kamikaze ferocity that day were four other ships. Seven more were so seriously damaged as to be useless.

While this part of the battle for Okinawa was being waged, Air Group Six was raiding Japanese airfields throughout the neighboring Ryukyus. At the end of April 6, Ted scribbled in his flight log:

Did a beautiful job on the airfield and its surrounding area. Counted over twenty Jap planes on the apron and in revetments—all were given a good going over. . . . We blasted a warehouse and Shaffer and myself both emptied our guns. On last pass we were not over 150 feet off the ground. . . . I blew the cockpit cover off a Togo and put fifty rounds of API [armor-piercing incendiary] into his engine. No planes lost but Lieutenant Crane's aircraft had a few holes—as usual he seems to consistently draw it.

Returning to their *Hancock* sanctuary, the flyers found no refuge from the frenzied kamikazes; "I saw a twin engine job completely out of control go in." And then with a prescience that only the morrow confirmed, he pleaded with Mars, "Just keep knocking them down and away from us—please." For Air Group Six, the Fightin' Hannah, and what was left of the Japanese fleet, 7 April 1945 turned out to be a fateful day.

Whatever the label, divine wind or floating chrysanthemums, Japan's naval leadership, once so prudent and methodical, had in the face of imminent defeat embraced a madcap scheme. They would dispatch their remaining super-battleship, the giant *Yamato* south to Okinawa on a suicide mission. With its eighteen-inch guns, the *Yamato*, like her sister ship the *Musashi* sunk in the Sibuyan Sea the previous October, was the largest battleship ever built. Accompanying this leviathan—its personnel numbered 2,760—would be a cruiser and eight destroyers. This sacrificial fleet, with a few notable exceptions, represented what remained operational of the Japanese Navy. Desperation may explain the admirals' recklessness; however, given the impending American invasion of their homeland and Japan's urgent need for fuel and fighting men, there had to be other reasons. One of them was the failure of the maritime mastodon to justify its great cost. The *Yamato* had been at Midway and then again in the Philippine defeat. In neither instance had the super battleship won any glory. Admiral Matome Ugaki had served with the *Yamato*; to send her to her doom can only have been a tortured decision. But the kamikaze ships and their valiant crewmen would die as samurai; Japanese honor would be sustained. And who could tell; maybe they really could create havoc throughout Okinawa's invaders before succumbing to the overwhelming might of the Americans.

United States submarines and aircraft denied the *Yamato* force any possibility of surprise. Early in the morning of April 7, word was passed to VT-6's aircrewmen what was afoot. It was too good to be true. In these waning days of the Pacific War, the employment of aerial torpedoes against actual Japanese warships had seemed extremely unlikely. Yet here was the enemy steaming toward them—and without any significant air protection. Tracking Vice-Admiral Seiichi Ito's fleet were Martin PBM patrol planes. To the south Admiral Mitscher waited impatiently. Ordnance men in each of his task groups rushed the preparation of their lethal loads: torpedoes for the Avengers and 1000-lb. and 500-lb. armor-piercing bombs for the Helldivers. Fighter planes shackled on an assortment of carnage creating munitions. Given the preponderance of American might, few doubted a slaughter awaited.

Hearing that only the more experienced VT-6 pilots would join the assembling air armada, Ted went to Chief Boone. If Witt was stuck on the *Hancock* maybe his radioman could find a torpedo-toting TBM that needed one. Moments later Hinckley asked himself why he had been so eager. With his inimitable laughter, Boone replied, "We'll see."

Air Group Six launched late. Indeed, by the time all of the *Hancock*'s dozens of aircraft had joined up and headed north to the target zone, exciting reports of the air-sea battle were coming in over the radio. Ted's pilot was Lieutenant (j.g.) Kresse, the same flyer who had lost his crewmen in the Hilo training accident. Not long after takeoff, Ted's mind commenced its usual speculations on being shot down or forced to make a water landing. Prayerfully Kresse had had his share of bad luck. Would a generous God preserve them from the torrent of defensive fire? A guesstimate of wounds from enemy flak were refigured in Hinckley's fearful calculations.

After over an hour in the air and with no indication that they were nearing the enemy, Ted relaxed somewhat. Perhaps the entire Japanese force had already been sunk. It wouldn't bother him at all if such proved to be the case. Almost three more long hours passed wandering about the East China Sea with Air Group Six repeatedly altering its course headings, vainly attempting to find the strike zone. Throughout the parade of planes, radio silence compounded ignorance and swelling frustration. With very mixed emotions, Commander Miller and his squadron commanders heard the jubilant shouts of other air groups throwing themselves at the listing *Yamato* and her pummeled escorts. But for Air Group Six to locate them and apply the coup de grace proved impossible. Miller must be about ready to rip off someone's head, Ted thought. What in the hell had gone wrong?

Flying back to the *Hancock*, its forlorn armada dumped every last bomb and torpedo into the ocean. A number of Ryukyu islands were passed en route. One, larger than the others, contained a sizable town. In his ignorance, Hinckley wondered why the air group had not unloaded their destructive cargo on such a community. Commander Miller might be a professional killer, but unlike the callow teenage coward sitting in one of his TBMs, he could distinguish between mindless killing and killing to end the killing.

Well before reaching Okinawa, the 68,000 ton *Yamato*, the cruiser *Yahagi* and four destroyers had been sunk. All told, 3,665 Japanese perished in what surely must rank as one of the dumbest sorties in military history. Had Air Group Six participated, there can be no doubt that Ito's suicide fleet would have been annihilated. Four destroyers escaped to stagger home to Japan. Nonetheless, Mitscher's men had executed a brilliant attack. Only four dive bombers, three torpedo bombers, and two fighters were lost. Regrettably, the triumph was marred by some fighter pilots who strafed the desperate Japanese survivors struggling midst the battle's flotsam.

Throughout the war Torpedo Squadron Six had been on other "group gropes," but this four-and-a-half hour flight of folly took the cake. In a lengthy bit of doggerel, Fighting Six pilot Lieutenant George F. Rogers recounted (here abbreviated) the mischance of war.

Weary and disgusted, Ted was relieved when Kresse swung their Avenger into its downwind leg. "Landing gear down, hook's down." But then instead of the sudden drop, plop, and scrunch of their hook grabbing the arresting cable, came the roaring surge of the engine. "Oh, shit! A wave off." As their plane roared down the port side of the Hannah, its engine fighting for more elevation to get back into the landing circle, Ted looked out his star-

We flew an even hundred knots
Till our aching balls were blue;
We flew in fog . . . we flew in rain
We flew throughout the day
While other Air Groups tallyhoed
Two hundred miles away.

And when at last it ended . . .
Sailing southward with the breeze,
The other Air Groups tallied up
Their countless D.F.C.'s

But Air Group Six had none of this
For nought had come to pass.
Instead we glumly tallied up
A blister on each ass.

board window. Then he took a second look and stared in disbelief. The *Hancock* had been kamikazed. The aft third of the flight deck had been charred black. The forward elevator was puffed up like the top of a Fourth of July tin can, and beyond it an ugly gaping bomb hole showed precisely where the attacker had scored. Hinckley didn't yet know the half of it. Another gruesome sight glimpsed from their Avenger: the motionless Bofors gunners seated at their mounts on the *Hancock*'s port side sponson. Instantaneous victims of the bomb's flash, they looked just like well-roasted pigs at a hellish luau. It was not a good homecoming.

Instead of hurrying off to VT-6's ready room, Ted walked up the scorched flight deck to survey the bomb damage. Welders were already sliding huge plates of steel into position over the hole. The mixed smell of burned wood, paint, and flesh was redolent; the odor had a sickening sweetness to it. Too many sailors were dead and missing, among them, two air group men. The cartwheeling kamikaze had crashed into the aircraft parked aft, igniting all of them. Up forward throughout the gallery deck, much not burned was wrecked.

Worried that their ready room had been torched, Hinckley hurriedly crossed the flight deck. Commander Miller, who had also landed minutes earlier, swept past him. As always, Miller's stride was rapid, his athletic carriage bent slightly forward. His face, while absolutely impassive, was resolute. Ted conjectured at the man's state of mind. Their CO, who had thus far played his role so well, had missed a crowning performance. Had Miller's moment of supreme glory eluded him?

The ready room had suffered only slight smoke damage, but death's perfume lingered about the forward part of the Hannah. The hangar deck was a mess. Near what remained of a melted plane by a port hangar bay, corpsmen were still laying out the bodies. A few creeps stood staring at the sprawled corpses. Encountering Jack Streeter, his face smeared with a ghostly green flash-burn preventive, Ted sensed that Jack had been in the thick of the fire-fighting. The conflagration created by the *Hancock*'s burning planes—thankfully empty of bombs—had spewed a huge pall of smoke. For a brief period, the black plumes had spread down the entire length of the flight deck, even blacking out most of the island. Airedales, air group ground personnel, and hundreds of ship's company had rushed to assist the expertly trained and equipped firefighters. Using state-of-the-art fire-fighting equipment and reinforced by the miscellany of men wrestling a spaghetti of fire hoses, the topside inferno was brought under control in less than thirty minutes.

Afterward, Ted heard about Jack's crisis-activated leadership. At one point in the fiery struggle, several men slacked off, arguing over who owned a piece of the kamikaze's fuselage. Apparently the souvenir had most of the red meatball painted on it. Jack kicked one of them in the butt, separated the other two, and threw the scrap overboard, shouting, "Grab those hoses and get your gawd damned asses moving." Such language from a characteristically gentle man had helped defeat the flames. Fortunately below the armored deck no destruction had occurred. Unlike the *Franklin*, and despite the *Hancock*'s immense pall of smoke, she had never been in mortal danger.

Superb fire control teamwork brought the Hancock's blazing topside decks under control in less than thirty minutes. However, the April 7th kamikaze had not only knocked CV-19 out of action but destroyed a number of aircraft and killed over sixty crewmen.

How about the VT-6 forward sleeping quarters? Surely their compartment must be torn up. On investigation, Ted was astonished to discover that except for the omnipresent sweet stink, nothing had been disturbed. Directly over them, however, the port catapult had been wrecked. As for the two adjacent Bofors quads situated at the bow, another ghastly sight greeted him. The attacker's straight in, bow approach had been probably less than a hundred feet off the water. When his bomb detonated, its flash had incinerated the gunners seated at the fo'c's'le 40 mms.

Lying in his bunk, and mindful of the *Hancock's* frightfully burned men writhing in agony in sickbay below, Ted asked his flight log whether "he could have been big enough to take the horrible pain some of those suffering men were enduring without moaning or asking to be shot." Late that night he was awakened by a deep groan from the man whose bunk was adjacent to his. "What's the matter, Dusty?" Ted asked. Dusty Rhodes had been a truck driver before the war. Older than many in the squadron, his quiet, kindly disposed manner was appreciated by all. Another pained sigh. "Ah, Teddy lad, we'll never have an opportunity like the one we missed today."

On April 9, the *Hancock* buried its twenty-eight confirmed dead. The port side, deck-edge elevator had been lowered half way, thereby providing an open sanctuary on which to stage the sobering ceremony. So positioned, sorrowing participants could stand either on the hangar deck or above on the flight deck and observe the officiating officers and men. Thanks to a magnificent Pacific Ocean day, their white uniforms almost sparkled as they performed the Navy's traditional burial at sea. The last rites included Bible readings, followed by a prayer for the dead. "Oh, God, whose mercies cannot be numbered: Accept our prayers on behalf of the souls of these servants departed, and grant them an entrance into the land of light and joy in the fellowship of Thy Saints, through Jesus Christ our Lord."

Taps floated across the serene sea. Then the actual committal of each body and the appropriate rifle salute. "Unto Almighty God we commend the soul of our brother departed, and we commit his body to the deep." Perhaps Ted's reaction was not uncommon. "It was a sad ceremony and damn brutal. Those white sacks had turned red in spots where the blood had started to come through, and when they slid over the side they made a splat and did not immediately sink, but floated the length of the *Hancock* before going under." The musicians struck up the Navy Hymn. "Eternal Father, strong to save, Whose arm hath bound the restless wave, Who bidst the mighty ocean deep, Its own appointed limits keep: O hear us when we cry to thee, For those in peril on the sea."

CHAPTER IX

"Whatta waste."

With his well-tanned body lying in the warm, soft sand of Waikiki, Ted knew he had to be one of the most fortunate men in the United States Navy. Before him extended Hawaii's famous beach. Immediately behind him lay a residence fit indeed for royalty, the Royal Hawaiian Hotel. Two weeks ago he had been surrounded by death; here in an unmatched R and R, everything celebrated life. Relishing Waikiki's wonderful rolling waves, he had bodysurfed until his muscles ached. Capping this bliss was the Royal Hawaiian's delicious food. Total freedom from fear, the freedom to sleep or read whenever one wished, and lots of dry land on which to walk, in Pasadena these had been mundane activities. Here they were positively sublime.

After a very brief stay at Ulithi, the damaged *Hancock* had headed back across the Pacific to Oahu's Ford Island Naval Air Station. Coming on top of their own losses, the sudden news of President Roosevelt's death compelled respectful reflection. Few knew very much about their new commander in chief. It augured well that Harry Truman hailed from Missouri. Writing to his parents, Ted opined, "It is too bad if a country like ours can only produce one great leader. I think Mr. Truman may surprise us all and turn out a good leader."

Thrice enroute to "Pearl," the Witt team had flown antisubmarine patrol. Otherwise Ted had done little more than write letters, read, and sunbathe. He had often heard how the spoiled aircrewmen hit the beach prior to the ship's docking. On that happy morning of April 21 he had lived it. Launched in the dark, their plane had flown east into the dawn. Climbing up into the observer's position directly behind Witt—so what if it had no safety belted seat—he had watched the rising sun set fire to Oahu's crenelated mountain ridge. What, Ted wondered, lay ahead? Would his orders for flight school finally come through? How nice that would be! How long would it require to get the *Hancock* patched up? Was there any validity to the scuttlebutt about Air Group Six returning to the states to prepare itself for the forthcoming invasion of Japan?

Shortly after their Avenger had landed at Ford Island and the nine-day Royal Hawaiian R and R had been confirmed, Ted got on the phone. Letters from home had informed him that Donald Green, a much admired Southern California cousin and now an Army Air Corps ACI officer, was an instructor at Hickham field. Reunion with Don was no substitute for a 1211 Avoca Avenue homecoming. Albeit, in the days ahead their shared memories of fishing at Three Rivers and hiking about Sequoia National Park meant a great deal. As with Bob Sands' friendship at Hollywood, Florida, Don's conversational level further convinced Ted how much he desired a college education.

Quickly finagling a jeep, Don provided an informative historical tour of the one-time Sandwich Island. Atop the Pali, Ted saw where King Kamehameha's men had driven opposing warriors to their deaths over the spectacular cliff. Weary of death, Ted much preferred Honolulu's arboretum, its Bishop Museum, and a stroll about the old Congregational missionary buildings. Predictably, the latter stirred memories of Father Serra's California architectural heritage.

At sea, Ted had thought a lot about both Pasadena and South Pasadena. Here at the Royal Hawaiian, relishing an absolutely hedonistic existence, he found himself dreaming entirely too much about the southland's fair sex. Lordy, what he wouldn't give merely to see a McKinley beauty frolicking on the Waikiki beach! One evening, joined by Katke, Patterson, and some other men, he strolled down Waikiki's main thoroughfare to Honolulu's fanciest movie theater. *The Very Thought of You* starred Dane Clark, Dennis Morgan, and eye-pleasing Eleanor Parker; the film's setting was none other than hometown Pasadena. As so often with Hollywood's home-front genre, the Warner Brothers show employed military-civilian stereotypes. Nevertheless, the catchy tune "The Very Thought of You" awakened Ted's sentimental melancholy. Certainly lovely Eleanor Parker compounded his nostalgia. Second only to his combat fears and potential loss of peer respect were those anxieties about unbridling his wild horses. Clearly God had created these enchanting two-legged creatures, but why women must awaken such bittersweet discomfort did seem unreasonable.

Devouring the daily Honolulu *Star Bulletin*, and the current weeklies *Newsweek*, *Time*, and *Life*, Ted and his squadron mates rejoiced that the Nazi thugs were finished. Thank God Germany had at last been brought to her knees. The revolting photos of German death camps with victims stacked up like firewood, the repugnant realization that their vast extermination of Jews really had been carried out as state policy stunned him. Weren't Germans renowned in archaeology, optics, music, philosophy, chemistry, and had not Protestantism been born in Germany? That was what he had been taught at school and had echoed at home. How prone to disciplined organization were these Germans. How else could they twice in the space of twenty-three years dare to fight France, England, Russia, and the United States. Ted knew nothing about Nietzche's superman nor Wagner's Götterdämmerung. How such an extraordinarily creative people could have crystallized the Nazi nightmare troubled and confused him. Germany's maniacal potentialities left indelible scars.

Despite his censored correspondence, Ted continued to communicate something of what he had been about. "Mr. Witt has been recommended for the Distinguished Flying Cross," he wrote his parents, "Shaffer and I have flown with him ever since we left Hilo." Deathly fear had spurred a powerful awareness that each day should be lived fully. "I sure love life and pray with all my might that if I am allowed to come through this mess that I will enter some field of human endeavor and go the limit." Having briefly experienced an aviator's half-fearful, half-ecstatic dance with death, he could "hold it against no one who is not eager to get in this hell." Hell? Compared with the squalid misery endured by Okinawa's ground forces, life on the *Hancock* had been a cup of tea: a daily shower, a clean bunk, lively ready room relaxation, and periodic movies. No, carrier war epitomized technology's sanitized insanity. As for old Pasadena friends fighting the war on America's campuses, "There is something inside me those chaps can never possess—and damn I don't mind telling you I am proud I had a part in it even though I was at times scared terribly."

Probably due to an administrative glitch, the aircrewmen's nine blessed days at the Royal Hawaiian became fourteen. One afternoon, shortly before their R and R ended, Ted found himself in a rather ticklish situation. Coming directly toward him through the hotel's beautiful gardens, was a brawny six-footer dressed in khaki. Three full rows of combat ribbons paraded across his chest. An officer, the first he had seen at the hotel, Ted prepared to snap off a salute. Even before his arm was up, he knew stormy weather lay just ahead. The man's face thundered anger; they were on a collision course and no matter what Ted did with his feet, the full-commander had determined on a bow-to-bow ram. Bad enough that he had the frame of a battlewagon, but with his glory bars, topped by a submariner's badge, this guy spelled trouble. Seconds before they collided, both men halted; clearly the submariner had recently dived in alcohol. "You gawd damned fly boys nearly finished me." And with that, he stomped off. Reports of Navy aircraft mistakenly bombing American subs were distressingly true. Although regretful of such awful blunders, Ted took a perverted degree of pleasure in the officer's alcohol-induced candor. For all the commander's glory bars, he, too, suffered from the tyranny of fear.

The Barbers Point Naval Air Station was home for Air Group Six from April 30 to June 6. To no one's surprise, and almost everyone's disappointment, the air group was not going stateside. Miller had apparently determined they had not yet completed their third war cruise. As at Hilo, few complained about the facilities. With decent food, a well-supplied beer garden, first-run movies, a range of nearby beaches for surfing, and Oahu's idyllic weather, this was "good duty." On 9 May 1945, he wrote his family, "Went swimming this afternoon, had dinner with Streeter, played game of baseball, had shower, now in sack. . . . Think of you folks all the time, all the time." Encountering some old gunnery school associates fulminating over their "imprisonment" within Barbers Point CASU, Ted discovered how too much of a good thing quickly paled. He had scrupulously refrained from even mentioning VT-6 and the big time. Nonetheless, the mere sight of his flight jacket's torpedo-riding Bugs Bunny had exacerbated the CASU captives' frustration. Envy of

On May 14, while VT-6 prepared at NAS Barbers Point for its second 1945 deployment aboard the Hancock, the redoubtable "Big E," suffered yet another battle wound. This time a kamikaze hit blasted the Enterprise's forward elevator skyward.

Hinckley's cocky, carrot-eating critter damn near precipitated a nasty quarrel.

As usual, the ARMs had too little to do. Except for some ACI sessions, occasional training exercises, particularly familiarization flights with the new PPI sweep-scope radar, time hung loosely. It hung too loosely for a few. One chief and his radioman frequently stunk of the witches' brew, while the squadron's most beleaguered alcoholic occasionally had to be assisted in and out of his Torpecker. Obviously this truly pitiable figure was not fit for sea duty, much less operating technical equipment in combat. One night, at about two in the morning, and out of booze, he stumbled across the naval station to secure some liquid reinforcement. His goal was the officers' barracks where he had heretofore replenished his whiskey supply. Not far from the BOQ were the WAVEs' quarters. Large two-story quonset huts, they were identical in design to the BOQ structures. The inebriated aircrewman staggered up the stairs to the second floor. Midway, a WAVE sentry did to him what the Japanese gunners had failed to accomplish: her shotgun blast removed a good portion of his tail.

Curious as to how the repair work was proceeding on their ship, several of the VT-6 men visited the *Hancock*. Much to their surprise, they discovered that not only had their ready room been relocated but their sleeping quarters had also been moved. Both had been placed beneath the armored deck. Ted never heard anyone express gratitude for this change. However, after the disaster aboard their late task group sister ship *Bunker Hill*, who can doubt that there were inward sighs of relief.

On May 11, while supporting America's Okinawa fighting men, and approximately one month after the *Hancock* had been knocked out of action, two kamikazes slammed into the *Bunker Hill*. But unlike the Hannah, much of her air group was aboard. For the latter in their gallery deck ready rooms, it proved disastrous. Over two dozen pilots preparing to take off were asphyxiated. Six hours were required to bring her fires under control; some six hundred of the ship's men were dead or wounded. From her hangar deck up, the carrier was a wreck. Her fighting days were finished. She, too, buried her dead, limped to Ulithi, and then headed east to Pearl.

Until this brutal mauling, the *Bunker Hill* had served as Admiral Mitscher's flagship. Wasting no time, he and his staff quickly transferred to the *Enterprise*; surely this premier carrier had suffered enough. No, just three days later the Big E once again felt kamikaze wrath. This time her forward elevator flew up into the air like some immense leaf lifted by an errant gust. The indomitable *Enterprise* had also ended her Pacific War service.

Suicide attackers had not succeeded in sinking any fast carriers during the Battle for Okinawa. Nor did their repeated disablement of these floating airdromes ever threaten to alter the battle's ultimate outcome. Nevertheless, the hard fact remained that the withdrawal of an inoperative flattop invariably weakened throw-weight in the air, on the sea, and ashore, thereby assuring the death of more American ground troops.

Mercifully, May marked the ebb of such kamikaze victories. Temporarily exhausted, Japan's Special Attack Corps would henceforth prepare itself for the coming invasion of their home islands. At the time, America's military leaders were not fully aware of Tokyo's altered priorities; while the intensity of suicide attacks waned, their daring persistence could never be discounted. Over fourteen hundred youthful Japanese had bravely sacrificed their lives, and thousands of American sailors had been killed or wounded. An exhausted Nippon was losing the struggle but remained capable of extracting a dreadful price in human lives.

Hoping that old friend, ARM Hageman, was aboard the recently docked *Bunker Hill*, and anxious to discover how he had fared and to tell him that Smitty and Ray Gumm were okay, Ted anticipated an operational-free weekend. He delayed too long. Wasting little time, the *Bunker Hill* and the surviving members of its air group were soon headed east to Washington's Bremerton shipyard. Not until long after the war was over did Ted learn what had happened to "short stuff Hageman." The wisecracker had not only won a Distinguished Flying Cross at the *Yamato*'s destruction, but, like Jack Streeter, he had become an instant volunteer fireman, an unsung hero fighting his ship's raging inferno.

But where there are strong principled men, one must also expect to encounter those who are weak and sometimes dangerous. Late one afternoon, just outside VT-6's Barbers Point ready room, situated on the second floor of a large concrete and steel hangar, Ted paused briefly at the balcony's edge to watch Shaffer and some other mechanics working below. Suddenly he felt a muscular, smelly force pressing against him. As in a huge vice, he found himself squashed against the balcony railing. Directly below him a knifelike propeller idled. Who was behind him? Whose two hands had locked on the railing? Whose encircling arms had totally immobilized him? Initially Ted had thought someone was having fun, but the unyielding force hurt. Who was this jerk? Seconds later he knew it was no jerk. "What's this you've been saying about me aboard the *Copahee?*" Rarely given to clever repartee or quick thinking, Ted gulped for air and shot back, "Whatever I said, it was a gawd damned lie." The pressure immediately terminated. However, the twisted face and sneering chuckle delivered a klaxon call of warnings. The leper had become a menace.

Barbers Point's neighboring beaches, its ship's service's infinite supply of chocolate malts, and the library's well-stocked collection of Daphne Du Maurier's novels—a shipmate had happily recommended them—made May 1945 pleasant enough. Two forces intruded to fracture Ted's sybaritic existence. Foremost was his gnawing realization how he dreaded a return to the cannon's mouth. This latent, embarrassingly persistent fear he kept entirely to himself. Hinckley's repeated inquiries of Lieutenant Fitzpatrick, "Where do you think my orders for flight school are?" said it all; despite his exterior confidence, Ted Hinckley's cowardice exceeded his courage.

A less serious but nonetheless pestiferous source of discontent were his damnable wild horses. To hobble them midst all these Navy nurses and WAVEs—the pretty ones invariably accompanied by officers—was never a simple matter. Aboard the *Hancock*, women had been the major topic of conversation, but lacking their actual presence, they could be treated abstractly and with levity. Here at Barbers Point that disconcerting minority was almost everywhere. Laughing, chattering, smiling, going about their work, and forever reminding him of all those Southern California beauties living a million miles away.

Although fear of death was never discussed among the aircrewmen, the fears and fun of heterosexual relationships were examined from every imaginable aspect. Unmarried or married, Ted's shipmates sublimated their sexual hunger with unending talk. A pre-Kinsey age, these discussions, while intriguing to Ted, were laced with misinformation. An awful lot of it dismayed Pasadena's untested lover. Descriptions of what inflamed a woman's sexual appetite seemed far-fetched. Lurid stories about San Francisco's black brothels chilled him. Such accounts surely roped in a wild horse or two.

An eminently more gentle wrangler assisted in removing other Hinckley stallions to their winter range. Judging from chow hall chatter, Judy Garland's utterly wholesome musical, *Meet Me in St. Louis*, offered universal approval. With a number of other vicarious love affairs, Ted had long cherished her company. In fact, he and Judy had grown up together. By the time she sang to him at Barbers Point's large outdoor amphitheater, what had once been a sibling relationship had become an uplifting, marvelously safe romance.

As did just about everything else in the Navy, movie-going at Barbers Point had a routine. Long since accustomed to Navy regimen, Ted found aspects of it rather appealing. For example, when each evening's film concluded, Rudy Vallee sang "Good Night Sweetheart." That sentimental recording, the clean ocean air, and the brief night walk back to the barracks promised pleasant fantasies of lovelies, real and cinematic. Preceding each film, movie goers would sit around the amphitheater and read that day's Honolulu *Star Bulletin*. Then shortly before the screen lighted up, a polished speaker summarized the news at home and abroad.

One evening while reading his *Star Bulletin*, Ted's attention was caught by a short column reporting that none other than Charles Lindbergh had shot down a Japanese airplane. Details were entirely lacking. Unknown to Ted, his boyhood hero's flight log also revealed misgivings at bombing and strafing enemy targets.

> Trees and ground rushing up at me. No sign of life. . . . I press the trigger. [He was flying a P-38 Lightning.] Long streams of tracers bury themselves in the roof and wall. Everything is still lifeless. . . . I hope there was no one in that building except soldiers—no women, no children. I will never know. There is no time to think about it.

Isolationism had ended with the attack on Pearl Harbor. That the famous Lindbergh was putting his life on the line heartened Ted. How was the one-time isolationist reacting to the formation of the United Nations Organization? News that San Francisco, California was hosting its founding conference, April 25 to June 26, gratified the Pasadenan.

The *Hancock*'s restoration had gone on night and day. Pained, in truth alarmed, at the realization he must return to war, Ted did what Navy life had now so effectively inculcated: accept the inevitable as gracefully as possible. Prayer and letters from home—visible answers to prayer—would prevent fear from disabling him. And despite the impending departure of their ship, there were reasons for celebrating. Two of Ted's "gruesome threesome" had departed for their well-earned retirement; thereby enabling John Burcham, Aviation Metalsmith 1st class, and Pop Varner, two hard-working squadron members with little time for surfing, to make chief. Furthermore, the Avengers' fancy new radar screens distinctly silhouetted ships and coastlines; while tightening safety measures and air-sea rescue procedures once again signaled how seriously the Navy cared about its aviators. Above all, at Barbers Point, no Torpeckers had been "creamed," nor men injured.

To double-check the *Hancock*'s recent repairs and better prepare her air group for what lay ahead, a brief shakedown was carried out June 7-11. With Hawaii's weather cooperating and all flight operations functioning smoothly, ship's company and aviators relaxed in self-congratulatory "well dones." Unfortunately, in wartime, fate abhors serenity like power a vacuum.

During a training exercise, and without any warning, a wing suddenly tore off of Eppler's Avenger. Fortunately for him, he had the altitude
to be thrown free of his cockpit and get his parachute deployed. Chappy
and Edward O'Connor, Eppler's radioman, never had a chance as their
maimed plane spun crazily into the sea. The loss of the greatly admired
Chief Chapman left Torpedo Six with but a single remaining aircrewman
who had flown in the squadron since Guadalcanal. Hearing of the tragic
accident, AOM 1st class Edgar Irwin waited only long enough for Eppler
to get a good night's rest. The following morning Irwin reported to him
in the *Hancock*'s wardroom. "Sir, we have seen a lot of this war together.
I'd like to be your gunner from now on." Forthwith, Irwin, who like
Chappy had flown from the doomed *Hornet*, flew behind probably the
squadron's finest pilot. Shortly after the *Hancock* docked, Eppler presented parachute rigger Cone a bottle of Scotland's finest.

Seated in the torpedo squadron's new ready room, and with less than
twenty-four hours remaining before they cast off, hoping against hope
for a flight school reprieve, Ted busied himself with his correspondence.
"How about a swim?" Looking up, and flattered that the conscientious
Jack Streeter had found time for leisure, Ted soon found himself in Ford
Island's swimming pool. Its bathtub dimensions bespoke prewar construction, but the pool had the great advantage of being within walking
distance of their ship. With departure so imminent, neither man had
any desire to find himself left on the beach.

"I've decided to fly with you guys. I'll be flying as gunner with
Bitzegaio." Dumbfounded put it mildly. Ted could hardly believe his
ears. Notwithstanding all his arguments why Jack, an outstanding ordnance man, should not fly and was indispensable on the deck, Ted simply could not dissuade him from becoming a flyboy. In essence, the
older man believed he "was not really doing enough." Watching the
Avengers depart on a strike, he felt he "had to be with them." And his
chagrined companion wanted to flee to flight school.

"California Here We Come" blared out across Pearl Harbor's waters.
Jubilant music for the men aboard an outward bound vessel steaming
home. However, for the men aboard the *Hancock*, especially its ship's
company, those lively notes aroused feelings of envy and justified self-
pity. On June 13, the Fightin' Hannah nosed down the channel and
headed west. Ted wondered if anyone else felt as wretched as he did.
Banter at morning chow with some Rover Boys (Katke's name for six
teenage VT-6 aircrewmen who hung around together: Frank Famera,
ARM 3/c; Bernard J. Lewis, ARM 3/c; Robert E. Lee, ARM 3/c;
Lawrence R. Sullivan, AOM 3/c; Coy C. Weaver, ARM 3/c; and George F.
Williamson, ARM 3/c) and several Bombing Six aircrewmen had not
helped matters. Clearly the VB men enjoyed jostling their VT counterparts. "We've had our share of bad luck; it'll soon be your turn." In
truth, no Torpecker had been shot down, no torpedo squadron personnel
had even been injured in combat during the March-April deployment.
On the other hand, Bombing Six had lost seven men and seen eleven of
their planes go in the drink. Nor was it that their pilots took more

chances. To some degree the blame lay with the white elephants they flew. Before breaking up their morbid breakfast discussion, everyone agreed, as Chappy used to say, "Don't discount the odds." Patently the odds on this deployment could not favor the men of Torpedo Squadron Six.

Ted's journal reveals that it was not just flying hazards that disturbed him.

No one feels at all comfortable—at the best we expect to be out here only a few weeks or so until we get hit again and have to return. The Japs are really perfecting their kamikaze weapons. We all hope that something like what happened aboard the *Bunker Hill* and the *Franklin* is not in store for the good old Hannah.

Accompanying the *Hancock* were five destroyers and the carriers *Lexington* and *Cowpens* (CV-25). Like the new blue-black Avengers parked on her flight deck, CV-19 no longer wore a light blue-gray camouflage; from bow to stern she had been painted a solid coat of dark

midnight blue. The Fightin' Hannah looked trim and smelled clean. In keeping with her renewal, a number of the VT-6 aircraft began to sport distinctive logos. Ted sought out the ship's painter-cartoonist; he and Al desired some sketch appropriate for "The Nit-Witt." A few days later Avenger No. 15 featured a pilot caricature; frowning and rolling up his sleeve, the aviator—the "Nit-Witt"—was preparing for a fight.

Despite ASP flights and the excitement of banging away at a towed spar, Ted's malaise lingered. Nor did news that they were to blister Wake Island on their westward voyage eradicate his self-indulgent anxieties. On June 19 he wrote: "F4U-4 fell apart in midair and

Insignia-cartoon for Avenger No. 15, Witt's TBM on second deployment, third war cruise of Torpedo Squadron Six.

took one of our best fighter bomber pilots to his death. Got briefed this evening for the 'Fuddle Strike' on Wake Island tomorrow. Would it not be the kiss off if VT-6 lost its first aircraft on this well-bombed atoll. . . . old lady luck is pushing the limit for us."

Witt had no need for a gunner, so his radioman had the thrill of seeing Wake get plastered from the turret. "The airfield and facilities were not touched, but the living quarters were really pulverized. . . . Three of our aircraft got hit but none shot down." Invisible fire did succeed in shooting down an F6F from the *Lexington*. "Another Lex plane made water landing off shore but pilot was picked up by rescue sub. . . . All in all the island took one hell of a beating."

A few days later on a practice exercise, Ted got his first view of the Philippine Islands. "A short bit of flying over the jungle spread out below and we headed back to the ship." Of course he thought of his dad's work there almost a half-century earlier. Steaming into San Pedro Bay (the northern part of the Leyte Gulf anchorage), the *Hancock* flotilla joined "nine big ones"; among these were the carriers *Shangri-La* and *Bon Homme Richard* (CV-31). Four tedious days were spent sweating in Philippine heat, partially relieved on the twenty-eighth by several hours ashore. "Beer and sandwiches for all the fellows. I am afraid I can't say much for Samar recreation center."

At Leyte Gulf as at Ulithi, a fearless pilot had slammed his plane into the jinxed flattop *Randolph*. However, this time it turned out to be a reckless American hotshot flying a P-38! Only Admiral Halsey's intervention prevented what might have become a serious inter-service spat. Having completed their resupply of munitions and fuel, and as part of Halsey's Third Fleet (TF-58 became TF-38), the *Hancock* upped anchor. The date was July 1; their destination Japan. Sister carriers in Task Group 38.1 were the *Lexington*, the *Bennington* (CV-20), the *San Jacinto* (CVL-30), and *Belleau Wood* (CVL-24). Ted guestimated there were approximately two dozen destroyers stretched out around their task group, along with battleships, cruisers, and the deadly, plane-killing antiaircraft cruisers.

En route to war, divine services were held on the fo'c's'le. Although miffed that God had not answered his prayers for flight school, Ted attended. Enjoying an unsurpassed setting of open skies, sparkling sea, and surrounding ships, perhaps the "Protestant Service of Worship" led by Chaplain (Lieutenant Commander) Joseph F. Parker eased some of Hinckley's shadowy forebodings. Prayerfully God sailed with them. However, just in case the Deity should favor some Divine Wind flyers, the United States Navy had installed a lot of fresh Oerlikons and Bofors. Quite possibly, the cacti of antiaircraft weaponry bristling across the surrounding fleet may have surpassed TF-58's during the Battle for Okinawa.

That ferociously fought contest had ended just a week earlier, on June 22. By then over 300,000 American troops had been committed to the struggle. Just before the final Japanese stronghold fell, the two commanding Generals, attired in their full dress uniforms, knelt before their headquarters cave and committed *seppuku*. The Americans had paid dearly in lives and equipment, but nothing as compared with the over 100,000 enemy dead. Estimates of Okinawa civilian dead ranged from 70,000 to 160,000. Approximately 7800 Japanese aircraft had been destroyed at a cost of some 750 American planes; over 400 vessels were sunk or damaged by Japanese aerial attack.

As Task Force 38 approached Japanese waters, two relatively new devices presaged future electronic warfare. Proximity fuses activated electric signals (within ten to one hundred feet) on nearing their target. When attached to either bombs or antiaircraft projectiles, the resulting fragmentation proved especially deadly. The other contrivance was a toy, an oversized, remotely-controlled model airplane called a drone. Utilized for target practice, they gave the gunners excellent practice. Ted wrote, "The [drone's] operator aboard ship really had it moving around, after about the tenth pass in firing range of the twenties" with tracers tracking it, the order was given to shoot it down. Within seconds the pretty red toy was destroyed.

On July 9, VT-6 was briefed for the Tokyo airfield strike on the morrow. "The object of the whole operation is to blanket the airfields around Tokyo, trying to keep the Nips on the deck and destroy them. We being the most experienced outfit in the task group have the toughest target— 65 miles inland." Expecting fighter opposition, Ted confessed, "I am really beginning to sweat." As it transpired, Witt "pulled down duty officer so we stayed on deck." To everyone's relief, "the ships of our group did not have to fire once today. We sure expected the worst and when the Japs did not come out in force we could hardly believe it was possible." Hundreds of enemy planes were destroyed on the ground. "All men made it back safe today." Two planes "were forced to ditch, but all personnel got picked up, and are in good shape."

On July 11, "Mines exploded all around the force today. . . . I wonder if the Japs are going to come out in mass or if they are waiting for the invasion. They might be low on gas, or even better yet no planes left of any consequence. Optimist!" Steaming north, Task Force 38 aimed its destructive might at Hokkaido, the most northern of Japan's four major home islands.

Thanks to his home collection of *National Geographic*, Ted was familiar with Hokkaido's exotic inhabitants. Old Pasadena chum Jim Downs had told him that its Ainu were actually Caucasians. "California had its Indians," Jim had commented; "Japan has its aboriginal Caucasians." How much better everything would be if he had some old friends to talk to. A recent letter from Stimmy voiced his disappointment flying C-47s. Apparently Louie Blatterman was headed for B-29s, and Kenny Wright was vainly trying to transfer from Occidental College to Navy Air. At this juncture, Ted would have gladly traded duty with him.

Due to the morning pea soup weather on July 14, the division in which Witt flew was forced to jettison their bomb load, but not before "Shaffer and I both got the wits scared out of us when two F6Fs flew on a collision course with us passing ten feet over and under us going in the opposite direction." The afternoon launch encountered improved flying conditions; The Nit-Witt's target was Nemuro Harbor on Hokkaido's east coast. A rising high overcast facilitated the port city's devastation. Awaiting their turn to dive down, dump their bombs, join up, and return home, the circling swarm of airplanes seemed like so many vultures.

> The ack-ack was almost nil—I imagine that they had moved all antiaircraft weapons south to the areas being attacked by the B-29s. The skipper peeled off and the next moment we were diving on some large warehouses along the waterfront. The round house was well taken care of by VBF and also the engines parked near by received a thorough going over. Other than an SB2C lost on take off this morning every plane returned. . . . Upon landing we made the first barrier crash of Witt's career—almost nothing—prop and hub only things badly smashed.

Cheers erupted throughout the *Hancock* that evening when the ship's music station announced that American battleships were actually standing off the Japanese coast and shelling the steel works at Kamaishi.

On the following day Hokkaido was again attacked. This time, however, VT-6 was ordered to locate targets on the island's west coast. After crossing spectacular snow-covered mountains, the Avengers dropped down to about 2000 feet. As they raced south along Hokkaido's shore, someone suddenly broke radio silence with an exultant shout, "There's a harbor filled with ships." Unfortunately division leader Lieutenant "Herbie" Hynd had already signaled his pilots to seek targets of opportunity. The advantage of a concerted attack had been lost. Nevertheless, an inviting number of cargo vessels were seen moored in Otaru Harbor.

> Shaffer and I were both screaming with delight at finding such a beautiful target. Before you could say 'Gosh' we were headed straight in on the harbor and only flying at about six hundred feet altitude. I sat by my gun and waited for a ship to slip underneath so I might get in some shooting. It seems the Japs had the same idea. Looking down on the water my first thought was that it was raining. When I realized that the many small splashes were falling slugs I really became afraid. Looking out my port and starboard windows I could see heavy black smudges cracking all around us. I knew they were firing at us for we were all alone. Just as the tracers were really closing in on us from all the ships Witt pulled . . . up into the overcast.

Blindly circling around in Otaru's overcast with streams of tracers greeting The Nit-Witt every time it approached a break in the haze, Witt decided not to be a hero. Informed by his radioman's radar that the harbor waterfront lay below, Witt promptly unloaded his four 500-lb. bombs. "Some people would call him a coward, but he probably saved our lives," Ted wrote. "I call him smart and thank God he had the sense to get the hell out of there."

Veteran pilot Hynd exhibited more grit. Ignoring the flak and yelling at his crew to hold tight, he dove his Torpecker down almost to mast height. One 5000-ton freighter was sunk and another left burning. "He will probably get the Navy Cross for this," was Ted's salute. Hynd's bravery was real enough. Who could forget what he had witnessed in Mid-

February 1944 at the famous Truk strike. Determined to plant his bombs on a Japanese freighter, Hynd's wingman, Lieutenant (j.g.) James E. Bridges, had also come in low on an anchored freighter. It turned out to be a loaded ammunition ship which disintegrated in one mighty blast. With the evaporated Japanese seamen, Bridges and his crewmen entered eternity.

Before departing the target area, Ted spotted a downed fighter pilot. On this strike Witt's plane had been designated to carry the large bag holding the four-man portable life raft. Struggling against the protesting slipstream, Ted wrestled the cumbersome canvas container out his hatch. When it finally did flop loose, the raft landed, as Witt groaned, "halfway to China." For the Nit-Witts, the flight home seemed distressingly long. "Our port wing was shot up and Shaffer and I really sweated it out." Passing close to the glistening mountains, "I could not enjoy their beauty in the least. They gave me the impression that they were reaching out for us and they would roar with delight if our fuselage would scrape the top of their peaks."

Two days passed, part of which was spent refueling the *Hancock*. *Life* magazine labeled the work of the seagoing fleet oilers "the Navy's secret weapon." Perfected during the Pacific War, this logistical breakthrough enabled ships to remain at sea far beyond their previous limits. From the oiler, huge rubberized pipes stretched across the foaming waters replenishing the *Hancock*'s indispensable supply of aviation and diesel fuel. It was dangerous work; throughout the refueling "the smoking lamp" remained out aboard both vessels.

But then in wartime mortal danger was never very far from an aircraft carrier. One day a Corsair inexplicably crashed into the sea on takeoff. Signed "Anonymous," an epitaph printed in the *Hancock*'s daily "Plan of the Day" was probably composed by the air group's poet laureate, George Rogers. Although they had flown on strikes together, Ted had never met the strikingly handsome Lieutenant William Eberle. Nonetheless, Roger's eulogy of Eberle so moved him that he clipped and preserved it.

> Rest Fighter! The final Guerdon gained!
> The last launch done—Tho fools say you are dead;
> We know—who saw the sun-splashed heavens stained
> Bright-Red—the color of your creed! !
> So rest—with the great sea overhead.
>
> The world for you shall never pale,
> Grow grey and dull and tedious in the end!
> Sweet wines of life shall not grow flat and stale,
> But all the memory—things that last,
> Their living sentiments shall lend!
>
> So rest Fighter—the last fight and the best
> Is over now, lay down the vengeful rod!

You've matched the goal and dwarfed the final test,
Now finishing—assume the victory poise,
And smiling rise to meet your God! ! !

Before becoming an air group ACI officer, Lieutenant Lewis E.
Anderson had been a botany professor at Duke University. Unlike VT-
6's more serious Sandy, Anderson laced his caveats about thwarting the
Japanese with off-color jokes. Despite his amusing briefing, the target
for the July 18 strike chilled Ted. Walking toward his plane, he admitted being terribly afraid. Their target was the Japanese battleship
Nagato, anchored at Yokosuka Naval Base bordering Tokyo Bay. "They
tell us the AA is the most concentrated . . . of any potential target in the
Japanese Islands." The Nit-Witt carried a strange bomb load; even
stranger were the orders issued to the dive bomber pilots. Shackled
within each torpedo plane were eight 240-lb. fragmentation bombs
tipped with the death-raining proximity fuses. "The [dive] bombers are
also carrying a new type fuse on their single 1000-pounder. It is a
hydrostatic fuse set to detonate just below the water line of the BB."
Instead of hitting the *Nagato*, the Helldiver pilots were to place their
bombs right along side the battleship, open her seams, and sink her
dockside.

Waiting for Witt and Shaffer to appear, Ted engaged in a conversation with some nearby airedales. Informed of the anticipated ground
fire, one of them offered Ted his general quarters steel helmet. "I'll put it
in by your gun; you may need it." The unexpected offer was a generous
one. Ted didn't demur. But Avenger No. 15 did, or more accurately, VT-
6's chief aviation machinist mate did. "Your major wing folding bar has
cracked apart." Three silent aviators stared up in astonishment at the
bar's quite visible separation. Was it a fatal fracture like this that had
cost Eppler his wing and the loss of Chappy and O'Connor? Whatever,
The Nit-Witt did not participate in the *Nagato* strike. Expressing their
gratitude for Chief Ira G. Tibbet's discernment, the three aviators
returned to their respective ready rooms.

Somehow all eleven of the Torpeckers got home. For his bravery and
leadership, Eppler was recommended for the Navy Cross. Torpedo Six's
fragmentation bombs had helped, but to totally suppress the numerous
guns implanted about Yokosuka Peninsula was quite impossible. While
VBs' bombs had scored, "All of the planes had many holes from shrapnel. . . . the AA was terrific. [VT aircrewman] Weaver had one slug go
two inches from the back of his head, and another just missed his legs."
Ted's journal all too accurately predicted: "We cannot go on much
longer without anyone getting killed. To date we have yet to lose a man
in combat, to have a water landing, or to even have a bad deck crash
with someone getting killed or hurt. We all know it has to come, yet we
all hope like heck that it might be possible to finish the cruise with all
hands."

Three days for refueling and repair of aircraft followed. An impressive air show was mounted for Secretary of the Navy James Forrestal

visiting aboard the *Ticonderoga* (CV-14). The Nit-Witts participated in what the flyers generally viewed as a waste of fuel. On returning to the ready room, everyone was cheered by mail from home. Except for Bing Crosby crooning "Don't Fence Me In," silence descended as the aircrewmen momentarily flew back to Pennsylvania, California, and two dozen or so places in between.

July 24, and "today the old law of averages caught up with us, or maybe I had better say it began to catch up with us." Having blasted Yokosuka, Task Force 38 unleashed its fury on Japan's great Kure Naval base located within her Inland Sea. Moored here were the pathetic remnants of Nippon's once-proud fleet: two heavy cruisers, some worn out battleships, several unfinished carriers, and a miscellany of smaller vessels. Two of the carriers had been covered with immense nets in a woeful attempt to camouflage them. Before the day ended, three VT-6 Avengers had flown their last flight. Shot down first was Lieutenant (j.g.) Teige. A one-time bluejacket, Teige seems to have had time to bail out, but held his TBM steady, hoping to see two parachutes blossom. His flaming plane crashed into a nearby hill. One man did survive: AOM 3rd class Luther Johnson. ARM 3rd class Jack Keeley never left his tunnel; perhaps he had been badly wounded. Once on the ground, Johnson sought to hide himself. Eventually some menacing citizens spotted him. Half-starved but luckily spared, Johnson was hauled off to prison.

Witt was assigned to the afternoon strike against Kure. En route his plane developed an oil leak and had to turn back. The TBM that promptly slid into The Nit-Witt's formation slot was piloted by Lieutenant (j.g.) William Callon. Much admired in the squadron for his joie de vivre,

Strike completed, and having entered the vast armada of Task Force 38, The Nit-Witt swings down into the Hancock's landing circle. Within Witt's Avenger crewmen Shaffer and Hinckley relax and speculate what might be that evening's ready room movie.

he was nailed by Kure ground fire as he nosed over into his bombing run. Afterward there was a debate whether Callon went straight in or was heard to signal a distress location. Missing with him were his two crewmen, ARM 3rd class John Scobba and Alton Porter, ACEM. As it transpired, no one survived.

Herbie Hynd somehow got his badly shot up TBM back to the *Hancock*. But then its landing hook stubbornly refused to release. Hynd wisely chose to ditch. Via a destroyer, the three men were soon back aboard the *Hancock*. Dazed by the vicissitudes of war, Ted could still brag, "Air Group Six was high scorer today."

The next day, and in the face of pessimistic weather reports over Kure, The Nit-Witt was once again on its way to the target. Hundreds of roaring planes soon stretched out on each side of their TBM in an awesome display of American might. Afterward, Lieutenant Anderson estimated that the spectacular sky mobilization exceeded a thousand carrier aircraft. Gazing in wonder at this profoundly inspiring pageant, if Ted didn't thrill to John Phillip Sousa's "Stars and Stripes Forever," he most certainly heard Kate Smith singing "God Bless America." Thereafter he understood the real strength massed within Alexander's Hellenic phalanx.

Instead of staying beneath the thick overcast, the strike commander directed his immense air armada into and then over the heavy cloud blanket. As the Helldivers, Hellcats, Corsairs, and Avengers began to disappear from each other, the entire formation quickly extended itself in order to reduce the likelihood of midair collisions. Three or four minutes passed immersed in wet isolation. Abruptly The Nit-Witt broke free of the cloud cover. Below the torpedo bomber lay an enormous white plain shimmering from the rays of the unobstructed sun. Except for a single airplane miles away, the vast fleet of airplanes had magically disappeared. That July 25 debacle may well have established an all time record for group gropes. Witt jettisoned his bombs in disgust—the radar indicated he was a few miles off the Japanese coastline—and headed home. But not Eppler; somehow he rounded up a few wandering Torpeckers, dived back through the pea soup, and discovered a moored 5000-ton freighter. Assisted by several fighter planes, the torpedo pilots sent the cargo ship to the bottom.

Ted's entry in his flight log for July 28 is confusing. A half-century later, he had no memory whatsoever of hitting Kure on that date, or at any other date. Why did his log state that Witt participated? Perhaps Ted was ashamed that on three occasions the Nit-Witt's team never actually struck the famous naval base and penned a blurred narrative. Did Witt fly without him? That seems extremely unlikely. What does seem obvious is that like a growing number of pilots, Witt was fast losing patience with bombing a defeated enemy. Kure had been turned into a graveyard for Nippon's Navy, but at a terrible cost of one hundred thirty-three American and British aircraft.

U.S. battleships and cruisers were bombarding Japan's coast. Attacks by U.S. submarines—during the Pacific War theirs was by far the greatest tally of enemy ships sunk—remained unrelenting. B-29s were methodically incinerating Japan's cities; some had begun dropping mines in Japanese harbors. On Okinawa and Guam, gigantic amphibious forces were being marshaled to invade their homeland. Couldn't Japan's leaders realize that continuing the war was absolutely nuts? !

If Hinckley's pride and/or memory muddled the record of what occurred on July 28th, his recollection of what happened two days later at Osaka remained grimly lucid. "Another pilot and his boys took the long trip today. My pilot's best buddy and one of my best friends, besides an old associate, were the ones picked." Torpedo Six had been "assigned to hit one of Osaka's largest airfields, doing all the damage possible to aircraft and facilities." Expecting a fierce retaliation by kamikazes, their task group stood well off the coast, just far enough to guarantee a safe round trip for the American war planes. Kamikazes still nibbled away at the outlying RAPCAP destroyer screen; periodically CAP fighters bagged a few. However, it was premature to take comfort in the fading threat of the suicide corps. Might the Osaka attack arouse fresh ferocity from swarming *kikusui*?

July 30, 1945 strike against Osaka airfield.
Minutes after this photo of Streeter's Avenger was taken, his TBM took its final dive.

At their various pre-strike squadron briefings, some of the ACI officers had briefly alluded to "five forbidden cities"; under no circumstances were they to be hit. Crossing Honshu, Air Group Six planes did indeed pass near one of these "five forbidden cities." Ted correctly surmised it was Kyoto. He then had little knowledge of Kyoto's preeminent cultural significance. Sure enough, the metropolis appeared totally unscarred by American air raids. Not until the first atomic bomb was dropped did Allied flyers perceive why these five places—which included Hiroshima and Nagasaki—were listed among the cities to be spared from

aerial attack. Wardroom conjecture figured they must contain large
prisoner of war compounds. In any case, no bombs fell on that "forbidden city."

This did not prevent the Japanese from firing away at the Americans
approaching Osaka.

> It was right in the formation and probably was radar controlled
> five inch. As we peeled off I attempted to hold on to the deck and
> take pictures through the bomb bay window. The next moment I
> found myself glued to the overhead. After quite a struggle I man-
> aged to get in position and commenced snapping off pictures as
> fast as possible. Right in the middle of the Jap airfield was a
> large outline of a B-29. The object I imagine being to get our fly-
> ers to go low to investigate and get blown to kingdom come by
> Jap fire.

After its 100-lb. bombs spilled out, The Nit-Witt pulled up from its glide-
bombing run.

> I felt completely satisfied that Witt was right on. But the next
> thing that came to my vision was terrible. One of our aircraft was
> going straight down into the middle of that blasting inferno on
> fire and with only one wing. . . . As brutal as it may seem I was
> hoping against hope that it might be some other squadron's air-
> craft, but all the time knowing it had to be one of our boys. . . .
> then Witt told us it had to be Bitz's [Bitzegaio] as that was his
> position in the attack. Yes, old Ensign Bitzegaio, his radioman,
> [ARM 3rd class John] VeHaun [whose company Ted had enjoyed
> since Opa-Locka], and a guy [Jack Streeter] who could have
> stayed on the deck but volunteered because "I don't feel like I am
> doing enough."

As always, the relief and shame of being glad it was someone else and
not himself tore at Ted. Could anyone have survived? "The pictures
showed their plane bursting into a million pieces upon impact . . . pictures taken a second later show bombs from the planes behind them
bursting all about them."

Some years after the war had ended, a family member discovered
that pilot Bitzegaio had miraculously escaped his flaming plane and the
bombs blasting about him. Violently twisting from the loss of its wing,
his "Black Cat" Avenger must have thrown him clear an instant before it
blew up. Mini-seconds before he hit the earth, his chute snapped open.
No one saw it deploy. Bitzegaio was less fortunate than Johnson. An
enraged Japanese civilian dispatched the pilot with a bamboo dagger
thrust to his neck.

With the rising number of missing in action, Torpedo Six's bonhomie
somewhat deteriorated. The question "Got a smoke?" instead of produc-
ing a cigarette might result in an acerbic rebuff. The ready room's
record player got less attention, the coffee became fouler, and foolish
pleasantries were fewer. Nor was it only the death of comrades.
Torpeckers were getting so chopped up by flak that, like Bombing Six's
Helldivers, they were ending up in Davy Jones' locker. When Lieutenant

"Duke" Du Temple went into the drink, he and his veteran aircrewmen, Gentzcow and Hardisty, kidded about their saltwater bath. Yet inwardly everyone asked himself how long before one of the squadron's TBMs crashed against an uncooperative Pacific Ocean swell? How long until a U.S. submarine or destroyer failed to locate some VT flyers futilely awaiting rescue in an inflated life raft? Everyone knew about Robert Trumbull's *The Raft.*

Ted found it difficult to concentrate; even his great joy in reading abated. Hardly one month back in combat and Pasadena's WASP warrior was afflicted by battle fatigue. Writing to his family, he vented his weariness.

When not occupied [flying] I try to sleep—beautiful sleep. You wander from the chow hall to ready room from ready room to quarters like a trapped animal. But that wonderful sack is always ready to give you a few precious hours of release. Release, oh for something to get your mind off this war. You try to read, finally you end up listening to the victrola playing "Moon Light Becomes You" and get home sick. In a bewildered, tired state of mind you find your legs transporting you from [there] to that haven of rest even though you know it will mean lying in a pool of sweat and waking up cramped all over. Above all it may mean dreams—a trip home, dancing with some beautiful creature, or maybe just standing on the soil of the good old U.S.A. If nothing else you are in a void where this present dilemma is nil. Thank God for slumber!

Ted knew he was not the only one depressed by war's deadly crap game. When a fellow aircrewmen began to act strangely, it disturbed but didn't surprise him. In this instance the man's tension sought release through petulance. Cleve "Clapp [ARM 2nd class] is taking the death of his pal Keeley badly and even looks sick. I understand that one of the fellows attempted to move into Keeley's sack and Clapp told him to get the hell out of there as Keeley would soon be back. Poor kid—he is the first one I have seen break down." Ted was ready to quit; he prayed mightily for flight school orders. "Scuttlebutt has it that we are to be relieved in the middle of August—I wonder—God I can't stand much more of this mess."

As a result of the July 17 - August 2 Potsdam meeting of Churchill, Stalin, and Truman, peace rumors rippled throughout the *Hancock.* Across Europe and the Pacific, Americans in uniform remained dubious. Must Japan, like Italy and Germany, be actually invaded to bring an end to the killing? Writing to his parents, Ted sought to check any ill-founded optimism. "Yes, I also pray and hope that this may take place but I am most certainly not counting on it. The Jap militarists are still in control and there is little doubt that they have complete authority over the nation. Japan is terribly mauled but it is nothing compared to what she soon will be unless she gets out of the struggle in a hurry."

The air group's August began with a week of relative inaction. On the fifth he wrote in his flight log, "The last few days have seen some bad weather, but there were times when we could have launched an attack. Something is in the wind." In the wind was a cataclysmic revolution in warfare.

News of the first atomic bomb sped through the ship. General skepticism greeted the initial August 6 report that Hiroshima had been swept away by a single bomb. Everyone in VT-6 hoped the astounding information was accurate. "Today this new atomic bomb made its debut," Ted wrote in his flight log, "and if we are to believe all reports, the war may soon be over. God have mercy on those poor Japs and please bring this war to a fast finish." This prayer would be answered, but not before Torpedo Six suffered additional losses.

To remove Navy planes from the region to be wasted by atomic bombs, Task Force 38 was dispatched north to strike targets in Hokkaido and northern Honshu. During her post-Okinawa deployment, the *Hancock*'s guns had rarely spoken. While the bulk of Japan's Special Attack Corps was reserving *kikusui* fury for the anticipated American invasion, a few persisted in their deadly work. And the roving CAP continued "scoring kills." Aboard the *Hancock*, Ted's relief was typical. "Keep knocking them down boys—just keep knocking them down." Aboard the radar picket destroyers courageously shielding Halsey's Third Fleet, relief remained sporadic. On August 9, it took only one well-aimed suicide plan to wreck the destroyer *Borie* and kill 48 of her men.

That same day, a second atomic bomb smashed Nagasaki. A day earlier, the Russian bear once again went to war with the samurai. In his diary, Admiral Matome Ugaki confessed how desperate was Japan's cause. "Now this country is going to fight alone against the whole world. This is fate indeed! I won't grumble about anything at this moment. I only hope we do our best in the last battle so that we'll have nothing to regret even if destroyed." Not long afterward Ugaki took off with some kamikazes and quite literally disappeared.

With two Japanese cities devastated by atomic bombs, not a few air group members groused at continuing their pinprick attacks on a defeated enemy. Wiser men appreciated how intransigent was Japan's military. No, the war must go on. Accordingly, on August 10, The Nit-Witt found itself bombing an already chewed up airfield at Matsushima not far from Sendai. There was no heavy flak; Witt came in low and laid his bombs across revetments cluttered with ruined Japanese aircraft. Right behind him was Lieutenant (j.g.) Joseph Newton. His Avenger "must have been hit just as they started to pull out. He leveled off for an instant and then plunged straight into the surf. The Japs sprayed the water where he went in . . . we don't hold any hope for them as we do the men lost over Kure."

Air Group Six fighter planes had better luck and discovered quite a number of camouflaged aircraft. During their firing/bombing runs, Ensign John Petersen's Corsair was hit. Having crash-landed, he signaled that he was okay. Eppler promptly asked for permission to land on Japanese soil and rescue him! Before that could be approved, infuriated civilians dragged Petersen away. They "appeared to take fiendish joy in humiliating him." Some, according to the Chicago *Tribune*, "threatened to put his eyes out with sharpened bamboo sticks. . . . They formed circles each one punching the captive as they passed. . . . He described the shameless acts of the women who were among his most insistent tormentors." Someone "offered a knife for Hara-kiri." Without the arrival of soldiers, Petersen's rustic abusers might have hazed him to death. Afterward the Illinoisan recalled how he played Scheherazade for his captors. "Japanese Army officers asked me interminable questions about our fleet and air force. They amazed me, too, by their abnormal interest in sex. They even wanted names and addresses of easy women in the United States and pressed me for all details of immorality there. I guess I told them some tall tales but they loved it."

To no one's surprise, Bombing Six also paid a price for keeping the pressure on the Japs. The same day as the loss of Newton and Petersen, Lieutenant (j.g.) J. E. Freemann's Helldiver was hit, forcing him to make a water landing. He and his gunner, the irrepressible Robert Molleston, ARM 2nd class, were promptly rescued by a destroyer. For Freemann's gunner it turned out to be a near thing. "Enemy fire over the target got Molly from Bombing badly shot up. The poor kid sure took his pain like a man. He will have a bad right leg for as long as he lives." For the air-crewmen who visited him in the *Hancock*'s sick bay—until Molleston was removed to a hospital ship—the ashen-faced, utterly helpless flyer was a sobering sight.

The deaths of VT pilot Newton and his two well-liked crewmen, gunner Tom Skawski, AOM 3rd class, and radioman Robert E. Lee, angered The Nit-Witt's aviators. And not for the usual reasons. "Ski and Lee did not have to go; their death in my estimation was the fault of some glory happy admiral who does not realize yet what the atomic bomb means." On the return flight to the *Hancock*, The Nit-Witt's intercom was as usual silent. Two harsh words from the plane's pilot said it all: "Whatta waste."

CHAPTER X

"You are the enemy."

It was 15 August 1945; the setting, a few hundred miles off Japan's east coast. Instead of an early morning launch against Tokyo's large Shibaru electronics factory, the panoply of warplanes had delayed and delayed. After what seemed an interminable wait, Air Group Six at last took off. Lying in The Nit-Witt's bomb bay was a 2000-lb. bomb; other destructive cargoes hung from the seventy-three planes accompanying her. Until the last, reluctant "Expedite Strike Charlie," everyone aboard the Fightin' Hannah had hoped to hear that supremely beautiful word: PEACE. Some days earlier Japan had apparently rejected the Potsdam Proclamation. But, peace talk persisted. "Our planes," agonized Zero designer Jiro Horikoshi, "can do little against the tremendous power of the enemy air fleets which completely control the air over Japan." Surely with the Soviets chewing up Japan's million-man Kwantung Army, and the nightmarish introduction of atomic weaponry, even brave Bushido warriors must accept defeat.

Al Shaffer was busy on the *Hancock*'s flight deck; Ted had the TBM's turret all to himself. There was only the remotest chance of Japanese fighter intervention. Less than forty miles from the target, his relaxed condition surprised him. "I really was not the slightest bit tense as would usually be expected starting out on a strike where yesterday the fellows had encountered such heavy ack-ack." Engrossed in the sky-scape's beauty, he at first missed the jumble of words that broke radio silence. Then Witt let out a yell. Not far off two Hellcats dove out of formation and commenced barrel rolls. "Let's go home, my boy," Witt cheered. "The war is over!" And then that formal command from afar, "Jettison load and return to base." Midst angry rebukes of "Let's have some flight discipline," and "Knock off the hijinks," Navy aircraft bobbed all over the place. A smiling Witt opened his torpedo plane's bomb bay doors and released their now useless freight. Watching that ugly, man-made creation drop into the Pacific, Ted thanked God.

Returns were always a pleasure, but none approached this rapturous flight.

> Good old Herbie Hynd turned the old gang around and we started home. We lowered to within fifty or twenty feet of the water and just fairly skipped the whitecaps in our great joy at that long awaited trip. . . . The fellows aboard ship did not know that the

war was really over until after our plane had landed. Capt.
Hickey passed the word over the loudspeaker and everyone went
crazy for awhile.

Predictably, there were Japanese elements that refused to "Bear the
unbearable," as the Emperor urged his people. Later it was revealed
that zealots had violently attempted to reverse his peace statement; fortunately they were crushed. Other blazing embers from a dying flame:
the last 48 hours of the war witnessed considerable air activity. Quite
appropriately, an Air Group Six Hellcat piloted by Lieutenant (j.g.)
Farnsworth shot down the Pacific War's last kamikaze.

His brain a Mix Master of emotions, Ted thought of his parents. To
them he wrote:

Well God was good and allowed me to live through this mess;
here is hoping I may someday justify His generosity. It is hard,
very hard to believe that it actually has ended. It is too big and
involved to come to a halt—it will be impossible to reconvert; can
it really have ended? . . . Above all I think of 1211 and all that
means. I don't guarantee you a changed son but I do think he
will have a great deal more patience and humility around his
mom and dad.

V-J Day, 15 August 1945, marked the end of humankind's most
ruinous war. All around the world millions of Second World War victims
hungered to escape Mars' every vestige. Aboard the *Hancock*, men's
thoughts and conversation eschewed war and eagerly anticipated the
sweet life in "the good old U.S.A." Within the ready room, the Andrews
Sisters' "Drinkin' Rum and Coca-Cola" soon gave way to the catchy
lyrics, "Kiss me once and kiss me twice and kiss me once again, it's been
a long, long time." Scuttlebutt that the Air Group was going "to occupy a
Jap airfield," got an amused response from ARM Hinckley. "I hope not, I
want to go home to my mammy."

Acutely aware that morale would take a nose dive if news arrived
that the *Hancock* was not going home, Commander Miller initiated boxing instruction. He challenged any and all to climb into the ring with
him. One had to admire a CO who would let himself be a punching bag.
However, Ted much preferred to use his leisure time refighting the
Napoleonic Wars with C. S. Forester's Captain Horatio Hornblower, writing letters, and crafting a brass lamp for his parents. To no one's surprise, the *Hancock*'s Marine contingent won top honors in boxing, as
they invariably did in every other shipboard athletic contest. Watching
the gyrenes drilling on the flight deck in preparation for possible occupa-
tion duty, aircrewmen ashamedly admitted how flabby were their own
bodies.

Mail delivery did little to raise morale. The war was over; paper
dreams no longer sufficed. Five days since the fighting had ended and
Ted confessed, "Golly this kid is homesick." But if Third Fleet officers
and men pined to return to their respective Pasadenas, Navy brass must
keep their immense battle fleet ready. As yet Japan had neither been
disarmed nor occupied. On August 22, Admiral Halsey ordered up

Exercise Tintype. For the operation, Bull Halsey bore the code name Seahorse.

It was "an immense air show . . . while all the ships of the fleet got together to have their picture taken. There were over a thousand planes in the air and it really took my breath away." Others reacted with less enthusiasm to Exercise Tintype. Standing below and glorying in the historic flyby, Admiral Halsey became agitated at the sloppy formation of one group of fighter planes. "This is Seahorse," he growled into his mike. "Get those fighters into tighter formation." To which an invisible aviator replied, "Fuck you, Seahorse." Not a few planes yawed up and down in mirthful agreement; the war was over, and to hell with Regular Navy chicken-shit.

The following day Ted finally got his longed for orders to report to flight school. Somehow they had been delayed. And for the rest of his life he would conjecture on the what ifs had he acted on this long dreamed of opportunity. What he did would have been inconceivable just two weeks earlier. Warned that with war's end, accepting flight school probably required Regular Navy status, his decision was easy. No thanks! He didn't need those golden wings. Like all the rest of the squadron, he hoped that the *Hancock* would be headed stateside in a few weeks. Surely civilian status would quickly follow. Chow hall and ready room discussions about discharges and postwar jobs melded with equally enticing talk of college education and marriage. In a couple of years, Ted promised himself, he too would march down the aisle. Now, instead of shiny bars and golden wings, the generous Servicemen's Readjustment Act educational benefits shimmered like a pot of gold at the end of a rainbow of peace. No, aircrewman Ted Hinckley would remain with the men of Torpedo Squadron Six until their air group was decommissioned on the West Coast.

On one hand Ted wanted to bid good-bye to the *Hancock* just as quickly as possible. On the other hand, he found himself curiously attached to her. No doubt some of this was inculcated routine and normal anxieties about homecoming. A half year had passed since he had first boarded this incredible steel labyrinth. Over the months, the Hannah had become his neighborhood and home. A number of her airedales had become acquaintances, a few good friends. Among the latter none was more refreshing to be around than a fellow Pasadenan and respected member of the ship's red-shirted ordnance gang named David Reineman. Like Ted, Reineman knew that Southern California was another name for paradise with Pasadena its Garden of Eden. As for the lovely Eves awaiting them there, the two men laughingly enlivened each other's fertile imaginations. Later Ted discovered that Dave was the brother of Dick Reineman, the crafts counselor he had so much admired at Pasadena's Y camp. On August 26, flyboy Hinckley enjoyed the rich satisfaction of sharing The Nit-Witt with airedale Reineman.

Having successfully dropped sea bags filled with medical supplies, candy, cigarettes, and magazines on Allied prisoner of war stockades in the Tokyo area, VT-6 was directed northward to Hokkaido to locate more isolated POW compounds. Since obtaining his well-deserved second-class promotion, Gunner Al was preoccupied with deck crew labors; obligingly, Witt okayed substitute Reineman. Their adventure, Ted wrote afterward, made "this whole damn war worth sweating out."

Four TBMs, each loaded with four large canvas bags of assorted goodies, launched early and headed across Hokkaido. The familiar Port of Otaru provided their geographic fix for ferreting out the incarcerated men. This time no one was shooting at The Nit-Witt. And sure enough, just off shore lay the freighter sunk by Hynd; all that was visible were its two forward king posts. Heading inland and skimming along at less than eight hundred feet, Ted was almost transfixed by the passing panorama. Japanese, real live Japanese, were working in the rice fields and strolling village streets. "All the people stood and gazed at us, some waved. . . . Some small boys threw rocks at us."

Heretofore Ted had been busy scrutinizing enemy terrain for antiaircraft positions and likely targets. Now he could leisurely appreciate the picturesque silver-green mirrors formed by the terraced rice paddies. "With the exception of the dirty industrial centers, the Japanese countryside is very, very beautiful. The unevenly spaced patchwork land with its rice paddies and varied shaded hills, and quaint roads and paths connecting everything makes one relax completely and enjoy its serene beauty."

He marveled at their parsimonious use of Nature's bounty. How stark the contrast between the giant hydroelectric dams of western America and the many small electric generators spaced along Hokkaido's streams. "Everything scattered across their countryside is primitive and appears to be handmade. The trains and their rails are small and old fashioned. The mills look slapped together, and even the largest towns have few modern constructions. How these people ever for a moment thought they could beat us is beyond me." Hinckley's conclusion probably voiced that of most of his shipmates. "Their leaders . . . knew the war was imminent and just took a big chance. They gambled everything before we could become fully armed, but in the end our industrial organization did the trick." Nor was this unadulterated jingoism. Ted's eyes told him what the anti-American militarist Ishihara Kanji had predicted immediately after the Pearl Harbor attack. "Japan would surely lose the war because it simply could not compete with America's material power."

Searching for the POW camp, the four planes came upon a good-sized Japanese Army training base. "The school had a complete battlefield located in the rear, caves, dummy tanks, gun positions, fox holes, trenches, etc. Out in front of the barracks was a field for drilling and tank maneuvers." Obliquely noted in Hinckley's flight log was a dishonorable action by the four cocky Navy pilots: their attempt to scatter and/or prostrate some columns of soldiers marching in white pajama uniforms. A year earlier such flat-hatting would have frightened Witt's radioman half to death. Now inured to flyboy hedgehopping, he could only shake his head and philosophize about the hatless, stern-faced troops who refused to break ranks. "The soldiers did not even look up—

Lord, how deep seated their hatred for us must be . . . they are humans
and I cannot hate all of them." Another booming low pass, a thundering,
ground-vibrating assault, but the soldiers "never once bothered to follow
us with their heads." Their country had lost the war; their collective
respect remained rock solid.

Forced by Hokkaido's low overcast to pursue almost a valley by valley
search, the *Hancock* flyers finally found what they sought. Racing over a
seemingly deserted POW stockade, the four Avengers rounded a hill,
lined up, throttled back, and came in at about two hundred feet.

> This second zoom found men all over the place. They were in the
> courtyard, on the roofs of the barracks, and even standing on
> each others shoulders waving and yelling at us. One chap had a
> Dutch flag and was waving it like mad. I never had a more proud
> feeling in all my life. Proud that after four years of confinement
> these fellows could show so much spirit, proud of our planes and
> pilots who had found these poor unfortunate devils, and most of
> all very proud to be a part of this.

Proving he was good for something, Hinckley spotted "the second
POW camp over to one side and not as conspicuous as the main one.
Witt then passed the word on to Waddell." So excited were the Nit-Witt's
aviators that they fouled up the bomb bay door closing procedure. "We
just pulled up in time to avoid going into one of the barracks and two
seconds later missed the top of one of the hills by inches."

The men of Torpedo Squadron Six never had the privilege of meeting
any of these POWs. Fate, however, soon communicated a warmly satisfying acknowledgment in a *Time* magazine "Letters to the Editor."

> Through the three and half years of misery, ghastliness and
> humiliation which is the lot of a prisoner of war in Japanese
> hands, I had clung to life with the hope of a return to a world I
> understood, but my imagination never rose to a conception of the
> heights of the reception which the American Army gave us. It
> started on August 26 when our POW camp of 509 British, Dutch
> and a few Americans in the center of Japan's Northern Island was
> visited by four torpedo bombers . . . they bombed us with food,
> tobacco, candy, *Time* and *Life*.

New Zealand Private David Marshall told how he was subsequently
"clothed, fed, deloused, bathed, injected, inoculated" and flown home by
a Liberator (B-24 bomber). "To a country which produces in its rank
and file such an innate sense of human decency" Marshall was forever
grateful. ARM Hinckley would be forever grateful for those shared seconds witnessing such unrestrained joy, POW jubilation for the white-
starred peace planes and what they represented.

Lying in his bunk and fuming that it would be at least another
month before they headed home, Ted sought surcease in Joseph
Pennell's *History of Rome Hanks*. An affectionate shout disturbed him.
"We've got room for you. It's the peace-signing aboard the *Missouri*.
We'll be flying right over Tokyo." Badgering him was the forever ener-
gized Paul Valenti, old Florida friend and the best checker player in the

Air Group Six passes over the battleship Missouri as a part of the roaring, multi-service air parade honoring the September 2, 1945 peace signing. Despite his excitement, the sight of the sprawling Tokyo carcass shook the author.

squadron. "Come on, get off your ass; you don't want to miss this." Reading about the Civil War seemed eminently more pleasurable than being crowded into a TBM bus for rubbernecking sailors. Fortunately, Valenti's cajoling got results and Hinckley joined the other sightseers. Their bus driver was owlish Ensign Paul White, probably the best of the Opa-Locka pilots. The September 2 joint Navy-Army Air Corps air show proved to be almost as memorable as Ted's recent POW flight.

For V-J Day's hundreds of Third Fleet airplanes, it was a short flight. Approaching Tokyo at less than a thousand feet, one quickly became aware of a strange, faintly pink haze overlaying the shattered capital. Only when on top of the vast carnage did it dawn on Ted what all this meant. Less a weather creation than a fog of human derivation, the haze's particulates were ash blown up from the enormous ruination spread out below. To his astonishment, American propaganda that the Emperor's palace had been spared turned out not to be propaganda at all. Miraculously, midst the miles of surrounding rubble, the hallowed architectural jewel remained unscratched by war. For the broken island people, it would prove to be an islet of hope. Silly wartime Navy palaver about seizing Hirohito's white horse for Admiral Halsey had ended. America wisely let the Emperor keep his throne.

Shaken by the vast desert of destruction, those within White's Avenger stared in silence. Ted wished that his boyhood friends had had a chance to get in on this. Feelings of triumph were diluted by reactions of shock and pity. Flying over the USS *Missouri* with its peace signers gathered amidships, Ted did sense a flicker of family triumph. Having graduated second in his class at Annapolis, cousin Ensign Nelson Upthegrove was somewhere down there on the "Mighty Mo" taking photographs of General MacArthur and Admiral Nimitz. Of course the public would accord them credit for winning the Pacific War. Ted and those who flew with him knew who really had made victory possible.

What had defeated Japan? Ten years later Japanese naval officers Captain Mitsuo Fuchida and Masatake Okumiya would offer their explanations.

> The root cause of Japan's defeat . . . lies deep in the Japanese national character. . . . A tradition of provincialism makes us narrow-minded and dogmatic, reluctant to discard prejudices and slow to adopt even necessary improvements if they require a new concept. . . . In short, as a nation, we lack maturity of mind and the necessary conditioning to enable us to know when and what to sacrifice for the sake of our main goal.

In the 1930s and 40s, Japan's primary goal had been imperial expansion. As for "conditioning" and "sacrifice," their 1945 purgatory had turned out to be unimaginably horrible. Historian Saburo Ienaga estimated that within their armed forces the price "paid for their leaders' folly" amounted to approximately 2.3 million lives.

On September 10, the *Hancock* dropped anchor in Tokyo Bay. "The CL *Pasadena* is two ships over from us. The *Missouri* is here and I wonder if Nellie [Upthegrove] will come over and see me." That effort failed. However, when an opportunity to go ashore availed itself, Ted grabbed it. After a wet passage aboard a rusting LCM, the *Hancock* men spilled out on Yokosuka Peninsula, down the shore from Yokohama and Tokyo. Almost immediately the smell of saltwater spray was supplanted by the stink of ruptured sewers. Ted had not walked more than two or three hundred feet when his eyes beheld a nauseating sight easily exceeding the odor attacking his nostrils.

Strung out from a long, low motel-type building were two extended lines of men. One was made up of officers in khaki, the other composed of sailors in liberty whites. For a moment he wondered what they sought. Then he recalled what he had heard back in Hawaii, how not until Honolulu's citizens rid themselves of neighboring houses of prostitution had they eliminated these unsavory lines. The appalling scene of human degradation on the shore of Tokyo Bay recalled the sordid brothel encounter in Remarque's *The Road Back*. In this subdued stampede of wild horses, men were permitting their bodies—worse, their minds—to be grievously branded. Ted hurried on, relieved that he had spotted no one he knew.

For nearly three hours he wandered about Yokosuka. Japanese civilians and uniformed Americans mingled unconcernedly; he might as well have been strolling on the streets of San Francisco's Chinatown. Blocks of burned buildings were being leveled and thoroughfares, although torn up, carried a surprising amount of traffic. Greatly improving his outlook were the large, robust American sailors posing for photos with their arms around the shoulders of diminutive Japanese—men, women, and children; everyone smiled as though they were old friends. In his hand Ted carried his flight bag. Before departing the *Hancock*, he had removed his pistol, goggles, sheath knife, oxygen mask, etc., substituting for them Lifebuoy soap, cigarettes, and candy bars. These he now intended to exchange for a beautiful Japanese kimono, the ultimate prize for every sailor with a girl back home. For her morale-boosting letters, sister Jane deserved only the best.

Two hours passed. There were no merchants with lovely kimonos for sale. In fact, there were few shops with anything attractive to sell. Desperation dictated resolve. Entering one place of business, undoubtedly a print shop, he approached a middle-aged gentleman, opened his flight bag, and commenced bartering. Immediately his flight bag received a shower of Japanese type and the cigarettes disappeared. "No, no, it's a kimono I want." A woman joined the conversation. Ted pointed to her colorless, tattered garment and held out four bars of Lifebuoy soap, exclaiming, "Kimono, kimono." She and her employer (husband?) promptly disappeared. The proprietor quickly returned. In his hand was the woman's recent attire, neatly folded with some kind of war medal laid across it. Embarrassed and confused, Ted took the package, dumped the contents of his flight bag on the counter, and fled.

On September 15, the *Hancock* departed Tokyo Bay; five days later Ted celebrated his fortieth carrier landing. About this time commendations for the squadron personnel were distributed; actual medals would follow. What a merry good time the men of VT-6 enjoyed reading to one another how heroic they were. "Dingleberry clusters" was how the old salts ridiculed the shower of air medals and DFC's. Their satire half-amused, half-surprised Ted. Certainly he was gratified to find himself a recipient of three air medals. His written commendations made him out as something of a hero. Hinckley's "courage and disregard for his own personal safety were in keeping with the highest traditions of the United States Naval Service." Would that it were so. Never had he shown a scintilla of genuine courage. Numerous Air Medals were awarded merely for finishing a prescribed number of attacks on the enemy. The Navy's unwarranted decorations befuddled him; the whole process smacked too much of eating innumerable dry cereals. However, now, instead of accumulating box-tops, it was missions flown. Dingleberry clusters, indeed.

Life was filled with so much pretentiousness, so much hot air. Yet, without self-congratulatory puffery, what happened? Lacking the "I think I can, I think I can" puffs by the Little Red Engine, where would he be, where would America be? It was all so mystifying, and his current reading about Rome Hanks wasn't helping much. Life was filled with Janus-faced scoundrels, evil men who would gladly run things if decent citizens did nothing. The fascist nations had convinced him of that. And now there was Stalinist Russia muscling into Central Europe. Worrisome talk about a possible war with America's recent ally disturbed him. Hadn't Mother Russia suffered enough? Ted sought out some well-

educated officers to get their opinions about the probability of yet another world war. "The only thing worse than winning a war is losing one."
Their gloomy assessments were anything but comforting. "The
Vibrator," as Katke delighted in labeling him, must soon have something
to keep his restless mind challenged or he would be in trouble. Did Ted
recall his mother's, "An idle mind is the devil's playground"? Damn, but
he was fed up with Navy confinement.

In truth, the Navy had liberated his mind. In 1995, a half-century
removed from his wartime experiences, Ted Hinckley was profoundly
grateful for his naval service. How manifest its lessons. War and
human folly were no longer abstractions. Decent men, like Jack Streeter
and Chief Chapman, made the pain of life well worth the cost. Most
important, the Navy had taught him a great deal about himself, teachings eight years of college-university study never could. There were, of
course, innumerable paradoxes that only future decades clarified.
Among them: the more one learns, the less he knows; women are
stronger than men; remarkably generous America suffers from a restless
selfishness; and that disciplined order and personal freedom form inter-
locking keystones in democracy's arch. As for the nation whose history
he so revered, and for which he had risked his life, there would be times
in years to come when he could not but sympathize with Edward Everett
Hale's Philip Nolan. But Lincoln had it right. For all of America's frail-
ties, its ugly scars, and costly blunders, the United States remains "the
last best hope of earth."

On September 30, the *Hancock* turned south. She was headed for
Okinawa to take aboard seventeen hundred troops on the "Magic Carpet
run." They really were going home after all! Home! That word tasted as
wholesome as peace. Of course none of the Avoca Avenue gang would be
there. With Philly now in the Army, both of the next door Marshall boys
were in uniform. How long before they and all the gang would be home?
How long before those nights on Raymond Hill with their dogs, laughing
at one another's grab-ass antics? But war had drawn its curtain on
their boyhoods. Ted at last understood Victor Herbert's lyrics, "Toyland,
toyland, mystic, wondrous boyland. Once you venture from it, you can
ne'er return again."

Four days later, Ted awoke to find himself a year older. "The bakers
prepared me a nice cake [Unfortunately he never did find out who
extended this kind act.] and all the fellows wished me a happy birthday."
He played the happy epicure well enough, but within him the blood of a
stoic ran just too powerfully. "Twenty years old today and I feel like I am
thirty. I wish that this were my fifteenth birthday. But as the poem
'Maude Muller' puts it, 'Of all sad words of tongue and pen the saddest
are these it might have been.'" What was he muttering about? Why in
heaven's good name did this Pasadena youth, who surely had it all at
the hoary age of twenty, believe he had so little to show for the last five
years of his life?

Was this angst a quite normal identity crisis? Fortunately, his WASP
nurture solidly undergirded him. As he admitted to his parents,

I have really been very fortunate as to my upbringing. I have a
wonderful mother and father and their guidance; never once was
I hungry or in want of clothes or normal luxuries. My life was
balanced and I had every opportunity to grow physically and
expand mentally. My environment in no way could have been
improved upon. Yes, I have lived a full life and I could ask God
for nothing more than that which He [has] already presented me
at 1211 Avoca.

In part, his hectoring conscience, his troubling disquiet was a neo-
Puritanism of his mother's molding. Mercifully, he was also his father's
son. Self spoofery was a life preserver. To himself he scribbled: "Ah,
well, lad you still have quite awhile yet, things could have been worse."

Lacking demanding psycho-physical stimulation, pushed about by
snowballing anxieties apropos his future, Ted prayed for guidance.
Direction arrived in the form of the *Hancock*'s Protestant Chaplain.

Well-educated, Lieutenant Commander J. F. Parker had joined the
Navy before the Japanese attack on Pearl Harbor. Earlier he had served
in the Virginia National Guard; he apparently enjoyed the sailor's life.
Plus a month, his tour aboard the Hannah coincided with that of Air
Group Six. Most definitely Chaplain Parker did not exude YMCA
Secretary Paul Somers' joyful Christian enthusiasm. Understandable, if
regrettable, Ted never exchanged ideas with the *Hancock* chaplain.
Rather than Jesus' forgiving, New Testament love, his Sunday messages
more often examined the grim prophetic warnings of the Old Testament
Jehovah; Baptist Parker's distrust of humankind was palpable.

America's employment of atomic bombs met the chaplain's harsh
condemnation. Those who heard his courageous sermon had to be
stunned. Jolted by Parker's candor, Ted wrote his parents, "I can only
say it means the end of the world unless some miracle occurs . . . these
terrible weapons, and another struggle among the nations of this world
will mean complete disaster for all of mankind." Thereafter the increasingly introspective Vibrator gave more attention to both his Bible and his
prayers, rarely if ever, missing Protestant services. Parker liked to cite
the works of Harry Emerson Fosdick, essays that Ted also admired. The
chaplain echoed Fosdick's warning in his *A Good Time to Be Alive*: If
America forgets its spiritual foundations, it faced collapse. Ted preserved Parker's printed admonishment.

The supeı ior equipment and the native intelligence of the
American people cannot be exceeded by any other nation. But
are we going to win the peace? The foundations of peace are spiritual. The nation is as strong as the characters of the people. No
nation can endure without God. Let us not ask God to give us
peace when we do not deserve it. Let us pray that by our deeds
and thoughts we shall be worthy of an abiding peace in our
hearts and in our world.

What were Hinckley's "deeds and thoughts"? How might he be "worthy"?

In 1945, Ted had only the dimmest notion what John Calvin represented. Perhaps the theological transmission was biological, more likely,

cultural; whatever, Calvin's skeptical view of humankind had already sprouted within Eunice Hinckley's son. One of Parker's final *Hancock* sermons laced together moral injunctions as well as encouragement. More subtle than "Sinners in the Hands of an Angry God," and presaging Reinhold Niebuhr's neo-orthodoxy, Parker used a nuanced military metaphor. Each of his listeners was both an enemy and a friend. "You are the enemy," he declared, but allied with God and by fighting the good fight, each of you will win many victories in the days ahead. Afterward, Ted noted with approval that some of Air Group Six's leaders joined the cluster of officers congratulating Parker for his well-selected words.

Two-and-a-half months earlier, in mid-July, as the proud *Hancock* had once again reentered combat, Ted had written his parents: "I am coming home someday and will get the opportunity to enter His work. I know it because of Matthew 21:22. 'And all things whatsoever he shall ask in prayer, believing ye shall receive.'" Now, four months later, and after an intensely moving moral imperative, he felt himself called to be a Christian minister, Although greatly relieved to have heard his calling, he was not elated at the prospect. "*Vaya con Dios*" did make sense—the world was so screwed up. And now there was this ominous prospect of another terrible war. Perhaps in studying God's design, Ted might comprehend where in the earthly jigsaw puzzle he fit. Surely one ought to be more useful as a clergyman laboring for peace than as a sham warrior attempting to beat back Soviet Russian expansion.

On 4 May 1946, aircrewman Hinckley received his honorable discharge; his quixotic pilgrimage had only begun.

EPILOGUE

Ted Hinckley would never wear a clergyman's collar. Given his self-centeredness, it would have choked him. His ministry would be in higher education, rather higher than The Nit-Witt ever reached, but a long way from the historical heights which he so glibly urged on his too patient San Jose State University students.

While failing to attain either the personal or professional esteem a Calvinist vainly seeks, he did win wings of a sort. In 1946, he earned his private flying license. That fall, just a year after participating in war's destructiveness, he had the satisfaction of joining the first four-year class (1950) to graduate from a brand new academic institution, today's Claremont McKenna College. Here a generous God introduced him to a most remarkable seventeen-year-old. Miracle of miracles, that Scripps coed combined the charms of an Osa Johnson and Judy Garland. Never very swift, it took him decades to fully appreciate his loving wife. But, again, fate was kind, and over the tough, grinding years, a polished jewel of a marriage shone forth. And, yes, his Missouri Minerva did successfully corral his wild horses. At seasonal roundups, Caryl Chesmore brought him five lovely fillies, two daughters and three granddaughters.

A half-century after the Californian had gone to war, he still wondered why he had been spared. With the longest flight no longer remote, he prayed for God's mercy and goodwill among humankind.

War's over and VT-6 poses below Air Group's scoreboard on flight deck of the USS Hancock. (Front row center, seventh from right Harold J. W. Eppler, perhaps the squadron's finest pilot.)

ROSTER OF VT-6 PERSONNEL
For Third War Cruise

Abbey, W. R.	Hinckley, T. C. Jr.	Pattee, S. A.
Abernathy, L. M.	Hoge, C. V.	Patterson, G. W.
Anderson, J. J.	Hood, R. B.	Paul, C. R.
Ashman, L. C.	Hoover, J. T.	Pierce, W. D.*
Babbitt, A. V.	Hynd, H. F.	Porter, A.*
Berryman, A. H.	Irwin, E. G.	Privette, W. G. Jr.
Berland, E. E.	Janschitz, F. J.	Pushigian, C.
Beyer, P.L.	Janson, R. C.	Puthuff, H. V.
Bitzegaio, N. B.*	Johnson, L. P. Jr.	Reardon, H. J. Jr.
Boone, R. A.	Junghans, R. J.	Rhodes, R. E.
Burcham, J. F.	Juvinall, O. E.	Sandidge, R. M.
Berkenbine, M.E.	Karstens, R. J.	Schneider, R. G. Jr.
Burrus, J.C.	Katke, J. B.	Schuetz, R. J.
Callon, W. C.*	Keeley, J. S.*	Scobba, J. J.*
Chapman, G. W.*	Kennedy, F.	Shaffer, E. P.
Clapp, C. E.	King, G. J.	Skawski, T. J.*
Clatty, C. R.	Kresse, A. F. W. Jr.	Smestad, D. L.
Cone, J. B.	Lee, R. E.*	Standen, B. J.
Crane, F. F.	Leitz, L. E.	Steele, W. B. Jr.
Crow, M. R.	Lewis, B. J.	Streeter, J. S.*
Dennis, T. T.	MacDonald, G. B.	Sullivan, L. R.
Donovan, G. C.	Macri, G.	Teige, C. A.*
Dry, E. E.	Madera, E. J.	Tibbets, I. G.
DuTemple, L. G.	Maxwell, J. E.	Valenti, P. I.
Eppler, H. J. W.	McCalley, R. A.	Varner, M. F.
Famera, F. J.	McCarty, A. W.	VeHaun, J. R.*
Fitzpatrick, W. H.	McConn, O. W.	Waddell, J.
Flohil, G.	McCormack, J. F.*	Walter, E. S.
Frink. G. W. Jr.	McGee, G. B.	Weaver, C. C.
Froetschner, E. G.	McLellan, D. W.	Weiland, M.
Gaffney, J. B.	Melson, J. F.	White, P.
Gallagher, W. P.	Mills, R. L.	Williamson, G. F.
Gentzkow, R. F.	Moore, J. E.	Witt, W. P. Jr.
Gillen, F. T.	Newton, J. R. Jr.*	Wolff, W. F.
Hardisty, M. A. Jr.	Nesbitt, R. S.	Yamrich, J. F.
Hill, J. G.	O'Connor, E. Jr.*	

*Killed in line of duty

BIBLIOGRAPHY

The author's wartime correspondence with his family and a copy of his radioman-gunner's flight log are often quoted in this book. Upon his death, these materials, as well as his Navy scrapbook will be turned over to an appropriate depository. In the interim, anyone who wishes to examine these personal papers is welcome to do so. Please contact him through his publisher.

Published literature on the Pacific War is now quite extensive. The following merely represents some of the major sources employed in this autobiography.

Angelucci, Enzo, and Matricardi, Paolo. *World War II Airplanes.* Vol. 2. Chicago: Rand McNally and Co., 1977.

Bailey, Ronald H. *The Home Front: U.S.A.* Alexandria, Virginia: Time-Life Books, 1978.

Blum, John Morton. *V Was for Victory: Politics and American Culture During World War II.* New York: Harcourt Brace Jovanovich, 1976.

Burns, Eugene. *Then There Was One: The USS Enterprise and the First Year of the War.* New York: Harcourt Brace and Co., 1944.

Caughey, John Walton. *California.* Englewood Cliffs, New Jersey: Prentice-Hall, Inc., 1960.

Corn, Joseph J. *The Winged Gospel: America's Romance with Aviation, 1900-1950.* New York: Oxford University Press, 1983.

Craig, William. *The Fall of Japan.* New York: Dell Publishing Co., 1967.

Dictionary of American Naval Fighting Ships. Vols. 1-6. Washington, D.C.: Government Printing Office, 1968- 1976.

Dull, Paul S. *A Battle History of the Imperial Japanese Navy (1942-1945).* Annapolis: Naval Institute Press, 1978.

Ewing, Steve. *USS Enterprise.* Missoula, Montana: Histories Publishing Co., 1982.

Fahey, James J. *Pacific War Diary, 1942-1945.* New York: Avon Books, 1963.

Feifer, George. *Tennozan: The Battle of Okinawa and the Atomic Bomb.* New York: Ticnor and Fields, 1992.

Flying, U.S. Naval Aviation at War-1944. (October 1944).

Flying and Popular Aviation. Special U.S. Naval Aviation Issue. (January 1942).

Francillon, Rene J. *Grumman Aircraft since 1929.* Annapolis: Naval Institute Press, 1989.

Fuchida, Mitsuo, and Masatake, Okumiya. *Midway the Battle That Doomed Japan.* New York: Ballantine Books, 1955.

Fussell, Paul. *The Great War in Modern Memory.* New York: Oxford University Press, 1975.

———. *Thank God for the Atomic Bomb.* New York: Summit Books, 1988.

Gandt, Robert L. *China Clipper: The Age of the Great Flying Boats.* Annapolis: Naval Institute Press, 1991.

Gerler, William R., and Fitzpatrick, W. H. *Carrier Air Group Six . . . Prepared by the Officers and Men on the Last Cruise.* N.P., ca. 1946.

Gow, Ian. *Okinawa 1945: Gateway to Japan.* New York: Doubleday and Co., 1986.

Gunnery Sense. Washington, D.C.: Government Printing Office, 1943.

Halsey, William F., and Bryan, J. *Admiral Halsey's Story.* New York: McGraw-Hill Book Co., 1947.

Hart, James D. *A Companion to California.* New York: Oxford University Press, 1978.

Hinckley, Ted C. "Depression Anxieties Midst a Pasadena Eddy," *Pacific Historian* 27 (Winter 1984): 27-32.

Hines, E. G. *The "Fighting Hannah": A War History of the USS Hancock CV-19.* Nashville: Battery Press, 1989.

Howarth, Stephen. *To Shining Sea: A History of the United States Navy, 1775-1991.* New York: Random House, 1991.

Hoyt, Edwin P. *Closing the Circle: War in the Pacific, 1945.* New York: Avon, 1982.
———. Pacific Destiny: *The Story of America in the Western Sea . . . 1800s to the 1980s.* New York: W. W. Norton and Co., 1981.

Hynes, Samuel. *Flights of Passage.* New York: Pocket Books, 1989.

Ienaga, Saburo. *The Pacific War, 1931-1945: A Critical Perspective on Japan's Role in World War II.* New York: Pantheon Books, 1978.

Iriye, Akira. *The Origins of the Second World War in Asia and in the Pacific.* London: Longmans, 1987.

———. *Power and Culture: The Japanese-American War, 1941-1945.* Cambridge, Massachusetts: Harvard University Press, 1981.

Ito, Masanori, and Pineau, Roger. *The End of the Imperial Japanese Navy.* New York: Macfadden Books, 1965.

Kuwahara, Yasuo, and Allred, Gordon. *Kamikaze.* New York: Ballantine Books, 1957.

Lindbergh, Charles A. *The Wartime Journals of Charles A. Lindbergh.* New York: Harcourt Brace Jovanovich, Inc., 1970.

Los Angeles Times.

Lotchin, Roger W. *Fortress California, 1910-1961: From Warfare to Welfare.* New York: Oxford University Press, 1992.

Lundstrum, John B. *The First Team.* Annapolis: Naval Institute Press, 1984.

MacDonald, Scot. *Evolution of Aircraft Carriers.* Washington, D.C.: Government Printing Office, 1964.

Miller, Henry L. "Transcript of Miller Reminiscences," typed manuscript. Annapolis: U.S. Naval Institute, 1973.

Milton, Joyce. *Loss of Eden: A Biography of Charles and Anne Morrow Lindbergh.* New York: Harper Collins Publishers, 1993.

Morison, Samuel Eliot. *History of U.S. Naval Operations in World War II.* Vols. 3-8, 12-14. Boston: Little Brown and Co., 1948-1962.

———. *Strategy and Compromise: A Reappraisal of the Crucial Decisions Confronting the Allies...*1940-1945. Boston: Little Brown and Co., 1958.

———. *The Two-Ocean War: A Short History of the United States Navy in the Second World War.* Boston: Little Brown and Co., 1963.

Mullins, William H. *The Depression and the Urban West Coast, 1929-1933: Los Angeles, San Francisco, Seattle and Portland.* Bloomington: Indiana University Press, 1991.

Nash, Gerald D. *World War II and the West.* Lincoln: University of Nebraska Press, 1990.

New York Times.

News-Pilot (San Pedro Daily).

O'Callahan, Joseph T. *I Was a Chaplain on the Franklin.* New York: Bantam Books, 1985.

Ota, Masahide. *The Battle of Okinawa: The Typhoon of Steel and Bombs.* Okinawa: Kume Publishing Co., 1984.

Pahl, Herschel A. *Point Option.* Privately printed, 1988.

Parker, Joseph F. *Prayers at Sea.* Annapolis: United States Naval Institute, 1956.

Pasadena Post.

Pasadena Star-News.

Polenberg, Richard. *War and Society: The United States 1941-1945.* Philadelphia: J. B. Lippincott Co., 1972.

Polmer, Norman, et al. *Aircraft Carriers: A Graphic History of Carrier Aviation and Its Influence on World Events.* New York: Doubleday and Co., 1969.

Pomeroy, Earl. *The Pacific Slope: A History of California...and Nevada.* New York: Alfred A. Knopf, 1965.

Potter, E. B., and Nimitz, Chester W. *Triumph in the Pacific: The Navy's Struggle against Japan.* Englewood Cliffs, New Jersey: Prentice-Hall, 1963.

Prange, Gordon W., et al. *Miracle at Midway.* New York: McGraw Hill, 1982.

———, and Chihaya, Masataka. *Fading Victory: The Diary of Admiral Matome Ugaki, 1941-1945.* Pittsburgh: University of Pittsburgh Press, 1991.

Pratt, Fletcher. *The Navy Has Wings.* New York: Harper and Bros., 1943.

Prisoner Sense. Washington, D.C.: Government Printing Office, 1943.

Reynolds, Clark G. *The Carrier War.* New York: Time-Life Books, Inc., 1982.

———. *Command of the Sea: The History and Strategy of Maritime Empires.* New York: William Morrow, 1974.

———. *The Fast Carriers: The Forging of an Air Navy.* New York: McGraw Hill, 1968.

———. *The Fighting Lady: The New Yorktown in the Pacific War.* Missoula, Montana: Pictorial Histories Publishing Co., 1986.

———. *War in the Pacific.* New York: Military Press, 1990.

Roberts, John. *The Aircraft Carrier Intrepid.* Annapolis: Naval Institute Press, 1982.

Rolle, Andrew F. *California: A History.* New York: Thomas Y. Crowell Co., 1963.

Safety Precautions for Fixed Gunnery. Washington D.C.: Government Printing Office, 1943.

Sakai, Saburo, et al. *Samurai!.* New York: Ballantine Books, 1957.

San Francisco Examiner.

Shark Sense. Washington, D.C.: Government Printing Office, 1944.

Spurr, Russell. *A Glorious Way to Die: The Kamikaze Mission of the Battleship Yamato April 1945.* New York: New Market Press, 1982.

Stafford, Edward P. *The Big E: The Story of the USS Enterprise.* New York: Dell Publishing Co., 1962.

The Hanalog (Ship's newspaper of the USS Hancock).

Thruelsen, Richard. *The Grumman Story.* New York: Praeger Publishers, 1976.

Tillman, Barrett. *Avenger at War.* New York: Charles Scribner's Sons, 1980.

Trumbull, Robert. *The Raft.* New York: Dell Publishing Co., 1942.

U.S. Navy Microfilm F-108, AR 57-79, World War II Aviation History, Action Reports CAG-6.

U.S. Navy Microfilm 1980-41, World War II Aviation History, Action Reports Torpedo Squadron Six.

Vatter, Harold. *The U.S. Economy in World War II.* New York: Columbia University Press, 1985.

Ward, John William. "The Meaning of Lindbergh's Flight," *American Quarterly 10* (Spring 1958): 3-16.

Webber, Bert T. *Retaliation: Japanese Attacks and Allied Counter-Measures on the Pacific Coast in World War II.* Corvallis: Oregon State University Press, 1975.

Wheeler, Gerald E. *Admiral William Veazie Pratt,. . .A Sailor's Life.* Washington, D.C.: Government Printing Office, 1974.

Wheeler, Keith. *The Road to Tokyo.* Alexandria, Virginia: Time-Life Books, 1979.

Wooldridge, E.T. *Carrier Warfare in the Pacific: An Oral Collection.* Washington, D.C.: Smithsonian Institution Press, 1993.

Unavailable for use during the preparation of this book but strongly recommended:

Daws, Gavan. *Prisoners of the Japanese: POWs of World War II in the Pacific.* New York: W. Morrow, 1994.

Gailey, Harry A. *The War in the Pacific: from Pearl Harbor to Tokyo Bay.* Novato, California: Presidio Press, 1995.

Kernan, Alvin. *Crossing the Line: A Bluejacket's World War II Odyssey.* Annapolis: Naval Institute Press, 1994.

Wheeler, Gerald E. *Kinkaid of the Seventh Fleet: A Biography of Admiral Thomas C. Kinkaid.* Washington, D.C.: Naval Historical Center, 1995.